Sarat Chandra Das (1849-1917) was born in Chittagong in East Bengal, now a part of Bangladesh, and studied civil engineering. In 1874 he was appointed headmaster of a school in Darjeeling; he was also a spy and adventurer, a linguist and Buddhist scholar. As a spy, he went to Lhasa twice—in 1879 for six months and in 1881 for fourteen months. The reports he wrote during these expeditions were published in 1902 as *Journey to Lhasa*. Other than this travelogue, Das wrote spiritual and scholarly tracts and compiled a dictionary of the Tibetan language. His house, Lhasa Villa, still stands in Darjeeling today.

Journey to
LHASA
The Diary of a Spy

SARAT CHANDRA DAS
Introduction by Parimal Bhattacharya

SPEAKING TIGER PUBLISHING PVT. LTD
4381/4 Ansari Road, Daryaganj,
New Delhi–110002, India

Edition copyright © Speaking Tiger 2017
Introduction copyright © Parimal Bhattacharya 2017

ISBN: 978-93-86702-05-0
eISBN: 978-93-86702-10-4

10 9 8 7 6 5 4 3 2 1

The moral right of the author has been asserted.

Typset in Adobe Garamond by Jojy Philip

Printed at Sanat Printers, Kundli

All rights reserved.
No part of this publication may be reproduced,
transmitted, or stored in a retrieval system, in any form or
by any means, electronic, mechanical, photocopying,
recording or otherwise, without the prior
permission of the publisher.

This book is sold subject to the condition that it shall not,
by way of trade or otherwise, be lent, resold, hired out,
or otherwise circulated, without the publisher's
prior consent, in any form of binding or cover
other than that in which it is published.

Contents

	Introduction	vii
I	Journey from Darjiling to Tashilhunpo	1
II	Residence at Tashilhunpo	45
III	Journey to Dongtse	71
IV	Residence at Tashilhunpo, and Preparations for Journey to Lhasa	108
V	From Tashilhunpo to Yamdo Samding, and Thence to Lhasa	127
VI	Residence at Lhasa	153
VII	Government of Lhasa—Customs, Festivals, Etc.	174
VIII	Return to Tashilhunpo and Ugyen-Gyatso's Visit to the Bonbo Sanctuary of Rigyal Sendar	199
IX	Funeral of the Panchen Rinpoche—Visit to the Great Lamasery of Samye and to Yarlung	217
X	Visit to Sakya and Return to India	238
XI	Social Divisions—Marriage—Funerals—Medicine—Festivals	246

Introduction

On the fringe of Darjeeling town, where the Hill Cart Road winds into a thick urban sprawl, is a neighbourhood known as Lhasa Villa. One needs to ask around to find the origin of this name, a nineteenth-century villa that still stands somewhere here. But only a dogged spirit with a pair of strong legs can find it in the forest of concrete and tin 50 feet below the road, at the end of a steep pebbled path. It is an old derelict cottage, the remains of what had once been a pretty structure, now indistinguishable from the tenements that have grown around it. One must exercise the imagination to remember that a century ago this was a place of solitude, filled with the call of crickets and murmuring pines, and that a spy once lived here. He was a spy who had fallen in love with the land of his mission and remained its lifelong lover.

But Sarat Chandra Das was more than a spy. Trained as an engineer, he went to Tibet in the late nineteenth century on a secret mission, became a well-known Buddhist scholar on his return, and even wrote a thousand-page dictionary of the Tibetan language. He also became a Rai Bahadur, a Companion of the Indian Empire, won a medal from the Royal Geographic Society and was supposedly the model for a character in a Rudyard Kipling novel.

Born in 1849 in a middle-class Bengali family in the

Chittagong district of East Bengal, now Bangladesh, Sarat Chandra Das studied civil engineering in Calcutta's Presidency College. A sharp and diligent student, he soon attracted the attention of his sahib teachers and, even before he had obtained the degree, was appointed the headmaster of Bhutia Boarding School in Darjeeling. It was 1874. The school had been newly set up to teach the rudiments of English and science, particularly the skills of cartographic survey, to boys in the hills. Darjeeling, too, was a new hill station surrounded by verdant mountains and the majestic Kanchenjunga towering in the sky. Coming from the flat Gangetic plains, young Sarat Chandra was captivated by such beauty. He explored the hills around town and made a trip to the neighbouring kingdom of Sikkim. But his destiny lay elsewhere, across snow-covered ranges to the north, in the mysterious land on the roof of the world. After he had read a book of travel into Tibet by two Englishmen in the eighteenth and early nineteenth century (the book was lent to him by the deputy commissioner of Darjeeling) Sarat Chandra felt 'a burning desire for visiting Tibet and for exploring its unknown tracts'. That is what he writes in his brief autobiographical sketch.

However, there was the larger picture. Across Tibet lay the two mighty empires of Russia and China, and the British were uneasy about their imperialist designs, particularly that of Russia. A thorough knowledge of this buffer kingdom—mostly unknown and ten times the size of England—was imperative for them to come to grips with the geopolitical reality of the subcontinent. But Tibet had always been wary of outsiders, except the Chinese, and the forbidding mountains and hostile tribes inhabiting its frontiers had kept it virtually cut off from the rest of the world. This had also deepened its mysterious charm. Since the early nineteenth century, the presence of foreign powers like Russia and Britain in Asia had prompted Tibet to tightly shut its doors to outsiders. It was almost impossible for Indians from the plains, let alone white-skinned Westerners, to enter this kingdom of snow.

But trade had been going on between India and Tibet along the high mountain routes since ancient times. It was monopolized by Tibetans and the hill tribes of the border region. The only other people who had access to these routes were the Buddhist monks, a tradition that had continued for centuries.

The British began to exploit this chink. They sent spies into Tibet disguised as Buddhist monks in secret and dangerous missions. These spies were called Pundits. Pawns in the so-called Great Game played by Russia and Britain on the high chessboard of central Asia, these men were drafted from among the hill people. They were given a basic training in land survey and specially made instruments that they could conceal in their baggage to hoodwink the border guards. With sextants and theodolites in secret chambers of their boxes, compasses fitted on walking staffs, paper and hypsometers tucked in hollowed-out prayer wheels, and rosaries with one hundred beads instead of the sacred hundred and eight, they measured distances by keeping count of their paces and mapped swathes of the Tibetan territory. Some of these Pundits had shown remarkable acumen and grit, a few had perished or been killed, and one of them, Nain Singh Rawat, had even won a gold medal from the Royal Geographic Society for exemplary work.

But these men lacked the formal education required to gather the kind of in-depth knowledge of the land, particularly its people and culture, that the British government in India hungered after. As an English-educated young man with a training in civil engineering, Sarat Chandra Das was cut out for the job. And his 'burning desire' for Tibet was matched by an eager nod from the top bureaucracy; it was never known which of these occurred first. But setting up a boarding school for hill boys in Darjeeling and installing a young Bengali engineer as its headmaster, must have been part of a larger design. The new school was on the radar of the government. It was patronized by Sir Alfred Croft, the director of public instruction and Sarat Chandra's mentor, and was even visited by the Viceroy.

Ugyen Gyatso was an assistant teacher in the school. He was a lama from the Rinchenpong monastery in Sikkim, which was affiliated to Tashilhunpo lamasery in Shigatse, eastern Tibet. It was Ugyen who procured from Tashilhunpo a passport for Sarat Chandra and accompanied him to Tibet. For the secret mission, Sarat Chandra's salary was raised from one hundred and fifty rupees to three hundred rupees a month. He was married. Before setting off, Sarat Chandra had told his wife that he was going to Shigatse for a few days on some official business. Naturally, she had no idea where Shigatse was or what was the nature of the 'business'; neither did she know that a pension of one hundred rupees had been fixed by the government for her if her husband didn't return from the mission.

Sarat Chandra went to Tibet twice; first in 1879, for four months, and then in 1881 for an extended stay of fourteen months. This book, first published in 1902, is based on the extensive notes he had taken during his second journey. Much of its materials—which he had used to prepare two reports for the intelligence and survey departments—were strictly classified until the end of the nineteenth century. Before him, other English travellers had written about their journeys into Tibet, notably George Bogle, an East India Company officer, explorer Thomas Manning and the great botanist Joseph Dalton Hooker. Sarat Chandra had read them carefully and had more or less followed the route Hooker had taken through Sikkim and Nepal during his foray into the Tibetan territory in 1849.

But Sarat Chandra Das's writing differs from that of his predecessors, though the narrative is strung together in the same journal form. Firstly, *Narratives of the Mission of George Bogle to*

Tibet and of the Journey of Thomas Manning to Lhasa was put together from the notebooks the two Englishmen had kept during their trips and that were never meant to be published. Their styles are necessarily unpolished and sketchy. Joseph Hooker, with his vast knowledge and experiences of travel from the Alps to the Antarctic, captures the Himalayan flora and other aspects of nature in vivid details in his classic *Himalayan Journals*. Sarat Chandra's account lacks its professional touch when it comes to describing nature and natural phenomena. But then in the *Journey to Lhasa and Central Tibet* there is a depth of insight, a sympathetic view into the lives of people and their culture, an imbuing of personal feelings and emotions, that are rarely to be found in the writings of Western travellers to Tibet, past and present.

One of the reasons for this was that Sarat Chandra often had close access to the lives of people in the villages along the route. Unlike Hooker and the others, he had travelled lightly, with fewer people and equipment; he was forced to, because of the meagre fund the government put at his disposal. He had stayed in the cottages of herdsmen and village monasteries, and had developed a warm intimacy with his servants and porters during the long and difficult journey. The book is full of rare vignettes of ordinary village life and lively portraits of common people. It also describes in graphic details the hazards of crossing the formidable mountain passes, that too in the month of November. Professional mountaineers would later marvel at the feat Sarat Chandra and his men had pulled off without adequate clothing and almost no gear.

But more formidable than these natural barriers were the people who inhabited the border region and fiercely guarded it against intruders. Here too Sarat Chandra passed the test remarkably well with his fluent Tibetan and schooling in Buddhism, and also a talent for impersonation. In Tibet, he had won the trust of Sengchen Dorjechen, a revered monk and the powerful prime minister of the Panchen Lama. This had opened for him the doors to the Tibetan society, and Sarat Chandra was one of the first Asians to have been able to visit Lhasa and have an audience with the thirteenth Dalai Lama, then a boy of eight. He also came in close contact with a number of noble personages, including a beautiful lady, and was offered rare views into the land's culture, its complex rituals and practices. Being an Oriental himself, Sarat could easily get into the skin of the Tibetan society with empathy and understanding, and yet his Western liberal education had afforded him an amused objectivity all along. This was surely a rare feat.

Lama Sengchen Dorjechen was an unusual man. Being a part of the ruling establishment in a land caught in a time warp—a land that did not have material uses of the wheel!—he had an avid interest in Western science and had procured through Sarat Chandra some of its wonders, including smallpox vaccine, a photographic camera, magic lanterns and even a complete lithographic press. While Sarat Chandra studied Buddhist literature in the lamasery's library, Sengchen took a sabbatical from his ministerial duties to learn arithmetic and English from him. He had even begun to write a handbook on photography in the Tibetan language.

Sarat Chandra was taken by the Tibetans as one among the long line of scholars who had brought new knowledge and wisdom from India, the land of the Buddha. He himself, on the other hand, had seen Tibet as a high and dry repository of priceless ancient texts and belief systems that had been ravaged in India by bigots and tropical climate. The fascination and respect was mutual. And he returned with two yak-loads of rare books and manuscripts, splendidly pulling off a mission fraught with great hardship and danger. He was feted by the British government for this, was sent to China as part of a diplomatic mission and he became quite a name in the Himalayan explorers' circuit.

But there was a dark aftermath. Soon after Sarat Chandra returned to India, his true identity and the purpose of his mission came to light in Tibet. The people who had hosted him and assisted him inadvertently during his stay were charged with sedition. They were arrested, mutilated and thrown into dungeons. Sengchen Dorjechen was drowned alive in the river Tsangpo in a public spectacle of capital punishment. Such brutality was wired into the Tibetan culture, and Sarat had witnessed it during his stay there. In this book there are descriptions of petty criminals begging on the streets of Shigatse—manacled, mutilated and their eyes gouged out. There are also other murky shadows of a closed theocratic society.

But that is only a small part of *Journey to Lhasa*. Page after page, what comes forth in this book is a spirit of inquiry and wide-eyed fascination for everything that the author had seen and come in contact with—from architectural details to aspects of cuisine, from customs of polyandry to etiquettes of drinking tea, from the rhythms of village life to the politics of Lamaism. And then there is the grandeur of nature, the animal world, the rich and varied aspects of Tibet's material and spiritual life. It all reads as if a besotted lover is recounting all the details of his paramour's beauty, spot by spot, but in a lucid and precise prose.

This lucidity and precision in describing a little-known land helped Francis Younghusband lead a military expedition there in 1903. Tibet was prised open like an oyster. Thousands of Tibetans defending their land with crude weapons were killed, the temples and lamaseries were sacked. And yes, a few of the still-surviving prisoners who had befriended Sarat Chandra were freed after thirty years of incarceration. This also ended the Great Game and drew a curtain on a fascinating chapter of espionage that had continued for most of the nineteenth century. Overnight, men like Sarat Chandra became redundant, forgotten, a relic from the past. We find him making an appearance in the caricature of an

English-educated Bengali spy in the figure of Hurree Chunder Mukherjee in Rudyard Kipling's famous novel *Kim*.

In the autumn of his life Sarat Chandra Das was a bitter man, recounting in his autobiography the raw deal he had been given by the British government and quoting stoical lines from Hafiz's poetry. He even sued the government on pension-related matters and published his autobiographical sketch in *Modern Review*, a mouthpiece of Indian nationalists. But Sarat Chandra also embraced Buddhism with zeal, wrote copiously on spiritualism and founded the Buddhist Texts Society. A year before his death, he visited Japan accompanied with Ekai Kawaguchi, a Japanese monk and a Tibetologist like him. Sarat Chandra's home in Darjeeling, named Lhasa Villa, was a most sought-after address for the scholars of the world who had anything to do with Tibet and Tibetan Buddhism.

As I write these lines, Lhasa Villa, or what has remained of it, still stands. But nobody remembers Sarat Chandra Das anymore, nobody knows what happened to those books, thangkas and manuscripts that he had brought from Tibet. Standing before the rickety cottage, it is now difficult to imagine that this remarkable man had spent the creative years of his life here. He had named it after the city of his dreams and had written here his books and a dictionary of the Tibetan language, in what was almost a Borgesian quest, cataloguing bit by bit the semantic dimension of a world that he had been able to trespass.

This book is a door to that world.

Parimal Bhattacharya
Kolkata

I

Journey from Darjiling to Tashilhunpo

November 7, 1881—On the night of my departure from Darjiling, the moon was shining brightly, though some dark clouds presaged a slight fall of rain. Our eyes often turned with anxiety towards the mountain-tops on the eastern outskirts of Nepal, to see if snow was falling on them; and the fear of death in the snows and the hope of overcoming the obstacles of nature alternated within me as I left my home in Darjiling, soon to bid a long farewell to my native land, with but faint hope that I would ever see it again.

I rode on silently, and, to my great relief, unnoticed by any one, save one or two Bhutias on their way towards Darjiling, and in the stillness of the night we could hear the songs of the workwomen of Takvar and the music of their pipes and drums. Coming to the river, which was rather broad at this season of the year, I met lama Ugyen-gyatso, who was waiting to help me across. Three or four bamboos loosely laid over the main stream enabled us to cross, though with some difficulty, and with the help of an intelligent Bhutia attendant I was able to push on over the narrow slippery path till half-past one, when I reached Gok, now a deserted village, where, in place of the dozen shops and pretty Buddhist shrine which formerly marked the place, I found but a cow-shed where a Nepali was snoring fast asleep. It was here that the up-country grain-sellers used to come to buy large quantities of Indian corn and cardamom seed to resell in the Darjiling bazar.

Spreading our rugs in the long grass near the cow-shed, we tried to rest for a while; but what with the unevenness of the ground, insects creeping over me, the prickly points of brambles and weeds penetrating the thin rug on which I lay, and a shower of rain which wetted us through, we could get no sleep, so we started again at four in the morning. The path, hardly a foot broad, was choked with weeds and long grass. Lighting my lantern, I followed Phurchung, my shot-gun tied across the top of the load he carried, and with many a slip and tumble we reached the valley of the Rummam at daybreak.

November 8—The Rummam, one of the principal feeders of the Great Rungit, rises in the Singli mountains, and forms the boundary between British territory and independent Sikkim on the north-west, all the country to the right (south) of it belonging to the former Government. We found it a raging torrent, and only spanned by a light footbridge of bamboo poles resting on a huge boulder in the middle of the stream, and held down by rocks. The Lepchas and Limbus catch fish, sometimes of considerable size, in the cold season in the pools in the riverbed, which the former sell in the Darjiling bazar. Sal trees were abundant, and on the hill-slopes we saw cardamom and cotton now ready to be picked. On the larger patches of cultivation, guards were stationed in bamboo watch-houses to scare away the monkeys and bears with bamboo clappers. I was told that a large species of monkey, besides the small variety of which we saw a few, are found in this valley, and that they are a terror to the peasants and to solitary female travellers. To kill these the Lepchas use dogbane and other poisonous roots, which they mix with cooked edible roots or rice.

On nearing the bridge, we fell in with some twenty men carrying oranges to Darjiling, but I was fortunately able to pass by unnoticed. After a short rest, during which I had some breakfast, and changed my Indian dress for a Tibetan one, we resumed our journey uphill, leaving the Mitogang road on our right. Antelope and wild goat abound hereabout, but the villagers shoot but little: they are so poor that they have hardly a dozen matchlocks among them all. Nepalese settlers are numerous here, and I noticed some Brahmans and Chetris who live chiefly by selling milk and butter. We passed several paddy fields made on terraces along the hillsides, where ploughs drawn by bullocks were used; but the Bhutias neither terrace the hillsides nor do they use ploughs, but keep to their time-honoured implements, hoes and clubs of oak, by which they get but scanty returns. The Limbus till the ground for three consecutive years, and then leave it fallow for three, when the weeds are cut and burnt, and it is again put under cultivation.

After ascending several hills by steep paths, we came to the top of a ridge marked by a *mendong* and a *chorten*, and from whence a picturesque view of the valley of Dhuramdien, dotted with numerous houses, and of the surrounding country is obtained. This spot is called *Mani-dara* by the Pahirias, and *Chorten-gang* by the Bhutias, both names meaning 'the ridge of the sacred *stupa*.' Here we halted by the side of a rill, and purchased two bottles of *murwa* beer and vegetables from some Limbus.

November 9—Our way led along an easy path by Limbu houses with sheepfolds and pigsties in front of them, and around which a few goats and cows were also seen. The Limbu fowls, by the way, are not so large as those of the Bhutias. As I journeyed on we talked of some of the Limbu customs, the most remarkable of which is that of beating drums on every trivial occasion. Every Limbu family, be it poor or rich, possesses, as a rule, three or four tambourine-shaped drums, which they beat on going out of or returning to their villages. The wife or children beat them in honour of the husband when he goes out, and the latter when they leave the house.

Crossing the range we entered a richer country, as was evidenced by the vegetation and the abundance of trees. We saw long canes growing luxuriantly, and there was quite a large grove of plantation trees, showing the warm climate the country enjoys.

November 10—The sky was cloudy and the atmosphere filled with fog when we set out. Along the banks of the streams we had to cross grew tall pines and giant ferns, while thick brushwood, ferns and rattans lined the banks, the water dashing down from the hill-tops in cascades. Pushing our way through the dense forests of the Hi range, the sky scarcely visible through the lofty oaks, pines and magnolias, we reached after an hour's hard ascent the Rishi *chorten*, near which is a moss-covered *mendong*. The Hi La commences here, and from it one commands an excellent view of southwestern Sikkim, including Tonglo and Singli, and the hills of Darjiling. In the thickets roundabout were to be seen the tracks of wild pigs, and the woods were alive with monkeys which feed on acorns.

At about 1 p.m. we reached the top of the range, some 6,000 feet above the level of the sea. Crossing a number of brooks which empty into the Rishi, we came to some cowsheds, where I would have liked to have rested; but no rest was possible, for I could see the leeches spanning their length with swift but measured paces, making for me with haste.

At 4 p.m. we commenced our descent from the top of the ridge, which is marked by a *lartse*—here a bush of dwarf bamboos, with scraps of red cloth tied to it, near which Phurchung uttered his *lha sol*, or invocation to the mountain deities. We halted for the night in a little clearing in the jungle at the foot of a gigantic oak, a few miles above the village of Lingcham. The giant nettle creeper here attains its largest growth, some more than 100 feet long. The tree nettle also abounds in this forest, and our servants found also the common nettle, the tender leaves of which make excellent soup.

November 11—The sky was overcast, and there was rain and sunshine at the same time, a phenomenon the Bhutias call *metog-charpa*, or 'flowery shower'. The village of Hi, by which we passed, contains several Bhutia, Lepcha and Limbu houses. The latter people seem to be prosperous; they cultivate rice on irrigated terraces, and use a plough drawn by buffaloes. A few hundred yards above the River Kalai (also called Kalhait) we saw cardamom patches carefully fenced. The Kalai river, which we found rapid at even this season of the year, rises in the Singli pass, and after a circuitous course of about 20 miles, empties into the Great Rungit near the foot of Tashiding hill. Villages are numerous along the river for many miles; they are situated on ridges, which look like lateral ribs of a range running on either side of the Kalai from west to east, generally sending out southerly spurs.

The Kalai is overhung on both sides by lofty trees growing on steep banks apparently inaccessible when looked at from the riverbank. The river is bridged by two long, stout bamboos resting on a huge boulder in the middle of the stream, and weighted down with slabs of stone.

In the shallow part of the stream piles have been driven to hold bamboo nets for capturing fish. This torrent is well known for its delicious fish; and we saw growing by some of the Limbu houses the *na-dag-shig*, a tree, the leaves of which are used to poison fish which swarm in the stagnant pools in the river.

There are five classes of priests among the Limbu people, who perform their religious and secular ceremonies. They are called *Phedangba, Bijuba, Dami, Baidang* and *Srijanga*.

The Phedangba enjoy the privilege of conducting the religious ceremonies, and of dealing in omens and fortune-telling. The Bijuba are trained to the Shamanic worship, of which fantastic dances are the characteristic feature. The third order practice witchcraft exclusively, and are said to be able to expel evil spirits through the mouth. The fourth class, called Baidang, are physicians, the name Baidang being undoubtedly derived from the Sanskrit *baidya*. The fifth, which is the most important of the five orders, has the exclusive privilege of interpreting the religious books, and of studying religious observances and rites. My informant, though a Srijanga, combined in his person the qualifications of the other four orders; hence his great reputation among the Limbus, who considered him endowed with divine attributes.

Leaving the banks of the Kalai, we pushed on uphill through long grass and reed thickets, where wild pigs were numerous and the porcupine abounds. The latter animal is said to do much harm to pulse and radish fields, and destroys a great many of the wild yams on which the people chiefly subsist. On ascending about 3,000 feet above the Kalai valley, we enjoyed distant views of Pema-yangtse, Yantang, Hi, Sakyang, and other villages on the high flat ridges on either side of the Kalai and Ratong rivers, and on our right was the village of Lingcham with its orange groves and numerous *murwa* fields. We halted near a Limbu house, and the coolies plucked wild onions (*lagog*) growing in the crevices of the rocks, with which they seasoned their curries. This *lagog*, though smelling like the common garlic, is not half so strong, and gives a peculiar flavour to meat. It is said to produce coughing.

November 12—We continued to ascend by a hardly discernible trail, passing patches of Indian corn and a few miserable Limbu houses. One woman we saw was carrying a basketful of wild apricots. At 2 p.m. we reached the top of the ridge, on the furthest extremity of which to our right was the Sangnag Choiling (pronounced Changachelling) monastery, while near the path we were following was an old moss-covered *chorten*.

Passing through dense woods of oaks and pines, and pushing our way through thickets of tree-nettle and underbrush, we reached, after two hours, the little village of Tale, where there are some twenty houses, and around which some mares, buffaloes, pigs, and a large number of cows were feeding. The inhabitants were anxious to get salt from us in exchange for *chang* for the October fall of snow had prevented the Yangpung salt dealers from reaching this place, and salt was in consequence scarce; but we had to decline their offers, as we had no more than we required ourselves.

November 13—Our way led us through the village of Tale to the Ringbi river, a stream as rapid as the Kalai. There is a strong bamboo bridge over it, but we crossed by some bamboos laid side by side where the river was narrowest. To the northwest of the village, on a parallel ridge trending northward from the same range of hills, is the village of Nambura. We followed the stream up for 5 miles by a circuitous trail, and then crossed over again to the right bank, a little below Nambura. The path led along the side of a cliff, and we had great difficulty in making our way along its slippery side, placing our feet in fissures of rocks and holding fast by creepers and grass. Then, following the course of the river, we ascended towards the village of Ringbi, and looking back we saw Tale, Nambura, and many other villages perched high up on the mountain sides several thousand feet above us.

Passing under a huge rock, below which the stream had cut gullies, we crossed over by means of bamboos and wooden ladders. Looking up once I saw some stuffed pheasants and a Tibetan shirt of red cloth hidden in a fissure of the rock, evidently by some bird-shikaris. Birds of various hues, especially several varieties of pheasants, abound in these woods, which are frequented by shikaris who earn a livelihood by selling stuffed birds at Darjiling.

A mile further on we came to the village of Ringbi, situated in a beautiful plain, behind which rose cragged rocks; to the north and east the Ringbi river roared far down below us. The wild plantain, a gigantic rattan, and numerous pines and oaks covered the hills on the other side of the torrent. There are here a half-dozen houses inhabited by Limbus, who raise rice, Indian corn, *murwa*, and other varieties of millet.

As soon as Phurchung had laid his load on the ground, he ran off to the house of an acquaintance to buy for me some bottles of beer, and presently returned with three, of which he well knew one would be given him. Our tent was pitched on the flat near the river, and my rugs being spread, I stretched myself at my ease, forgetting the fatigues of the journey. The servants had dispersed, some to collect firewood, some to pick edible wild plants, others to buy vegetables for our evening meal—nothing broke the silence save the sound of the rushing torrent below. I slept soundly, my mind more occupied with the future than the past.

November 14—The morning was clear, the view on all sides superb, and, though familiar with mountain scenery, my eye never tired of its wild grandeur. We waited and waited for hours for Phurchung, whom I had sent to Nambura to buy provisions, but, as he had not appeared by noon, we had to give up all thoughts of travelling that day. In the afternoon he made his appearance, loaded with rice, maize, *murwa*, eggs, vegetables, etc., and leading a ewe, which he said had cost him Rs 4. He was very drunk, but conscious of his condition. He begged to be excused, and, after numerous salaams and lollings of the tongue after the Tibetan fashion, he vanished from our sight.

We were asked by the Limbus to exchange salt, of which they stood much in need, for *tsao*, a dyeing creeper which grows here in abundance, and of which they had collected many large bundles; but again we had to refuse.

Phurchung much regretted that one of his best friends among the Limbus of this place had gone to a distant village to attend a marriage, for he might have rendered great assistance in many ways.

The marriage customs of this people are very curious and interesting. Some among them at the time of marriage consult astrologers. When a man and a girl think of marrying, they meet, without consulting their parents, at some place—a market, if there be one near—in order to sing witty songs, in which test the man is required to excel his fair rival. If he is beaten in this contest by the maiden whose hand he covets, he runs away in deep shame at his defeat; but if he wins, he seizes her by the hand and takes her to his home without further ceremony, but usually accompanied by a female companion. If the man has had some previous knowledge of the girl's superior attainment in singing, he sometimes bribes the maiden's companion to declare him the winner in the singing competition.

Another means of wife-winning is by courting her in the house of her parents, to which free access is readily gained by presenting the girl's nearest relative living in the house with a pig's carcass, a present called in their language *phudang*. When the marriage ceremony takes place, the bridegroom, if rich enough, kills a buffalo or a pig, which is presented to the bride's parents, a silver coin fixed on its forehead. Among the lower people, the parents of the bride seldom know anything about the marriage till the return of the girl from her victor's house. Then the marriage ceremony takes place. The friends and relatives assemble in some spacious courtyard, each bringing a present of a basket of rice, a bottle of *murwa* or arrack. The bridegroom then beats a drum, to the music of which the bride dances, outsiders also taking part in the dance. This over, a Phedangba priest conducts certain religious ceremonies beginning with the following mantra: 'According to the commands handed down to us from ancient times and the doings of the patriarchs, we bind our son and daughter to-day in marriage.'

As the priest repeats the formula, the bridegroom places his palm on that of the bride, holding at the same time a cock, and she a hen, which they afterwards hand over to the Phedangba. When the above formula has been recited, the fowls' throats are cut, and they are thrown away for any one to pick up and keep, and the blood is collected on a plantain leaf, and from it omens are drawn. In another leaf is some vermilion paint, in which the bridegroom dips his middle finger, which he passes across the forehead of the priest to the tip of the bride's nose. The bridegroom then says, 'Henceforth, maiden, thou art my wife;' and shouting repeatedly, 'Maiden, thou art my wife,' he puts a vermilion mark on her brow.

The following morning the priest invokes some friendly spirit, and says to the newly married couple, 'You two should henceforth live as husband and wife as long as you remain on this earth;' to which the parties suitably reply, 'We will do as you command.' Unless this period of a lifetime is mentioned, the marriage is held to be unlucky; and to make it fortunate further ceremonies, which open new sources of profit for the priest, are considered necessary.

At the marriage feast, where first *murwa* is served to each guest, the meat is generally pork, and finally a dish of rice is presented to every one of the party.

When the marriage ceremony is over, the bride, released from her captor's hands for the first time, returns to her parents, who are supposed to have been in ignorance of the previous proceedings. Two or three days after her return comes a go-between, or *parmi*, to settle differences with the bride's parents. He brings, as a rule, three things—a bottle of arrack, the carcass of a pig, and a silver coin, as presents to the bride's parents. Just as he is about to make them the presents, they are bound to fly into a passion and threaten to beat him, whereupon he entreats them not to do so, and tries to pacify them with the present of another rupee. Then they ask him in an angry tone, 'Why did you steal away our daughter?' and such-like questions. When their anger has subsided, he pays the price of the bride, which, according to the wealth of the groom, varies from Rs 10 to Rs 120, or the equivalent; but in all cases a pig is an indispensable part of the price. Then a further present of usually Rs 12, or its equivalent, is made to the *soffas* (subahs) and village headmen.

This present is known in Limbu as *turayimlag*, meaning satisfaction to the parents for stealing their daughter; and though it is really due to the bride's parents, it is nowadays appropriated by the village officials.

Like the Tibetans, the Limbus present white cotton *khatag* to all who are interested in the marriage. When the time comes for delivering up the bride to the *parmi*, the parents must say, 'Oh, our daughter is lost! She is not to be found! Some one must go and find her!' Then a couple more silver coins are paid, and one of the relatives discovers the lost bride, who has usually hidden herself in the storeroom, and she is handed over to the *parmi*. Nowadays, however, it is more common for the bride to come forth herself as soon as the money has been paid, but not before.

November 15—The villagers tried to dissuade us from attempting to cross the passes where the paths were hidden by the snow, saying that it would be more convenient to stay at Ringbi, where provisions were easily procurable. If I remained here, however, various reports would be spread to prejudice the frontier guards of Tibet against us, and we would, moreover, be unable to ascertain when the snow should have hardened sufficiently to admit of our setting out on our journey, as the passes were three or four days' march from the village. We determined to try the Yampung la, which still remained free from snow. Our coolies gave the villagers to understand that we shikaris (for Phurchung, with his fowling-piece and load of cartridges, was enabled to pass us off as such) had very little to do with the passes, except for going to Kangpa chan, where game was more abundant: if we failed entering Namga-tsal, we should most probably return by Jongri to Darjiling.

We passed behind the village, where there are some tall cypresses and a solitary juniper tree, which the people erroneously call chandan, or sandalwood. A short distance from the village we passed the road leading to Dechan phug, 'the cavern of bliss', a huge rock, the hollow in which is haunted by numerous demons and evil spirits. Now and then we saw Limbus making bamboo mats or collecting osiers to thatch their houses. The road along the river was easy, the rills falling into it bridged, and the steep banks carefully crossed by stone dykes, while steps were cut in the rocks where necessary.

By one o'clock we reached Paongtang, where, in a wretched shed for travellers (*dong-khang*), we made our camp. A light rain was falling, so we had to cook our food in the miserable shed, where we could not stand erect, where ants and centipedes were creeping over everything, and the smoke and dust raised by the bellows nearly suffocated us. Though we had a tent, the obstinacy of my servants compelled me to forego the comfort it afforded, for to them the *dong-khang* was a comfortable dwelling, and they insisted that I should enjoy it too.

Phurchung bought some milk, cheese, *murwa*, and excellent fish from one of the neighbouring herdsmen, a cousin of his; and when we had refreshed ourselves with the beer, we sat listening to two of our companions, Jordan and Tonzang, as they sang and declaimed over their drink. Though these men carried our loads, they were men of much respectability in their own country, and had been induced to do menial work only to oblige me, as I did not care to trust outsiders with the secret of my movements. I amused myself listening to Jordan, and really wondered that even among the uncivilized dwellers of the hills wine could inspire such eloquence. Among the volleys of his eloquence were quotations from a book called *Rinchen Tenwa*, or 'The Precious Rosary'.

> 'All here assembled, pray attend.
> 'The eagle is the king of birds; when he rises, all rise.
> 'The lion is the king of beasts; when he leaps, all leap.
> 'He who drinks is the prince of speech; when he speaks, all hear.'

Here Jordan's analogy broke down, for he should have said, 'When he speaks, all speak' but as his were quotations, he could take no liberties with the text.

November 16—After having started Jordan and Tonzang to Darjiling with letters and my Indian clothing, we resumed our journey, and after a mile along the course of the Ringbi we climbed the Lungmo la, which is thickly covered with dwarf bamboos and mossy oaks of immense size.

At 2 p.m. we came to Chonjom, the junction of the two head-streams of the Ringbi, where there is a well-made bridge across the river with strong boulder-made buttresses; its bed is here covered with thick green moss. A little later on we halted at a place called Keta, in the midst of dark woods, the abode of bears, pigs, and Sikkim leopards. As I had sent my tent back, we had to make a shelter against the inclemency of the weather by a contrivance made with our bed-clothes, and on the branches of a neighbouring tree we hung our meat and fish, which attracted owls and mice during the night.

November 17—Our hearts quaked as we continued our way through the dense wood and thick undergrowth, for a man-eater was reported to have killed two Nepalese wood-cutters in the Singli la. The year before last a tiger came up to Jongri, where it killed a dozen yaks, and we feared lest now it might have come back to make havoc on the Yampung yaks. While crossing one of the numerous fences dividing different pieces of property, we found a pheasant caught by the neck in a hair-trap. The way was steep and stony, and the cold piercing.

At noon we reached the zone of rhododendrons, and, passing through the pines, where we startled pheasants and some other birds of beautiful plumage, we came to a snow-covered ridge. Then we began the ascent of a steep spur, where we were told the Lepcha troops of Sikkim had repelled the Gurkha invaders, shooting their arrows at them, and then rolling rocks down on the enemy. After this difficult piece of road, the ascent became more gradual and easier. On the way we saw some beehives, which differ in shape from those of the plains, being like great white fungi projecting from the rock.

At 2 p.m. we reached the Dok of Yampung, situated on the lee side of the range. Long *mendong* mark the approach to the village, and flying flags show the whereabouts of the yak-sheds and houses; patches of snow and ice glistening in the sun gave, from a distance, a fine appearance to the village, but, on approaching, the beauty vanished, as we perceived the forlorn and deserted condition of the place. Not a living being, not a yak, nor a dog, only some hungry crows perched on the flag-poles and the roofs. The village is composed of a dozen houses built very rudely of loose stone slabs, the roofs made of long pine planks kept in their places by stones. The larger houses were locked up, and the doors of those without locks were sealed by strings. Heaps of red dye-creepers were in every house, which the people exchange for salt brought here from Eastern Nepal in the summer months and in November after the first snows. The Limbus and Lepchas of Western Sikkim come here annually to buy salt, wool, tea, and Tibetan earthenware, in exchange for *murwa*, maize, dye-creepers, and other little commodities of the Darjiling bazar.

November 18—The Yampung la, though not lofty, presented much difficulty in the ascent, the vegetation on its sides not so luxuriant as that on the Jongri la, which is nearly of equal height. To the north the range skirts the snows of the famous Kangchan, the dreaded Khumba Karna of the hillmen. The eye, on all sides but the east, met only snow, and as I descended to the southwestern flank of the Du la, 'Demon Mount', I looked down towards the deep gorge through which the Ringbi leaps with ceaseless roar. The snow-streams from the Yampung la flow into a lake some half-mile in circumference, called Tama chu, on account of its crescent shape; the Nepalese call it Lampokri.

With the Du la the difficulties of the ascent began. Ugyen complained of headache and shortness of breath, and said he was sick with *la dug* (mountain-sickness); and to add to our troubles, such a gale was blowing that I was thrown to the ground several times. One of the coolies fell helpless to the ground, his feet frostbitten. I gave him my shoes and Kabul socks, putting on myself a new pair of Tibetan boots. The direct way to Gumo tang was blocked with snow, so we had to make a detour by the northern and western flanks of the pass. The snow was frozen, and walking became very dangerous.

I made my way as best I could, using both hands and feet. The gorge along which we advanced was so deep that the eye tired of following its windings. The snows from the pass supply the headwater of the Yong-dso chu, which runs past the Jongri la. The descent was even more dangerous than the ascent; my coolies, used to such work, had soon left me far behind.

Leaving the snows of the Du la, we again came in sight of deep gorges filled with pines, with here and there bits of pasture-land overhung by rugged cliffs.

Again we had to cross a spur, beyond which lay Gumo tang, our next halting-place, in a deep gorge, some 2,000 feet below us. We followed a glacier, and by six in the evening I reached the beautifully wooded Gumo tang gorge, and found it flooded by a torrent coming from the melting snows to the north-east. On the other side of the precipice which overhangs Gumo tang is Lachmi pokri, 'The Lake of Fortune', said to contain gold and precious stones. It is a mile in circumference, deep black in colour, and in its depths are water-elephants, the people say.

November 19—Crossing a stream, with water knee-deep, flowing eastward to feed the Ratong, we began the ascent of the Bogto la. Firs and junipers of various species overhung our way, which lay along the sides of a dry, glacial channel, with a stream flowing down it, and debris on either side. There are two tracks from here leading to the only shed on the slope of the Bogto; one follows the course of the stream which comes down from the Tsonag lake, and is usually taken by the Yampung herdmen and the salt traders from Yangma; but the one we followed is not liked by them, as there grows along it a plant called *Dug shing*, a deadly poison if eaten by yaks or sheep. Pheasants were feeding on the rhododendron berries, and we also saw herds of wild sheep; but before we reached the summit the rhododendrons and junipers disappeared, and we only saw now and then some lichens or moss-like vegetation in the clefts of the rocks.

Reduced for the last few days to a miserable diet of rice and tea, we were but ill prepared to go through the exertion of climbing up to such high altitudes. I pushed on for half a mile, my head aching violently and with continual retching; I finally fell to the ground, and lay there breathless and utterly exhausted. The coolies suffered even more than I, for while I had only my heavy clothing to carry, they had their loads besides. The wind was piercingly cold, and clouds scudded across the sky. One of the men prepared some tea; I drank a little, but I had no desire for food, though Phurchung insisted on my eating a frozen egg and a little dried fruit. Wrapped in all my blankets, I lay prostrate, my feet resting against one of the loads to prevent me rolling into the abyss. I passed the night in a troubled sleep, while close by me my companions were snoring in deep slumber.

November 20—The sky was overcast and a gentle breeze was blowing, and the guide, who saw signs of a snowstorm, took up his load reluctantly, after chanting some mantras; and, leaving this dreadful place called the Noga slope, we began the ascent of the pass.

A few hundred yards of ascent brought us to the Tso-nag tso, a lakelet now frozen to the bottom, of oval shape, and about 400 yards long and 200 broad; passing this we crossed from ridge to ridge, each covered with sheets of ice, the scenery of the wildest grandeur, the solitude appalling; no sound of water, not even the fall of an occasional avalanche was heard, no one spoke, all were intent on making their way over the slippery surface.

After a mile's ascent we reached another frozen lake. The guide ran forward, and, collecting some snow and pieces of ice, he sprinkled them across the lake to show us the path and prevent us from slipping. This lakelet, of about the same size as the one just referred to, is held in the sacred books of the Sikkimese to be an object of special sanctity. It is called Tso dom-dongma, 'The Lake of Peacock's Spots', and the eye of the enchanted devotee can see something like spots in the bubbles in the icy sheets of the lake. The glorious peak of Chum-bok la rose right before us. Clouds now swept swiftly across the sun, and within half an hour the whole vault of heaven was hidden from our view. Courage then failed our hitherto intrepid guide. 'Why proceed further up, sir?' said he. 'Death awaits us in this desolate place. One hour more and we shall be gone.' 'What do you mean by this, Phurchung?' said I. 'Where see you death?' 'Sir, look at the sky; those clouds will shortly fall in heavy snow on us, from which no human means can enable us to escape. If you escape the snows on this side of the path, you cannot do so on the other.' He trembled and looked pale and depressed. He cried, and said, 'Oh, sir, we *pon-yog* [master and servant] will perish if we go not back to Bogto. The skies are ominous, and tell you to return towards the Bogto la.' He repeated his entreaties with childish tears, but in vain. I told him and the coolies that I was determined not to retrace a single step, and that all his entreaties were to no purpose. In an hour's time we could scarcely reach Bogto, and if the snow began falling in the meantime, we could hardly escape; besides, such a course would not lessen our troubles, as we should have the risk of recrossing the distance we had now travelled over. There might be a second snowfall, when we should again have to turn back.

Ceding finally to my arguments, Phurchung pushed forward. I took the lead, and with fresh energy clambered on, till after an hour we stood on the pass. The skies had cleared up, the azure heavens again smiled on us, and the welcome reappearance of the brilliant sun dispelled all our fears. To our left was Sundub phug, to the right the towering pinnacles of Kangla jang-ma, while the rounded form of the lofty Lap-chyi in the Shar-Khambu district of Nepal rose above the haze. The valley of the Chum-bok la is called Chu lonkyok, 'The Water-spoon', because it receives the waters of the surrounding mountains in a spoon-like basin.

I had hardly time to congratulate myself on having reached the summit, when our guide, now smiling, put his arms in the straps (*nambo*) of his load, and uttering the usual prayer (*lha sol*), resumed his journey. The descent was fraught with immense dangers, for it lay through trackless snows. The guide sounded the snow everywhere for a path, and not finding one, he took a circuitous direction which seemed practicable to his experienced eye.

After walking about an hour we found we had made but little progress, when we came on the tracks of a Tibetan long-tailed leopard (*sah*). I wondered how the animal had been able to walk along over the soft snow without ever sinking in it, but my men explained this by attributing supernatural powers to this beast, which they said was indeed the goblin of leopards. An hour's struggle in the snow exhausted my strength, and I could proceed no further. The guide opened the loads and repacked them, putting all the breakable objects in one, all the clothing and provisions in the other. The latter he threw down the slope, and it ploughed a path, down which I followed till the load brought up against a rock. Then I let myself slide down the half-hardened snow, guiding myself with my elbows so as to escape any crevasse across my path.

By 3.30 p.m. we had descended so far in the gorge of Chu lonkyok that patches of grass showed here and there amidst the snow, and I saw an alpine shrub called *upala* with large pink leaves at the top like those of the water-lily, waved in the wind, which had again begun to blow. The coolies now pushed rapidly ahead, leaving me far behind, but the gradual reappearance of grass, rhododendrons, and juniper bushes revived my spirits as I walked on, frequently halting to catch my breath. Continuing down the gorge through rhododendrons, junipers, and several species of prickly, sweet-scented shrubs, we finally reached, about dark, a great boulder, underneath which we camped. In front of it ran a brook about 4 feet wide, said to be the head-stream of the famous Kabili of Nepal, which receives the waters from the Chum-bok and the Semarum mountains.

November 21—Though I still felt, when I awakened, greatly exhausted, I had to start without breakfast, as the coolies had left early, fearing lest the fine morning might be followed by a bad afternoon. Dressed very lightly in order to be able to climb more easily, I set out, following in Phurchung's footsteps. The trail at first presented no great difficulty, though it was continually up and down over mountain ridges five or six hundred feet high; but our previous day's experience made us think little of such a road. After a few miles we reached a kind of gateway lying between two rocky cliffs, where began the region of scanty vegetation that invariably is found just below the snow-line. Here we halted for a while and drank some tea; then, resuming our journey, we reached the summit of Semarum after a couple of hours of most trying climbing over ice and melting snow. The pass is protected to the south and west by a very rugged cliff resembling the outspread wings of an eagle both in colour and shape, and inspired me with a strange feeling of dread. Sitting on the summit of the pass, I enjoyed, though tired and unwell, the grandeur and sublimity of the scene. No poet could adequately describe Nature's exploits in this part of the world, no pencil could delineate these romantic scenes.

Legend has it that many years ago, on this very pass, a certain cunning and designing Limbu of Tambur Khola concealed under the rocks a red earthen jar filled with charcoal, with the object of establishing his heirs' right over the whole easternmost part of Nepal, called Yangoro, which includes Singli la, and in his will he made mention of this bequest. A few years later hostilities broke out between the Limbus of Tambur Khola and Yangoro, which lasted for nearly twelve years, during which time the Gurung were the chief sufferers. Pasturing their cattle on the disputed land, both parties stole them as a rent for the right of pasture. Finally the Chambisi Rajah, who ruled at Bhatgaong, settled the dispute in favour of the Yangoro Limbus, the trick of the Tambur Khola Limbus having been found out.

From the Semarum pass I saw the Choma Kankar, or 'Lord of Snows', the famous sacred mountain of the Buddhists which overhangs Lap-chyi, the highest of its three peaks, dome-shaped, the two others standing side by side, of truncated cone shape; then to the north-west of these appeared the Shar Khambu Mountains, half lost in the rising mist; to the west, beyond the great chasm formed by the Tambur valley, were the valleys of Feylep, Yalung, Dhunkota, all indistinct in the general haze.

Phurchung endeavoured in vain to find a way down through the deep snow which everywhere covered the ground, and finally we had to slide down through the snow for several hundred feet; and then, finding a foothold, we waded on, dragging the loads behind us. I saw tracks of rabbits, snow-leopards, and a species of bird called *chamdang*, probably the snow-pheasant. After a little while we could advance no further down the slope, so Phurchung made a detour over a ridge to our right, its summit a huge bare rock some 40 to 50 feet high. From this we descended with great difficulty, throwing the loads down ahead of us and sliding down ourselves in the deep, soft snow.

By 4 p.m. we were clear of the snow, and once more found vegetation. After a short rest we resumed our journey along the gentle rill which leaps down from here with a pleasant murmur, and is known as the second headwater of the Kabili, although the brook which we followed empties into the Namga stream which rises in the Kangla Nangmo pass near Jongri. The snow, reaching several miles below the Kangla pass on either side of the Namga, showed us that this pass was inaccessible. These early snows are called *shingsa pahmo*. The road led through dwarf rhododendrons, bushy junipers, and prickly shrubs bearing a red fruit. The river was frozen over, except in the narrow parts. In the distance the pine-clad flanks of Juonga, through which the Yalung dashes, were seen resplendent in the rays of the setting sun. We plodded on to 6 p.m., when we reached a broad flat called Namga tsal, 'The Grove of Joy', and shortly after crossed the river by a wooden bridge of the East Nepalese type, and some 40 feet long, and came to the halting-place under the widespread branches of a high *dung shing* or cedar. Namga tsal received its name, I was told, from Lhatsun, the great Buddhist patriarch of Sikkim, having spent a few days here to rest from his fatigue when travelling for the first time from Tibet to convert the Lhopas (Southerners). He so enjoyed his rest here that he ordered his disciples to hold the place sacred, and to celebrate their annual inaugural religious ceremonies at the cavern in which he had spent a few days. We could see the cave from where we were camped, and were told that the Buddhists of Sikkim and Eastern Nepal still resort to this place on pilgrimage.

November 22—Crossing two streams with swampy banks, the way led uphill for a while through thickets of rhododendrons, where we saw numerous green pheasants of the colour of a green parrot, with spurs on their legs and a deep, thick red line round their eye. In size they were larger than a domestic fowl. Next we came to the Yalung river, which we crossed by a substantial bridge of cedar logs and silver-fir planks, and then we began the ascent of the steep and lofty Chunjorma, or 'Collection of Cascades'. In the wooded solitudes on the lower slopes of the great Kanchanjinga stood the little monastery of Dechan rolpa. The predecessor of the present abbot, it is said, was able to visit Na-Pematang, the Lepcha Paradise, which has only been entered by seven families, and which lies between the Cho-kanchan and Cho-kanchanjinga.

Some 3 miles to the west of the Dechan rolpa gomba is the village of Yalung, where twelve families live who spend their summer in tending yaks at Yalung, and their winter at Yanku tang, in the valley of the Kabili.

Passing by the two lakelets of Tso chung donka, we ascended the mountains of the same name, and finally reached by the Nango la the summit of Chunjorma, which name applies to the portion of the pass between the Nango la and the Mirkan la, where the road from Nepal by Khan-do-phug joins it.

From Mirkan la we passed some lofty crags, called Ta-miran kukyab, the principal of which is said to be the image of the horrible deity Tamdrin, or Haryagriha. In shape it resembles a horse's head (Ta-mgrin) facing towards Kanchanjinga. Descending, we found grass growing on the Pangbo la, and on the Zinan la were junipers and rhododendrons. At about 7 p.m. we reached Mudang phug, Phurchung carrying me on his back for part of the way.

November 23—Our way led along an extensive moraine, the huge reddish boulders of which were covered with creeping tamarisks and dwarf junipers. After about a mile we reached Manda phug, a hollow between two gigantic boulders, the one inclined towards the other; and here we took our breakfast of rice and buttered tea. The vegetation improved as we neared Manda la, and the sight of thick forest growth in the deep glens refreshed our eyes, so long tired with looking on barren rocks. From Tama la, where we saw some shepherds tending their flocks and some yaks, one descends the Yamatari valley, the top of the slope being held sacred to the dreaded Mamo goddesses; on the rhododendron bushes were white and red flags offered to them by wayfarers. From this point I obtained a good view of the Kangpa-chan valley.

Finding that I was greatly exhausted, Dao Namgyal, Phurchung's brother-in-law, took me on his back and carried me till we reached the northwest flank of the Tama la. Soon after this we came to a flat, grass-covered valley with tall rhododendrons and ferns growing about. Phurchung held this spot to have been a singularly lucky one for him, for it was here that his parents had met Hooker some thirty-five years ago, while the great botanist was exploring Nepal. Phurchung's father, suffering from snow-blindness, was led by his wife to the Doctor, who not only gave him excellent medicine, but presented her with a pretty coin to hang about the neck of her child, Phurchung, then a baby in arms.

At about 2 p.m. we reached the Yamata ri, formed by the streams which issue from Kanchanjinga. The gorge in which this river flows is singularly beautiful. Above the steep crags on either side were blue glaciers, and at their feet forests of native firs and larches, covered with pendant mosses waving like feathers in the breeze. Just before reaching Kangpa-chan (Gyunsar) village, the Yamata ri river is crossed by a little bridge, and then the village with its wooden huts comes in view. Some of the houses were empty; a few old hags with goitre sat on their thresholds basking in the sun and spinning.

Phurchung had reached this, his native village, ahead of us, and he now came, much the worse for drink, to greet us, and led us into his mother's house, where a fire of rhododendron boughs and aromatic firs blazed in the middle of the room. *Chang* was ready in wooden bottles, and his mother poured some boiling water into them as soon as we were seated on the cushions placed for us. Some dry junipers and pines were burnt as incense, and two joss-sticks smoked before us. Then two brass plates full of boiled, red-skinned potatoes were offered us, followed by rice and boiled mutton, the rice being served wrapped up in the broad leaves of some kind of hill plant. When night came on we sat around the fire, each with a bottle of *murwa* before him; but drowsiness soon overtook me, and I fell asleep.

November 24—The village of Kangpa-chan is built on several terraces facing the southwest, the houses enclosed in low stone walls. Several small streams empty into the Kangchan below the village, and mountains covered with snow and ice rise precipitously on either side of it, their lower slopes clad with thick forest growth of moss-covered silver firs, deodars, and larches. Juniper and rhododendron bushes surround the village. Round about it are patches of barley, from one to the other of which flew flocks of wild pigeons.

Coming back from a stroll, I found two men waiting to invite me to drink *chang* at their houses; and having accepted their invitation, I went first to that of a man called Jorgya. Taking my seat on a thick mattress-like seat covered with a piece of Khamba carpet, a bamboo bottle filled with *murwa*, with a little piece of butter placed on top of it, was set before us. Tea was first drunk, the housewife serving mine in a china cup, a form of Tibetan politeness only shown to persons of superior social standing, those of equal or inferior rank to the host using the wooden bowls each one carries about in the breast of his gown. After this, a brass plate filled with potatoes was placed before us on a little table, together with parched Indian corn, milk, and butter, of all of which we ate heartily.

Our host advised me not to attempt to go by Wallung, as I would be sure to meet with much difficulty, but rather to enter Tibet by Yangma and the Kangla chen pass, which was still possible, he said, even at this advanced season of the year.

I next went to the house of Pemazang, Phurchung's uncle, which I found well plastered and with a tastefully painted chapel. His son and wife received me at the head of the ladder, and led me into the house. Pemazang had long, thick, and tangled hair. He wore gold earrings in the shape of magnolia flowers, and his looks and talk were grave and serious. He often sits in deep meditation for the purpose of arresting hail or other storms by the potency of the charms he is able to pronounce.

Leaving Pemazang, we crossed the river and paid a visit to the Tashi-chos ding monastery, which we found nearly deserted, one or two old women here and there turning the prayer-wheels outside the temple. Ascending two flights of ladder-stairs, we entered the lama's house. He and his *ani* received us most kindly, and the latter asked me for some medicines for the old gentleman, who was suffering with dyspepsia (*pakan*).

Returning to our lodgings, we found that the lock of the bag in which I kept my money had been tampered with, but I did not open it, as six other persons were living in the room we occupied, and I feared lest they might see the contents. Whatever the loss might be, I made up my mind to bear it silently, and keep my suspicions to myself.

November 25—Phurchung's brother-in-law, Dao Namgyal, brought me a quantity of presents—potatoes, *murwa*, millet, butter, and last, but not least, a kid, for which I gave him a return present of five rupees. The poor people of the village all followed with various presents, not that they had any great respect for me, but solely with an eye to return presents, which they hoped would be greater than the value of theirs. Fortunately there were but few people in the village, otherwise they would have drained me of all my cash.

By noon Phurchung had sufficiently slept off his drunkenness to procure for me several pairs of *kyar* or snowshoes, from the people of the village. I had learnt from a newly engaged coolie that he had lately crossed the Kangla pass on *kyar*, and had reached Jongri, where he had met Captain Harman, who had been much struck by the great usefulness of this rude contrivance.

In the evening the men killed two kids; the blood was poured into the intestines, which had been washed and cleaned, barley-flour (*tsamba*) being mixed with it. These blood puddings were boiled and packed away with the tripe in a small wicker basket for my use on the journey.

It is told of the upper Kangpa-chan valley that it was first peopled by Tibetans, called Sharpa (Easterners), whose original home was in the mountains of Shar Khambu, or Eastern Kirata. Lower down the valley lived the Magar tribe from Nepal, whose chief extended his sway over the Sharpa, and exacted such oppressive taxes from them that they decided to avenge themselves. The Magar chief, going to the village of Kangpa-chan, he and his followers were murdered, and their bodies buried. No clue could be had of the missing men, so the chief's wife went herself to Kangpa-chan, but she also failed to discover what had become of them. While going along the river bank, a boulder, undermined by the current, tumbled down, when a swarm of flies flew buzzing out. Attracted by this, the queen had the earth removed, and discovered the bodies of her husband and his followers. Returning home with the chief's body, she ordered great funeral ceremonies to be held at a place some 6 miles up the river, near the Rapa-chan torrent, midway between the two great villages of the Kangpa-chan valley—Gyunsar and Yarsa, as being more accessible for the people, for whose entertainment great bowls of wine were to be provided. In the wine poison was mixed; and as soon as the Magars had finished drinking, they passed it to the Kangpa-chan people, who drank deeply, and fell asleep to awake no more. Nearly a thousand people were in this way done to death, and the babies were carried away by the queen's followers. The place where this foul deed was done became known as Tong-shong phug, 'the place which witnessed a thousand murders'.

The few who escaped carried the news to Tibet, and soon returned with a large army to wage war against the Magars. The queen shut herself up in one of her castles, and, though ill-prepared to stand a siege, she and her people defended it for three months. The Tibetans decided to reduce the place by famine and by cutting off the water-supply. Then the queen, to deceive them, opened the reservoir in the castle and let the water flow towards the Tibetan camp; and the enemy, thinking that she must have a great store of it and that their attempt was vain, raised the siege, and withdrew to a distance. The queen now attacked them in turn, but fell in the first skirmish, fighting valiantly. The Tibetans finally expelled the Magars from the Kangpa-chan and Tambur valleys, and restored them to their former possessors.

It was among the Kangpa-chan tribe that I had found Phurchung, the most devoted and faithful of all the men I ever came across in the Himalayas. Although Ugyen distrusted him, and he abhorred Ugyen, yet I placed implicit confidence in his loyalty and ability, and his devotion and fidelity to me were boundless.

November 26—We left Kangpa-chan, our party now comprising four coolies. Phurchung marched along with my gun as a sign of his importance, but its red cloth cover, its principal beauty, had been stolen the night before; his younger brother, Sonam-dorj, carried his pack. Ugyen-gyatso and I rode ponies, hired for eight annas each, to take us halfway up the Nango la. The old women (*ama*) of the village awaited our approach at the east end of the bridge to give us the stirrup cup (*chang kyel*) (a custom invariably observed in Tibet at the parting of friends setting out on a long journey), with bowls of wine in their right hand, and plates full of parched barley flour (*tsamba*) in their left. Each of the old women poured a little wine into a china cup, to which a pinch of flour was added, and we were asked to take a sip, with the wish of 'May we offer you the like on your return.' We thanked them for their kindness, and put a couple of rupees in one of their plates, to be divided amongst them.

We rode slowly on by the bounding river, into which a number of little rills empty, flowing down from behind the monastery, and over which were several prayer-wheels turned by the water. Our way lay amidst thick woods up to Daba ngonpo, where the natives used to get blue clay to make images. This clay they held to be exceptionally good, as it came from the summit of a holy mountain. From this point we followed up the bed of a former glacier, passing Kamai phugpa, and reaching at Khama kang tung, the timber line. A mile beyond the latter place we came to the end of the pasture-lands on this side of the Nango la, not far from which we saw a flock of spotted birds, called *sregpa*, which Ugyen tried, without success, to shoot.

The ascent of the Nango la now began over deep snow, in some places its surface frozen, in others so soft that we sunk knee-deep in it. I soon became so exhausted that I had to get one of the coolies to carry me on his back, and so we reached the summit of the pass.

Two miles to the west of the pass is Sayong kong, a plateau whence there is a direct road leading to Yangma. A mile below this place is Sayong-hok, where vegetation begins again, and gradually increases as one advances along the Lungkyong chu. We camped on the river bank under a great boulder, spreading our rugs on beds of long dry grass, which covered, but very imperfectly, the rough, stony soil.

November 27—We followed down the Lungkyong chu (the only way of communication between Kangpa-chan, Yangma, and Wallung), the mountains on our left nearly hidden in the morning mists. For part of the way our road led along a steep path through thick woods of firs, feathery larches, and deodars, amidst which I saw many pheasants and other kinds of birds, and the coolies told me that musk deer and wild sheep were also found there.

About 2 miles above the junction of the Yangma with the Lungkyong, we crossed the former stream by a wooden bridge, and finally arrived at the village of Tingugma, where we rested a while and ate a light meal.

Shortly after starting again we met a party of Yangma natives driving before them a few sheep and a dozen yaks laden with blankets, yak hides, barley, and salt. They were going to a village called Chaini, in the Tambur valley, to exchange their goods for rice and Indian corn. Phurchung asked them if the Kangla chen pass was still open. Some said we could easily cross it; others expressed doubts about it, for they said 3 feet of snow had fallen on it a few days previously.

Passing by Maya phug (a cavern sacred to the goddess Mamo), we crossed a little juniper-covered plateau called Shugpa thang ('Juniper plain'), and after a short but steep climb reached the summit of the pass, from whence I had a most extended and beautiful view of the surrounding country—behind me great reddish granite rocks, looking like the ruins of gigantic ramparts; before me a plain some 2 miles long, the bed of a former glacier, encircled by snowy mountains rising the one above the other; while to the south-east was the Nango la, and behind it the plain of Sumdongma. Crossing the Djari thang, or 'Plain of Gravel', and the Do la, or 'Rocky pass' (round the base of which the Yangma flows), I reached by dusk the monastery of Yangma, or Manding gomba, situated on a broad, shrub-covered terrace some 40 to 50 feet above the stream; where Phurchung found me lodgings in a wretched cell, where I settled myself as best I could for the night. He obtained a few eggs and some milk from the lamas; and while one of the nuns (*ani*) helped Dao Namgyal to cook the food, another blew the bellows. The lamas were engaged in their annual reading of the Kahgyur, which occupied them daily from five in the morning to 7.30 p.m., when they retired to their respective cells. There were fifteen monks and seven *ani* in the lamasery.

Ugyen had been suffering most of the day with violent pains in the bowels; he now wrapped himself in all the blankets I could spare, and lay groaning and crying, '*Achi-che apa-ouh*!', so that I felt grave apprehensions for him, and feared that his illness might oblige us to stop over in this wretched place.

November 28—Phurchung had been away on a drunken bout all night, and I arose full of fear lest he might have disclosed our plans to his companions, and Ugyen shared my alarm. After a while Phurchung and Phuntso appeared, and with much salaaming and lolling of the tongue asked me to wait here a day, the latter assuring me that he hoped to obtain, without much difficulty or the payment of custom duty (called *chua* in this part of Nepal), permission for us to proceed on our journey. Shortly after the elders arrived, the richest man among them recognizable by his *tamuski* hat, a long earring, and a deep red serge robe of *purug*. He had come from the village of Yangma riding a half-breed yak (*jo*), which, with the saddle still on its back, stood tied at the gate of the monastery. I anxiously awaited the result of their conference with my men, and in great anxiety prayed to the Supreme Dispenser of our destinies that nothing might happen unfavourable to ourselves and our enterprise.

The Manding gomba, or Nub Man-ding gomba, 'The Western Flying-Medicine Monastery', owes its name to the fact that lama Lhatsun once lived for three years in a cave close by called the Zimphug, to discover medicines of wonderful potency, and that he there obtained three wonderful pills. One came to him through the air, falling on the spot where the lamasery now stands. The second pill fell a little above the monastery, where the people of the village now burn their dead; and the third alighted on the spot where the great *chorten* now stands.

Manding gomba is held in great sanctity, for it is one of the first cis-Himalayan lamaseries founded by the great red-hat Lama Lhatsun; but Wallung ranks first, and Kangpa-chan second, in point of wealth and power. Manding possesses a fine copy of the Kahgyur in 125 volumes.

The *Lha-khang*, or temple, has massive and neatly painted walls and doors, after the manner of the Sikkim *donpa*. The huts or cells of the monks in its immediate vicinity, all painted red with clay obtained from the adjacent mountains, are of irregular and ugly style, the doors, windows, and cornices being roughly made; each house has around it a low stone wall, inside of which the sheep and yak find shelter.

After a little while Phurchung and Phuntso came back to me in high spirits over the result of their conference with the village elders. They had told them that I was only a pilgrim (*nakorpa*) who spoke Tibetan and dressed in Tibetan fashion. The head lama said that he knew of no order from the Nepalese Government for stopping pilgrims on their way to Tibet, and that he would certainly not prevent me doing so, as I spoke Tibetan with greater fluency and accuracy than many Nepalese. The headman (*gopa*) asked that Phurchung should give bond, holding himself personally responsible for my character as a traveller, and a custom duty of eight annas a head was levied on our party. Phurchung also told me that the headman and head lama were coming to bid me farewell, and that I must not forget, after exchanging compliments with them, to say *sangpoi ja chog*, 'May we meet again next year'.

In a little while the big men arrived. The headman, conspicuous by his earring, boots, and red serge robe, nodded to me slightly, and took off his hat. He asked me why I had chosen such a bad season for going to Tibet. I told him that I did so in obedience to the command of our holy and learned chief lama (*Tsawai*), and not by my own wish. His object in coming to see me was to find out if I spoke Tibetan and understood the Buddhist religion. My fluency in Tibetan, and the citing of one or two proverbial sayings in course of conversation, made him form a high opinion of my knowledge of the sacred texts and histories, as well as of my character and holiness. '*Laso, laso*' (yes, yes), he said, and then he apologized for not having brought me some presents; but I answered him that our acquaintance was only just begun, and there would be time in the future to cultivate it, and, handing him a scarf (*khatag*), I expressed the hope that we might meet the next year (*sangpoi ja chog*). Many of the bystanders made wishes for our welfare, but someone in the crowd said that I was certainly not a Tibetan. Then another swore I was an Indian; and a third said that they would soon have news of me: 'That Hindu will surely die in the snows, and his servants will soon return here with the news of his death.'

It was past noon when the coolies picked up their loads, and I set out in excellent spirits, having now escaped the much-feared obstruction from the Yangma people, on whose mercy and goodwill our success entirely depended.

We passed by some *mendong* and *chorten* at the entrance to the convent, and then followed up the course of the Yangma, passing by a pretty lakelet, the Miza, or 'man eating', now filled with ice, and seeing on the way some very high *chorten*, known as *thongwa kundol*, 'bringing deliverance when seen', which had a few years previously been repaired by the head lama of Wallung. Near these we saw a half-dozen wild sheep (*nao*), but we gave up all idea of shooting them when told that the Yangma people think the gods of the land and mountains (*Shi-bdag, ri-lha*) would be deeply offended if anyone molested them.

By 3 p.m. we got sight of the village of Yangma, whose houses could only be distinguished from the boulders everywhere strewing the ground by the smoke issuing from the roofs. There were not more than a hundred houses in the village, and the fields round about were enclosed within low stone walls. Buckwheat, barley, turnips, radishes, and potatoes are grown here, and rice brought from Yang-ku tang and other villages in the warmer valleys is procurable. The village was founded by Tibetans from Tashi-rabka, one of them having discovered the valley and its comparative fertility while hunting for a lost yak calf. The name Yangma was given it on account of the breadth of the valley.

The male part of the population is idle in the extreme, but the women are correspondingly busy; some I saw were threshing corn, some gathering fuel, others engaged in various kinds of household work.

By 5 p.m. we got off from this wretched valley, where Phurchung and the coolies, by the way, were most desirous to remain to continue drinking *chang*, though Phurchung showed unmistakable signs of having already imbibed too much. After an hour's march we reached Ki phug, where we found, under an overhanging rock, a bit of ground free from snow on which to camp; but Phurchung remained behind in Yangma, in a helplessly drunken condition.

November 29—The way lay along the Yangma, which was scarcely visible, snow and ice covering entirely its bed. There was nothing to give life to the scenery; the river flowed into a deep gorge, or else opened out into lake-like expanses; on either side the mountains seemed to reach to the sky; not a bird, not even a cloud in the heaven, not a sound save that of our feet crushing the light dry snow. It was 11 a.m. when we came to an unfrozen pool, by which we ate our breakfast of tea and last night's meal. This place, which is in a broad portion of the valley, is a favourite summer pasture-ground (*tser chan*) for the Dokpas, who, from July to September, bring their herds of yaks here.

Po phug was reached after a march of 3 miles through the snow, then the ascent became steeper and freer from snow, and we came to Luma goma, 'Fountain head', the source of the Yangma river; and after an easy ascent of half an hour we arrived at Tsa-tsam, the limit of vegetation.

Here we began climbing a huge glacier, a quarter of a mile wide and more than 3 miles long, the Chyang-chub gya-lam, or 'Highway to Holiness', over which I was carried on Phurchung's back wherever the snow lay deep. Then we climbed a huge mass of bare black rocks (*Dsama nagmo*), and darkness had overtaken us before we reached the 'White Cavern' (*Phugpa karpo*), where we proposed passing the night. The fog added to the obscurity of the night, our feet were benumbed by the cold, and we frequently slipped into crevasses or between the clefts of rocks. Finding it impossible to reach the cavern, we scraped away the snow from between some rocks, and there I sat, my knees drawn up, hugging myself during the long night.

How exhausted we were with the fatigue of the day's journey, how overcome by the rarefication of the air, the intensity of the cold, and how completely prostrated by hunger and thirst, is not easy to describe. The very remembrance of the sufferings of that dreadful night makes me shudder even now, but I quickly recover under the inexpressible delight I feel at the consciousness of my great success. This was the most trying night I ever passed in my life. There was a light breeze blowing, attended with sleet, which fortunately weighed my blankets down and made them cover me closer than they otherwise would have done. And so with neither food nor drink, placed as if in the grim jaws of death in the bleak and dreary regions of snow, where death alone dwells, we spent this most dismal night.

November 30—The coolies once more picked up their loads, and our guide began in his gravest tones to recite his *Pema-jung-ne samba duba* and other mantras. The morning was gloriously radiant, and the great Kangla chen glittered before us, bathed in a glory of golden light. Fortunately for us, there was no fresh snow on the ground; for, had there been any, we could not possibly have advanced. We found that we had stopped not more than a furlong from the *Phugpa karpo*, which, by the way, is not a cave at all, but only a crevasse between two detached rocks. Our guide, leaving his load in charge of his brother, took the lead, driving his long stick into the snow at each step, and digging footholds in the soft snow. From the White Cavern the top of the pass bore due east, and was distant about 2 miles. Just at the base of the final ascent there is a little sandy plain, in the middle of which is a huge boulder: this is the 'Place of Salvation' (*Tarpa gang*), thus called because, when once this point is reached, travellers may be confident of attaining the summit of the pass.

I steadily followed in the footsteps of the guide, and would not let him take me on his back; for if I succeeded in ascending to the highest summit of Kangla chen without any help, I could look to the achievement with greater pride. Ugyen here gave out, and it was with difficulty that I persuaded Phurchung to carry him on his back, for they were far from being on the best of terms. An hour's hard climbing brought us to the summit of the pass. The sky was cloudless and of the deepest blue; against it a snow-clad world of mountains stood out in bold relief. Far beyond the maze of snow-clad peaks we saw in the northwest the mountains of Pherug, in Tibet, while those of Shar Khambu stood gloriously out to the west.

The summit of Kangla chen is a plateau, some 2 miles from east to west, and one mile and a quarter from northwest to northeast; it inclines towards the west, while to the northwest it is bounded by a mountain of considerable height. Our snowshoes (*kyar*) now stood us in good stead; unfortunately we had but three pairs, so Phurchung and I had to wade through the deep snow in the footsteps of the others, with many slips and more than one narrow escape from falling into the deep crevasses. On all sides there was nothing visible but an ocean of snow. Innumerable snowy peaks touched with their white heads the pale leaden skies, where stars were shining. The rattling roar of distant avalanches was frequently heard; but, after having succeeded in crossing the loftiest of snowy passes, I felt too transported with joy to be frightened by their thunder.

These splendid scenes of wonderland, the grandest, the most sublime my eyes have ever beheld, which bewildered me so that even now my pen finds no words to describe them, inspired me with feelings of deep gratitude to Heaven, by whose mercy my life had been spared thus far.

We camped on a rock bare of snow, and passed another miserable night with nothing to drink, and but a couple of dry biscuits to stave off our hunger. To add to my misery, Ugyen was still suffering, and I had to give him half my covering, for he had none of his own; and so, with not even enough room to lie down, we passed the night huddled together, the loads placed on the lower side of the rock so as to prevent our falling off in our sleep.

December 1—'Twas not yet dawn when all were on foot and busy packing up. The track was hardly visible; below our path lay the great glacier, extending for miles, which feeds the Tashirabka river. The snowy sides of the mountains beyond this were furrowed by glacial streams, very noticeable in their varied shades of blue and green, and on the surface of the glacier itself rose huge rounded surfaces, or hummocks, evidently produced by boulders concealed under the ice.

Following carefully in the footsteps of Phurchung, we crossed some six spurs of the Dorjetagh range, and then came to an easy path down the central moraine of a former glacier, now only a huge heap of boulders and debris. The mountains lost, as we advanced, the whitish colour peculiar to the Indian ranges, and assumed the blackish or ochre colour distinctive of the Tibetan region. 'Twas with a feeling of intense relief that we finally discerned vegetation and heard the babbling of a little brook, near which flew birds feeding on rhododendron and juniper berries, and a little way off we saw some herds of yaks grazing, and smoke rising from a campfire. Here we stopped at the foot of a great rock, and enjoyed, after our long fast of two days, a meal of rice and buttered tea.

We continued down the course of the stream, passing with some apprehension near a huge bull-yak or *shalu*, though low stone walls separated us from him and kept him away from the she-yaks (*di*) in the adjacent pasturage. This part of the valley is frequently visited by packs of wolves, which kill large numbers of yaks, but the bulls are able to drive them off with their long sharp horns.

At 3 p.m. we passed Dsongo, the extreme border of the district of Tashi-rabka, and where are the ruins of a stone house built on a huge boulder. This was formerly a stage-house used by the Sikkim Raja's people, when the Yangma and Wallung districts still belonged to him, when going to or returning from Tibet. A little way beyond this point we met some herdsmen, who made inquiries as to whence we came and where we were going. Nearby were their tents, where I noticed two swarthy women and a fierce Tibetan mastiff. Phurchung entered one of the tents, sat down to chat and drink a cup of *tara*, a sort of thin curd.

Ugyen was much preoccupied about our getting by Tashi-rabka and escaping its headman (*Tongzungpa*). At about 6 o'clock we were close to the village, and so we hid till dusk in a gully, where we boiled our tea and ate some *tsamba*. The moon shone out brightly when we resumed our march and passed along a portion of a high stone wall, erected by the Tibetans during the Nepalese war, when, it is said, they put up 5 miles of it in a day under orders of their general, the Shape Shata. This wall is carried across the river on a bridge, where it has eight small watch towers. It crosses the whole valley, its ends being high up on the sides of the mountains. On the farther side of the wall is the village.

Ugyen and Phurchung stood trembling, not knowing whether to turn back towards the Kangla chen pass or to proceed onward towards the *chorten*, near which the headman resides. Phuntso alone was equal to the occasion. 'If the guards are awake, we will sing some of our national Wallung songs, and pass ourselves off for Wallungpa.' After a few words of encouragement to the others, we set out. Before we had reached the *chorten*, a voice from a yak-hair tent cried out, 'Whence are you, and where are you going?' To which Phuntso replied that we were Wallungpa going to Shigatse, asked them where they were going, and without waiting for a reply we hurried on and passed by the dreaded headman's house without awakening anyone, not even the fierce mastiffs tied up in front of the dwelling.

About 30 yards beyond the house we came to the bridge, a rough structure of logs and stone slabs. The Tashi-rabka river was partly frozen, and its swift current was sweeping down blocks of ice. We crossed over unnoticed, and I then broke the silence with thanks to merciful God who had enabled us to overcome this, the most dreaded of all difficulties, one which had frightened my staunch friend Phurchung, that the snows of the Kangla chen had not daunted.

We followed the river in an easterly direction, passing on the way two poor traders (*Gyagar Khamba*) who were going to Wallung to sell a wild sheep (*nao*) they had killed. Then we came to Ri-u, where is a large Nyingma monastery, and 3 miles further on to a bridge over the two branches of the river. 'Twas nearly midnight when we reached a sand-covered hillock called Shara, where we halted for the night, and slept in a sheep-fold, near which two hunters with a hound (*shyakhi*) were also camped.

December 2—At sunrise we resumed our journey, and after an hour's march got sight of the village of Guma Shara, at the foot of a range of mountains trending northwest and southeast. Leaving this village some miles away, we turned a little to the north and made for the Langbu la. There was not a soul to be seen on the vast table-land we were traversing, only a few little birds like swallows twittered on the hillsides by the way, and some kites were soaring in the sky near Guma Shara. We ascended steadily till we came to the foot of the pass, from which point the summit was reached by a zigzag cut in the rocks, the whole surface of which was inscribed with the mystic syllables, *Om mani padme hum*. I became so fatigued before the summit (some 700 feet above the plateau) was reached, that Phuntso had to carry me up; and Ugyen also made the ascent on Phurchung's back, as he was still feeling very badly and was quite unable to keep up with us. From the summit we could see due north, perched on a lofty peak, the Lhakha of Sakya, and to our west were snow-clad peaks of the lofty Pherugh mountains.

On the northern slope of the Langbu we found much drifted sand, and a short distance from the foot of the pass we came to the source of the Ge river, where we met a party of rice-collectors (*dadubpa*) on their way to Tashi-rabka with a dozen yaks and some donkeys, there to buy rice from the Wallung traders. While Phurchung talked to one of them, a former acquaintance, I slipped by without attracting their attention; for had they spoken to me, they would certainly have detected my nationality by my appearance and speech.

Proceeding onward, we met other parties of swarthy Tibetans, in which the women were conspicuous by their headdress (*patug*). Their dirt-covered faces, their white teeth and eyeballs, made them look exceedingly wild. Crossing the rivulet by a bridge made of two stone slabs, the valley broadened as we advanced, till we found ourselves on a plateau several miles broad, where the rivulet turned to the west, to empty probably farther on into the great Arun. Phurchung here pointed out a place where there is a large underground monastery, the chief temple (*tsugla khang*) of which is cut out of the massive rock. There are twenty inmates to this lamasery, and the church furniture and images are said to be of great antiquity.

Fording the little Tibgyu chu, said to rise in the Chabug la, we proceeded in an easterly direction, and passed the little village of Wena, a mile from which stands the village of Chani, where lives the Chyugpo mepang family, or the 'rich men who never reply nay'. When travellers passing by this way have asked the rich men (*chyugpo*) if there was such and such a thing to be had at their place, they have never replied in the negative. One day, in the month of August, a traveller who had heard the story concerning this family came to test its truth, and asked the housewife to give him a piece of ice, when she at once produced a piece from the butter-cask. On another occasion a traveller asked for a chile pepper in February, and the mistress of the house gave it to him at once.

December 3—At about a mile from our camp of last night we came to a rivulet some 15 feet broad, flowing in a northeasterly direction. We selected a shallow part of it, across which Phurchung waded, carrying me on his back. Irrigation ditches led the water of this stream on to the neighbouring barley fields. We stopped towards 7 o'clock at the camp (*dok*) of Pole, situated in the middle of a plain extending from east to west some 10 miles, and bounded to the north by the Arun river. There were several sheep-folds with walls of sun-dried bricks 6 or 7 feet high and 2 feet thick; in the corners of these folds were turret-like houses, in which the shepherds sought shelter from the severity of the weather. Here we hired two yaks for a *tanka* a-piece to carry us to the village of Tebong, about 6 or 7 miles away. This whole plateau was covered with a species of briar, amidst which grew long fine grass, on which cows and *jo* (half-bred yaks) were feeding, and whence innumerable hares and foxes ran, startled by our approach. Midway between Pole and Lebong, but on the mountain side, lies the village of Mug, with some forty families (*mitsang*). Before reaching Tebong, which is the first village this way on Tashilhunpo soil, we crossed the dry bed of the Chorten

Nyima river, forming the boundary, and which I had already passed over on my first journey to Shigatse in 1879. Near here we were overtaken by a violent dust storm, which hid the whole country from our view and forced us for a while to remain motionless.

Once on Tashilhunpo territory, all my fears of being arrested were over, and I walked on to the village of Tanglung with a light heart. An hour's walk brought us to the door of my old acquaintance, Nabu Wanga, who led me with much ceremony into the best room of his home, apologizing for his not being able to lodge me in his chapel, which was filled with carcasses of sheep and goats drying for winter use.

December 4—Our host appeared early in the morning to inquire what we required in the way of food for our journey, and Ugyen gave him a list of articles, comprising mutton, barley-meal (*tsamba*), butter, etc. He also undertook to procure us three ponies, for which I was to pay Rs 4 each as far as Shigatse. While we were breakfasting a number of old acquaintances came in, bringing me presents of *tsamba*, mutton, butter, and *chang*. One man, a doctor (*amchi*), brought a fox-skin cap of ingenious make, which he offered to sell me. It was so contrived that it protected every part of the head, leaving only the eyes and nose exposed, or it could be turned up and used as an ordinary hat.

In the evening Delah Tondub, the head of the militia or village police (*yulmag*), received an order from Khamba djong, which he brought me to decipher. It was to the effect that he must hold himself and force in readiness to proceed at once to the Lachan boundary, fully equipped with matchlocks, lances, swords, slings, etc., in view of the fact that a 'very important European official, deputy of the Lieut. Governor of Bengal, was on his way to the Tibetan frontier. This information was communicated by the frontier guards, in consequence of which necessary precautions were urgently needed.' I told them that the official referred to was probably Captain Harman of the Survey Department, with whom he was acquainted, having met him the year before at Tangu, near Lachan.

December 5—Our arrangements being completed and the ponies at the door, we hastened to finish our breakfast. From the sheep-pen close by the house we saw some fifty sheep led to the slaughtering-place behind the village. The butchers mutter some mantras over each one before killing it, and they receive as their perquisite the heads.

Following the same route I had taken in 1879, we left the village of Mende on our left, and, crossing several frozen streams, we came to the village of Targye, where we stopped in the house of an old man, who invited us to be his guests in the hope of getting some medicine for dyspepsia from which he was suffering. He put us up in his storehouse, amidst his barley, yak-hair bags, farming implements, etc. He had manufactured some rugs, and I bought one from him for a couple of rupees. The villagers, hearing of my purchase, brought me a number of their choicest carpets, but the price asked was larger than I cared to give.

December 6—I learnt with pleasure from my host that the Minister of Temporal Affairs (*Kyab ving*) of Ulterior Tibet (*Tsang*) was Phendi Khangsar, to whom I was well known. My host and his wife came and begged some medicine, and I prepared for him an effervescent draught, which the old man swallowed with much difficulty. 'Oh, sir,' he exclaimed, 'it boiled and foamed even as it ran down my throat; it must be a medicine of wonderful potency! I never took such a drink in my life, nor heard of its like before!' And the spectators all said, in amazement, 'This *amchi* is a miracle-worker (*tulpa*); his medicine boils in cold water.' And so my fame was noised abroad.

Crossing the Yaru la, we made for Kurma, before reaching which place we experienced some difficulty in crossing the broad bed of the frozen river. Near the village we saw in the fields several wild asses (*kyang*), some wild goats (*ragyo*), and wild sheep (*nao*). At Kurma we put up in the house of a doctor, an acquaintance of Phurchung, who had brought him a quantity of medicines the *amchi* had the year past commissioned him to buy at Darjiling. Our supply of meat being exhausted, Ugyen bought a sheep's carcass (*pagra*). When the sheep get very fat, the people, for fear of losing any of the fat by skinning them, roast the whole as they would a pig.

December 7—Leaving Kurma early in the morning, we arrived at Iago by 6 p.m., where we got accommodations in the house of a rich farmer, paying him a *tanka* as room-rent (*nala*). I had been feeling very badly all day, but Phurchung whispered to me to let no one know I was ill, as sick men are not admitted into people's dwellings in this country.

December 8—By 10 a.m. we reached Tamar, in the valley of the Re chu, here thickly dotted with hamlets. Numerous flocks of pigeons and swallows were picking worms and grain in the fields, and Ugyen told me that the pigeons were a serious nuisance to the people, for they are not allowed to kill them, animal life being held sacred.

We passed the foot of the hill on which the Regyinpai lamasery is situated, and by 2 p.m. came to Labrang dokpa; but finding all the houses closed, we continued on to the Nambu la, crossing which we reached the village of Nambu, where we stopped in the house of a friend of Phurchung.

December 9—We arose by 3.30 in the morning, and put on our best clothes, for to-day we were to enter Tashilhunpo. Travellers were more numerous now; we met several parties of traders with yaks and donkeys or laden sheep going to or coming from Shigatse. The day was cold, and there was a light wind blowing. I alternately rode and walked, and though I was by this time greatly reduced in flesh by the hardships I had had to encounter, I was in high spirits at the success which had so far attended me. Not so Ugyen: he was ill, and fretted fearfully, his appearance was repulsive, and his language to the Tang-lung men, whose ponies we rode, was most abusive, but they bore patiently with him. At 9 o'clock we passed through Chuta, and an hour later came to the village of Jong Luguri, where I was most kindly received by my former host of 1879, Lobdon puti. I ate a couple of eggs and drank a few cups of tea; then, reloading our ponies, we paid our bill (*jaltse*) and set out for Tashilhunpo, where we arrived by half-past four entering it by the small western entrance marked by two *chortens*.

II

Residence at Tashilhunpo

We entered the monastery of Tashilhunpo by the little western gate, in front of which stand two *chortens*—one very large with a gilt spire, the other smaller but neatly constructed. I walked along the narrow lane, lined on either side by lofty buildings, with the measured steps and grave demeanour which all wearers of the sacred costume are supposed to have. The rays of the setting sun shone on the gilded spires of the houses and tombs in the monastery, and made a most enchanting picture.

The minister, I learned from his head cook (*Machen*), whom I now met, had gone to Dongtse, his native town, but he had left instructions that I be lodged in the Targod chyi-khang until his return.

Though the news of the absence of my friend Phendi Khangsar somewhat damped my spirits, yet the pleasing thought of having been able for the second time to visit Tashilhunpo was a source of infinite gratification. The Machen opened the padlock which closed the great door of the house, and ushered me in with outstretched hands and greetings of '*Pundib la, chyag-pheb nang*', 'Welcome, Mr Pundit'.

The building was a three-storied one, the ground floor, adjoining which were two stables, being used as a godown. The rooms on the first floor were spacious and neat, but very cold on account of the height of the roof and the absence of sunlight. The third story, though it looked snug, was exposed to the wind, and therefore uninhabitable. The minister's steward (*Nerpa*), coming in while we were looking over the house, recommended the first floor for our residence, as it would be warm in winter, when much air is not desirable. Having made up my mind to occupy it, he had the rooms dusted, and removed some 200 volumes, a pile of printing-blocks, boards, and tables with which the rooms were encumbered; and then, some thickly stuffed cushions having been spread, on which our carpets and rugs were placed, he begged us to be seated. Cups were placed on some small tables before us, and tea was brought from the minister's kitchen and served us by the head cook. A few twisted biscuits, some pieces of mutton and *tsamba* were put before me, and from another teapot tea, of evidently an inferior quality, was served to my companions.

The Nerpa told me that we were to be lodged here by the minister's order, but if we did not like the place we might write to him on the subject, and he would have the letter forwarded to Dongtse. The remoteness of the house, with only that of the minister near it, and, above all, its location near the western gate, gave it peculiar advantages, which appeared to me very essential for my purposes, and we had every reason to be delighted at the forethought of our patron, who had shown himself so anxious about our safe arrival and comfort.

When the Nerpa and Machen had left us, I consulted with Ugyen about making presents to the servants of the minister and to our former acquaintances. Money, being very scarce in Tibet, is valued above all things, so that for the renewal of our former acquaintance we could do nothing better than to make presents of silver coin and scarves (*khatag*).

Later on in the evening we returned the visits of the steward and his comrades, and presented them with rupees, eight-anna or four-anna pieces, according to the importance of their respective offices. With difficulty we persuaded them to accept the presents, for they feared lest the minister might be vexed at their taking money from me.

December 10—Ugyen and Phurchung were up by daylight, arranging things and buying firewood and other necessaries. Shortly after I had arisen the men we had hired at Tang-lung to lead our ponies came in for their rewards. I gave each of them six *tankas*, and some twisted biscuits to carry home to their children, all of which pleased them greatly. It felt strange to me not to have a day's journey before me, so accustomed had I become to daily travel, instead of which I could sit peacefully reclining on my cushions on the balcony, lighted up by the rays of the morning sun. Phurchung was the only servant I now had to attend on both myself and Ugyen, so it was decided to hire a man to help him in fetching water and in blowing the bellows. We had to wait till the Shigatse market (*tom*) opened at 11 o'clock before we could get any breakfast, for our provisions were exhausted. Both Ugyen and Phurchung went to the market, from which they shortly returned with butter, salt, mutton, *tsamba*, *phing* and a few Chinese cakes for me. They had been surrounded on the way by two parties of beggars (*Rogyaba*), who, recognizing Ugyen as a new arrival from Sikkim, had by alternate threats and solicitations succeeded in squeezing from him several silver pieces. They had also seen an altercation between a woman selling salt and some Khamba traders. One of the latter had bought several seers of salt from the woman, and had offered her a debased *tanka* in payment, which she had refused. The Khamba would not return the salt or pay in better coin; he called six or seven of his friends to him, threw the salt on the ground, and wanted to beat the woman, whom there was no police to protect. It ended by the savage Khamba walking off unmolested, and the poor woman losing her salt. Ugyen was greatly surprised at the lawlessness of the people in the market, their violence towards the helpless, and the absence of police supervision. I smiled at his fears, and told him to take a hearty breakfast. In the evening I called at the Phuntso Khangsar, and learnt from the steward that Kusho Tung-chen, the minister's secretary, would be back on the following afternoon.

December 11—My breakfast consisted of a cup of broth (*tugpa*), with *tsamba*, radishes, marrow, and minced mutton, a little salt and some dried cheese (*chura*) in it. When it was over Ugyen and Phurchung went to market, and on the way they met Choi-tashi, a Mongol monk, whom I had once helped at Darjiling with food and money. The faithful Mongol had not forgotten my kindness: as soon as he saw Ugyen he threw his arms around him and led him to his home in the lamasery. Ugyen learnt from him of the whereabouts of some of my old acquaintances—Lobzang Tanzing and other Mongol friends. Lobzang had failed to pass his final examination for admission into the monastery, in which it is required of candidates to repeat without a single omission or mistake 120 pages of selected sacred texts, so he had been deprived of subsistence allowances, and had seen his name struck off the roll of monks. He had in consequence left Tashilhunpo four months before my arrival for his native land, proposing to visit Lhasa on the way.

In the market Ugyen met another old acquaintance, the Chinese head of the Shigatse police, who invited him into his house, where his mistress (*ani*) served them *chang* and a dish of vermicelli (*jya tug*). Then the Chinaman told Ugyen of the recent row in which the junior Amban had been involved, and of his own incredibly swift ride to Lhasa to carry dispatches to the senior Amban. As the senior Amban, together with the Shape Sa-wang rampa and Lhalu, had come to Shigatse to settle the trouble, the head constable claimed for himself no small share in the successful termination of the affair. It was also said that the Shape, together with the Amban, had decided to enforce the circulation of every kind of silver coin, no matter how debased. The distinction made in the Shigatse market between good and bad coin was considered to be productive of much inconvenience to trade, and so they had forbidden it. The same order had been recently enforced at Lhasa, to the great convenience and satisfaction of the people. Secret orders were issued to arrest the few respectable monied men who might offer objections to the enforced circulation of debased coin, by which means all trouble in the matter, it was hoped, would be averted. In consequence of this Ugyen took care not to get into trouble by changing our Indian coins for Tibetan *tanka*, by exchanging them in the monastery itself.

In the marketplace my men saw several parties of prisoners loaded with chains weighing 20 pounds and upwards. Some had their hands manacled, others their arms passed through blocks of wood, not a few had their eyes put out. The Government does not provide these miserable wretches with food, but lets them beg their sustenance in the marketplace. They are more troublesome than even the Ragyabas, and pour out curses and vile abuse on all who do not at once give them alms. At 4 p.m. I was told that the minister's secretary, the Kusho Tung-chen, had arrived, and wanted to see me; so I dressed myself in my lama costume, and, accompanied by Ugyen carrying a few coins and some *khatag*, I went to the Phuntso Khangsar.

Being conducted into his presence, I presented him with a scarf and a couple of rupees, and Ugyen did the same. We were then given fine *khatag*, and asked, with an air of genuine cordiality and kindness which greatly pleased me, to be seated beside him. A stuffed raised seat, covered with a Chinese rug, was given me, and a small table placed before me. Ugyen occupied a lower seat, and the table given him was also lower than mine, to show the difference of rank between us. Plates of dried and boiled mutton, together with bowls of *tsamba*, were served us. An attendant then brought from the minister's shelves handsome china cups, and, filling them with tea, asked me to drink with '*Pundib la, sol-ja-*

she' ('Please drink, Mr Pundit'), at which I drank about a third of the contents; for it is customary in Tibet not to drink more than this at first, while to drink less would be a reflection on the cook or the host. After a short conversation of no importance I returned to my dwelling.

December 12—The secretary sent to inform us that he would be despatching a messenger to Dongtse in the evening, and that if we had any letters to send they should be ready before noon. We at once applied ourselves to drafting a letter to the minister, which was no easy matter, as the form of the paper, the margin to be left at the top and bottom of the sheet, and the choice of complimentary words at the beginning, had all to be carefully weighed. We tried to convey to the minister how sorry we were in not having had the honour and pleasure of meeting him at Tashilhunpo, and how thankful we felt to him for his great kindness in arranging for our comfort and accommodation. We begged him, if possible, to return to the capital for the good of all living beings, and particularly for ourselves, who depended solely on his mercy for the security of our lives. We also told him that the lithographic press he had ordered me on my first visit to buy for him in India had arrived at Lachan, where it was held by the prefect of Khamba djong. Ugyen wrote a separate letter to the minister, and then we took them to the secretary, who added a few lines to our notes, asking his master to vouchsafe his sacred protection and mercy to us who had come so far and had encountered such incredible hardships and dangers.

Returning home, I found Lupa gyantsaan, a former acquaintance, awaiting me. He presented me some provisions and other things, and offered his services to buy what I might require, and see that I was not cheated. He also agreed to send me a good servant.

In the evening I called on another old friend, a most respectable man, Kusho Dechang. He was delighted to see me. Rising from his cushion, he begged me come in, saying, '*Chyag-pheb-nang-chig.*' The steward (*solpon*) then served tea, replenishing my cup from a silver teapot (*chambim*) as soon as it was about a third empty. Kusho Dechang then questioned me concerning the present condition of affairs in Aryavarta (India), and about its government under the *Frang* (Europeans). The conversation then turned on the recent row with the Chinese and its settlement, reached to-day.

The two Chinese Residents at Lhasa inspect each year in turn the Nepal-Tibet frontier, in order to ascertain the discipline of the garrison at Tingri and the state of the defences and military resources of the several frontier posts. As the task is a most tedious and fatiguing one, owing to the desert-like condition of the country, the Ambans draw lots to find out who is to go on the inspection tour. In the latter part of October of this year it fell to the junior Amban's lot to visit Tingri djong and Shigatse. He started accordingly, accompanied by an experienced Tibetan civil officer with the rank of Tsipon (accountant), who was to arrange, as usual, for the transportation of the Amban and his retinue by sending messengers (*ngondo*) ahead to the different stations along the road. The Amban decided to follow the northern road (*chang lam*) via Toilung Tsorphu.

Now, according to pre-established custom, the Tibetan treasury has to pay the Amban a daily travelling allowance of four *doche*, or Rs 500; but the Government of Lhasa, instead of paying it out of the Government treasury, raises it from the people at the time of the Amban's journey and along his route. The obligation of raising the Amban's allowance then devolved on the Tsipon Kong chyanglochan. On arriving at Shigatse, the Amban demanded six *doches*, or Rs 750, instead of four. The Tsipon notified the people (*misser*) between Shigatse and Tingri, and when they refused to give this amount, the headmen (*tsog-pon*) were flogged, and their ponies and property sold to make up the amount.

Returning to Shigatse on his way back to Lhasa, the Amban stopped there several days, during which he insisted on a daily allowance of Rs 750, which, the people protesting they could not pay, the Chinese soldiery, by various oppressive means, tried to squeeze out of them. The Tsipon tried to resign his commission, and then the Amban visited his anger on him. In the meantime the people combined in a body to resist the exaction, and, with the connivance of the two prefects (*Djongpon*) of Shigatse, openly refused payment of the Amban's unjust demands. The Amban, furious, ordered his Chinese soldiers to arrest the *Djongpon* and put the Tsipon in irons; but the former fled, and the soldiery were stoned by the mob. The next day the Tsipon was tied to a pillar of the Amban's house and flogged. After he had received some fifteen cuts, volleys of stones were thrown, and the Amban severely hurt before he could escape into the house, and he was only saved from the infuriated populace by the prompt arrival of the Tibetan general (*Dah-pon*) with the troops under his command. Then it was that a messenger was sent post-haste to Lhasa, and the senior Amban, the ministers (Shape) Rampa and Lhalu having arrived, formed, with the temporal minister of the Tashi lama (*Kyab-dvang chenpo*) and the paymaster of the forces, a commission to investigate the matter.

Their judgment in the case was made known on the 12th. It bore that the two Djongpon of Shigatse should be degraded from the third to the fourth class of Chinese official rank, losing also their position as Djongpon for that of Djongnyer under new Djongpon; and that, furthermore, each of them should receive two hundred blows with the bamboo. The village headmen (*tsogpon*) were to receive four hundred blows with the bamboo, and be imprisoned for two months in the jails of Re and Khamba djong. Eight elders (*gampo*) were to receive fifty blows of the bamboo, and wear the cangue for six months.

As to the junior Amban, it being proven that he had attempted to extort more than his allowance from the people, the Commissioners decided to petition the Court of Peking no longer to allow the payment by the Tibetan people of the Chinese travelling allowance (*jya-tal*) in such cases, only supplying the usual travelling facilities. To obtain this concession, it is said that two Lhasa Shape paid the Amban fifteen *doche*, or Rs 1,875.

Dechang then inquired what medicines I had brought, as he was suffering from a cold and cough, and I promised to give him some later on. Then, pouring the contents of my cup into the slop-bowl (*shalu*), as a sign of taking leave, I arose and went home.

December 13—To-day some 15,000 persons assembled at noon in the marketplace to see the arrival of the Kashmir Envoy with his guards and escort in military dress. All the alleys of Shigatse, the courtyard of Kesar Lha-khang, and the adjacent gardens were filled with people all eagerly waiting for the *temo* (sight). There was the Envoy of the Maharaja with some fifty sowars, all in uniform, besides a hundred mounted followers of various nationalities, some Sikhs, some Mohammedans with flowing beards and white turbans, Ladakis in clumsy lambskin dresses, Murmis from Nepal, Dokpas from Chang, a few Nepalese, and some Tibetans from Kirong. There were also with the Envoy a number of merchants dressed in princely style, and attended by servants in liveries of silk and broadcloth. Some of their ponies were also richly caparisoned with ornaments of silver and brocade of gold. The Kashmir Government, I learnt, sends an envoy to Lhasa every three years with presents (called tribute) to the Grand Lama. The Tibetan Government, on receiving notice of the proposed setting out of the mission, has relays (*ta-u*) of ponies and mules about 500 head, and also coolies, prepared at all the towns and post-stations along the road from the Ladak frontier to Lhasa. Although so large a number of ponies and men is hardly necessary for the Envoy, who only brings presents of precious things of little bulk, the party avails itself of the privilege for the carriage of personal property and merchandise to and from Lhasa.

As the mission passed by, we heard the people remark that all this splendour and ostentation was at the expense of the Government of Lhasa, and to the ruin of the poor people of Tibet.

The origin of this tribute from Kashmir to Lhasa is as follows: After the conquest of Ladak, Balti, and Skardo, Zorwar Sing, the famous Sikh general of Maharaja Golab Sing, turned his arms against Rudok and Gar in the year 1840-41. These two provinces, which produce the finest wool of Tibet, and contain the wealthiest and most sacred of its monasteries, were held by the great Buddhist ruler of Tibet as his most valued possessions, and the Sikh general, by attempting their conquest, excited the wrath of the Lhasa Government, who, applying to their suzerain, the Emperor of China, was able to put more than 10,000 men in the field. Zorwar Sing, with some 5,000 men, invaded these two provinces, and the governor (*garpon*) fled to the Chang tang, leaving the fort and the whole country at the mercy of the enemy. The general established himself near the sacred lake Mapham (Manasarowar), and sent detachments all over the country to pillage and spread desecration in the holiest of Buddhist sanctuaries at Mapham and Kailas; and one body of troops he posted at Purang, near the Nepal frontier, to watch the Lhasa forces. The combined forces of Lhasa and China now marched on Rudok under the leadership of one of the Shape; and Zorwar Sing, whose contempt for the Tibetan soldiery was great, and who underrated the strength of the forces opposed to him, sent some small detachments of his troops to oppose their advance. These were cut to pieces, when he himself, at the head of his troops, advanced to encounter the Lhasa forces. The two armies fought for two days and nights without any decisive result, but on the third day the Sikh general fell, and victory declared itself for the lamas. The defeat was complete, and the number of slain on both sides immense. The victorious troops now threatened Ladak, and the Maharaja sued for peace. A treaty was concluded by the agent of Golab Sing and the Government of Lhasa, of which one of the terms was the payment of a triennial tribute.

Talking with the Kusho Tung-chen of the severity of the punishment inflicted yesterday on the Djongpon of Shigatse and the circle headmen (*tsog-pon*), he told me that, besides those mentioned above, the Djongpon had had the flesh and skin stripped off their hands. The *tsog-pon* had offered to pay the mandarin Rs 2,000 apiece to escape the 400 blows of the bamboo, but the Chinese had been inexorable.

December 14—The Tung-chen sent me one of his acquaintances, Norpu Tondub, a Donyer of Dongtse, with a request that I would let him have some medicine, as he was suffering from dyspepsia. At first I refused, as I had but very few drugs with me, and only in quantity sufficient for myself; but, the Tung-chen insisting, I took my medicine-chest with me to his house. Lifting up the lid, I displayed the various bottles with their sparkling contents, the secretary, his friends, and the servants all looking on with amazement, while Norpu Tondub, at the very sight of the bottles, seemed to become certain of recovery, and said he would pay as much money as I might ask. I replied that even then I could not let him have any medicine, as no amount of money could get me a fresh supply of drugs from India once these finished, for the passes were all closed by the Tibetan Government. At this the Tung-chen looked anxious, so I opened one of the bottles and called for a china cup, and three or four persons ran to the kitchen and brought me half a dozen large and small ones. I weighed the medicine in my brass balance; the drams and scruples, which glittered like gold coins, perplexed them much, as they thought I was a miracle-worker who used gold coins for weights. I now told them that the two medicines when mixed would boil. The very announcement of this filled the spectators with mute amazement, and made the patient tremble with fear; he looked at the Tung-chen and then to heaven with anxiety, evidently repenting him for having pressed me for medicine, and seemed anxious to escape from my hands. The secretary, too, looked aghast; but the medicines were mixed, and to his mind they were too valuable to be thrown away so, having examined if the two mixtures were hot, and finding that they were not, he encouraged the patient, saying that I was a great physician, and he had no cause to apprehend danger from my hands. I told the patient that he could depend on me that I was not going to administer poison to him, and to be ready to take the draught as soon as it frothed up. All waited with eager expectation to see the phenomenon, when lo! the mixture foamed with a hissing noise, which made the patient shrink back. I told him to dip his finger in the boiling mixture; and when he found it cold he uttered the mystic sentence, *'Om mani padme hum'* and swallowed it, and said it was agreeable and refreshing, he then drew from the breast of his gown a *khatag* and a few coins, and offered them to me, laying the scarf on the ground before me. 'Great physician,' he said, 'accept this little token of my gratitude, though it is not worthy of your acceptance. Considering, however, that you are a pious man to whom money is of no value, I venture to hope you will accept it.' I declined the money, but at the request of the Tung-chen accepted the scarf. With looks of open-mouthed astonishment and feelings of endless admiration for the marvellous properties of the medicine and for the wonderful *amchi* (physician) who disdained money, the little circle of spectators returned to their houses and work.

    The punishment of the Djongpon had filled the people with fear of the Chinese. They apprehended new insults at the hands of the Chinese swaggering about the streets of Shigatse. People who had come to the market from a distance to sell their goods were packing them up to hurry off home. No provisions could be had, no purchases could be made. Ugyen met some grain-dealers whom he knew, and begged them to sell him some rice, but none would acknowledge even that they had any for sale. An old woman who had sold us rice on our first visit here said, 'Do not talk of rice before the Chinese and their friends, for they will come and take what I have away and throw some bad coins in my cloth. Come in an hour or two, when the rascals have gone away, and I will let you have what you want.' On one side of the marketplace is a large *zakhang*, or restaurant, where Phurchung and Ugyen went to appease their hunger. While they were busy with their chopsticks the proprietor came in. He was a nobleman of Tashilhunpo, head of the Tondub Khangsar family, and held the office of Chyangjob of the Tashi lama. He asked Ugyen whence he had come, where he had put up, and what merchandise (*chong*) he had for sale. The lady, under whose immediate supervision this establishment is, is no less a personage than the wife of this dignitary. Her manners were gentle and dignified, and she spoke in a sweet and polite manner. Her headdress was covered with innumerable strings of pearls, worth certainly not less than Rs 3,000), and besides these there were on it coral beads, rubies, turquoises, and other precious stones. Although she belongs to one of the richest and noblest families in Tsang (Ulterior Tibet), besides being connected with the family from which the Tashi lama has sprung, yet she does not feel it beneath her dignity to keep the accounts of the inn and superintend the work of the servants.

December 15—To-day was the twenty-fifth of the tenth Tibetan moon, and one of the greatest holidays of the Gelugpa Church, being the anniversary of the death of Tsongkhapa. It is known as *Gadan namchoi*. In every chapel new *torma* of *tsamba* take the place of the old ones, which are now thrown away.

Late in the afternoon the Mongol monk Lobzang Tanzing, to whom I have previously referred, came to pay me his respects, and presented me a long *khatag* and the carcass of a large sheep. He had only a few days before been released from a two-month's imprisonment, under suspicion of being implicated in a case of forgery, and had been repeatedly flogged. His tutor had been sentenced to three years of imprisonment, and had been sent to the prison of Khamba djong.

In the evening the monks of Tashilhunpo busied themselves illuminating their chapels. Hundreds of butter-lamps were tastefully placed in rows on the roof of every building in the lamasery. The Government supplies butter to every house in the town and to every resident monk, to enable them to contribute towards the illumination. From the roof of my house I saw the illuminations to great advantage. The fantastic roofs of the four tombs (*gyophig*) of the Tashi lamas were beautifully lit up. The mitre-shaped spires, the upturned eaves of the temple looked most gorgeous, and resembled the illuminated tajiahs in a mohurum procession in India. The great monastery of Tashilhunpo, situated as it is at the foot of a hill, presented a magnificent appearance. For an hour the illumination was beautiful, but towards 7.30 p.m. the wind began to blow a gale, and had soon extinguished all the lights and driven me into my house shivering with cold.

One of the newly incarnated lamas of Tashilhunpo, who had just arrived from the province of Tu-kham, in Eastern Tibet, took advantage of to-day being a holiday to get himself admitted into the tu-kham tsan order of monks. He invited the Panchen from Kun-khyab ling, and presented to 3,800 monks a *tanka* each, making also large presents to the Grand Lama, his court, and the College of Incarnate Lamas. At about 8 a.m. his holiness, the Panchen, arrived, and was received with due honours by the monks and State officials. The road for about 300 yards was lined with red broadcloth and banners. Some old lamas stood in a profoundly reverential attitude on either side of the road, bearing divers sacred objects to receive the Panchen's *chyag-wang* (blessing). Chinese trumpets, melodious flutes (*gyaling*), and great resounding horns (*dung ch'en*) sounded in his honour. He took his seat on an altar in the grand hall of worship (*Tso khang*), to preside over the inaugural ceremonies. By 10 o'clock the ceremony was over, and we saw the monks returning cheerfully to their cells, each bearing a large flat cake, sticks of candy, and strings of beads. The new incarnation, now admitted as a novice in Tashilhunpo, had gone through the usual course of moral discipline and study like any other monk. Within a year from the date of admission, every monk is required to pass an examination in selections from the sacred books, of which he must repeat from memory, and without a single mistake, 125 leaves. Candidates coming from outside Tibet are generally allowed three years to prepare for their final admission, which gives them the privileges of a resident monk, with an allowance of food. Any one failing to pass the final examination forfeits his rights to residence and his allowances. Once admitted, the monk may rise, by dint of industry and study, to the various degrees of lamahood.

At noon there was a large crowd between Tashilhunpo and the Shigatse *djong* (fort)—men and women in holiday dress, monks from the lamaseries, and not a few Chinese—to witness the annual rope-dancing. A long rope was stretched from the top of the fort to the foot of the lower castle bridge, a distance of 300 feet or more. Then an athlete appeared, a white *khatag* tied around his neck, and took his place at the upper end of the rope. With his face turned upwards, he invoked the gods; then, looking downwards, he invoked the nagas of the nether world, raising his voice to its highest pitch, and at times shrieking in a terrific manner. Then he scattered flour on all sides, and sang a snatch of a song, to which someone in the crowd sang out a laughable reply. He then let himself slide down the rope, exchanging jokes thrice with the crowd on his way down, and finishing with a shriek.

Phurchung and Ugyen, whom I had sent out to buy books for me, returned towards 2 o'clock with a quantity, and later on, while I was sitting making my choice of volumes, the bookseller's son came in to carry back those I did not require. I had a talk with him about different books, and he gave me some very interesting information.

I engaged also, to-day, a new cook in place of Phurchung, whom I proposed sending to Khamba *djong* to arrange for the conveyance from the Lachan barrier to Khamba of the lithographic press bought for the minister.

December 16—Getting up from bed at 7 a.m., I spread two mattresses on the third floor, opened the shutters, and, while basking in the sun and sipping tea placed on a little table before me, began to turn over the leaves of one of my newly purchased volumes. The residents of the neighbouring houses peeped out from their windows to observe my manners and habits. Henceforth I was careful to conduct myself like a good *gelong* (priest). Reading attentively, writing and making notes was the chief occupation of my days. It was not my habit to chant mantras, or hymns, or say my beads, for in the former practice I was never proficient, and with my beads I could only separate one bead from another without any knowledge of the prayers meant to accompany that mechanical action.

The new cook has proved no improvement on Phurchung; he is a sloven, and though I promised him a reward for cleanliness, he neither washed his face nor cleaned his teeth, and always smelled most offensively. Finally I got Phurchung to make him wash his clothes and face. Our breakfast usually consisted of a few pieces of bread, tea, and one or two cups of a thin paste made of boiled *tsamba*, mutton, and dried milk called *yatug*. In the evening I met the Tung-chen, the minister's secretary, and talked to him about getting the lithographic press here. Two of his friends were sitting with him, one of them engaged in munching a piece of boiled mutton. He told me that the Tung-chen had toothache, caused by worms in the root of a tooth, and could only eat hashed or pounded meat. The secretary showed me the cavities made, he said, by thread-shaped worms (*ringpa*). He had killed several, he added, by inserting red-hot pins in the cavities.

December 17—A messenger arrived from Dongtse with a letter from the minister asking Ugyen and me to come to Dongtse, a distance of about 40 miles, which town he was unable to leave, for various reasons, for some time to come. Before leaving I was anxious to start off Phurchung for Khamba *djong*, and also to get winter clothes for myself, as the cold was getting keener every day. Our house, like all houses in Tibet, had no chimney, and as the ceiling was covered with fine Chinese satin, dung-fuel was most objectionable, so I had charcoal burnt in the room in nicely made earthen stoves (*jalang*), paying about a rupee four annas a maund.

At about noon a great procession arrived from Dechan Phodang to pay homage before the image of the Emperor of China kept in the monastery. From the roof of the minister's house I commanded an excellent view of the southern and western quarters of the town. The Tung-chen told me that to-day was a Chinese holiday, the anniversary of their present Emperor's accession to the throne, when all Chinese and subjects of the Emperor are required to offer him homage and to pray to Heaven for his long life and prosperity. Within the monastery there exists an image of the Emperor of China, probably Chien-lung, to pay reverence to which the procession I now saw, headed by the Lhasa Shape, the Ambans, the Shape Bora of Tsang, was advancing. Flag-bearers and a mounted troop came first, then Tibetan officials, in their best apparel of brocaded satin (*kinkab*), painted with the dragon of the Tartars, and Chinese satins of various colours and patterns, riding on richly caparisoned ponies, were marching slowly and solemnly towards the western gate of the monastery. The Chinese were conspicuous by their pigtails and petticoats, and, though very well dressed, were all black and of villainous appearance, greatly contrasting with the respectable Tibetan gentry, which forced me to think that they were all recruited from low-class people from

Western China; and the Tung-chen told me that these men were noted in Tibet for their dissipated and licentious habits.

Some men carried boards about 2 feet square, on which were written the Amban's titles and his commission to supreme authority over the whole of Tibet. Some of these inscriptions were in Chinese, and were carried by Chinamen; others, in the Tibetan language, were carried by Tibetans. The Shape also rode, their advance heralded by two men who warned passers-by to keep out of the way. Each was escorted by three mounted men, one on either side of him, and one marching in front, keeping off the crowd with whips, which they freely used, while two grooms ran behind holding his horse's tail. There were about 300 dignitaries and gentlemen of the provinces of U and Tsang, besides the followers and retainers of the Ambans. The Ambans' sedan chairs were carried by eight Chinese soldiers to each, and some fifty Tibetan soldiers helped to drag them with long cords attached to the bars of the chairs. After paying homage at the sacred chapels and tombs of the departed saints, the procession came out of the monastery by the eastern gate, and, headed by the Shape Bora, marched across the marketplace towards Kun-khyab ling. First came the officers of state, then followed the paymaster's (*Pogpon*) party, then the Chinese officials, followed by the chief Amban in his state chair. The flags, carried in tasteful array, were all of China silk, those at the point of the lances of the guard being of brocade, and inscribed in Chinese and Tibetan. Throughout the march the Tibetans occupied a subordinate position, and the Chinese displayed their superiority in every possible way. Though the crowd had reason to fear a whipping from the Chinese, who ran on all sides, they did not suffer from the Amban's guard. The junior Amban, as he followed on horseback, seemed pleased to see the heavily chained prisoners, the recently punished headmen groaning under the weight of their cangues. His sedan chair was carried by the same number of soldiers as that of the senior

Amban, and his retinue and followers resembled his. Then came the other Shape with their respective retinues. The guards were all armed with Chinese matchlocks and long spears. Following them came the captains and lieutenants of the army, with a hundred men; and behind these marched the yellow and black turbaned officers of Labrang and the Djong. The Ambans were received by his Holiness, the Panchen, with due honours, and they paid him the reverence due to his exalted position and holy character.

In the evening I saw the Tung-chen, who gave me a very valuable manuscript entitled *Dsamling gyeshe*, or 'General account of the world'. I carried it off with me to my house to read.

December 18—The Tung-chen sent one of his storekeepers, Tsering-tashi by name, to Tondub Khangsar to get a passport (*lam-yig*) to enable me to send Phurchung to Khamba *djong* and Lachan, to bring here our heavy luggage. The tailor came at 7 o'clock this morning to begin work on my winter clothes. We kept ready for him a kettle of tea on an earthen stove. A cup, a few pieces of boiled mutton, and a wooden bowl filled with *tsamba* remained all the time before him, and he drank some tea every hour or so, making also three meals a day. His breakfast consisted of mutton, *tsamba*, and tea; at noon we gave him a dish of rice and mutton curry, *tsamba*, and tea; and at 6 o'clock he ate a few balls of *tsamba*, put on his yellow turban (*bakto*), and, making a low bow, walked off towards his home at Tashi-gyantsa. I was much pleased with his steady work, which had earned for him the proud title of Uje chenpo, or 'head craftsman', and secured for him a-*tanka*-a-day wages, exclusive of food.

December 19—Tsering-tashi was despatched again after the passport. The delay in securing it was occasioned by the Tung-chen not having tipped the clerks and officials who had charge of the matter. The senior Amban started to-day for Lhasa via Gyantse and Nangartse *djong*. All the ponies of Shigatse had been requisitioned to supply his numerous retinue with riding and pack animals, so the junior Amban and the Shape could not get off for want of *ula*, and the local authorities of Gyantse were ordered to supply what they could to them as soon as the senior Amban reached their place. In the meanwhile the Chinese were strolling about the Shigatse market, carrying off the best of everything, paying nothing, or only a nominal price for the things they took. People coming into town saw their ponies seized by the *ta-u* officers for the Amban's service, and started off with loads to Gyantse. My men could buy nothing, for most of the people had packed up their wares and fled; but they managed to purchase some mutton and rice inside the monastery, and we found out that good things could be had there at comparatively moderate prices.

December 20—I passed most of my day reading a collection of hymns, the composition of the second Dalai lama, which I had bought from a Lhasan bookseller. To-day there arrived five men from Gyantse, whose advent was at once detected by the Rogyabas, for these pests are always on the lookout for newcomers, whom they at once surround with clamorous solicitations for alms. Few can escape from their hands without paying them something. As soon as the Rogyabas saw these Gyantse men, they informed all the fraternity of the new prey, on which vulture-like they pounced. Well do they deserve their name, which means 'corpse-vultures', though, to speak the truth, they prey on the living. These Gyantse men brought news about the orders issued by the Lhasa Government stopping the egress and ingress of all traders at the frontier passes. The two Djongpon of Phagri were busy executing these orders; no one, it was said, had eluded their vigilance and reached Darjiling. Even some Bhutanese traders on their way to Lhasa were stopped at Phagri; but another party of these people had started out, in defiance of the Djongpon, for Lhasa. The Bhutan Government resented such unusual interference on the part of the Tibetans in a trade which had been carried on from ancient times.

December 21—To-day is the new moon (*nam-gang*, or 'full night'), one of the holiest days of the month. The conch-shells called loudly the lamas to prayers. From break of day to an hour after sunset large numbers of men and women circumambulated the monastery, some carrying strings of beads, others prayer-wheels. Early in the morning the Nepalese, beating cymbals and chanting Sanskrit mantras, walked around the great monastery.

Towards 10 o'clock my attention was attracted by an unusual scene to the east of the monastery, where the entire space between the great *mendong* of the marketplace and the eastern gateway of Tashilhunpo was filled with beggars, both men and women. Among them were people from Amdo and Khams, whose eyes had been put out for crimes such as murdering lamas; some were cripples and walked with crutches, some in heavy chains and drawn on wheelbarrows, some maimed, others deaf and dumb, others, again, still bearing traces of the torture to which they had been subjected—a vast concourse of misery and pain. In their midst stood the well-known Lhagpa-tsering distributing alms, an anna to each one. For ten years past he had done thus on the first of every moon. The circumstances which led this worthy man to undertake giving alms to the indigent is very remarkable and instructive.

Lhagpa-tsering had been a silversmith, and had by patient work amassed such wealth that he established himself as a jeweller and banker. His business prospered; in his shop were all kinds of goods—fine china, besides pearls, coral, turquoises, and jade; and here came all the great men of the country. He became noted also for his munificent gifts to the lamasery of Tashilhunpo. Some ten years ago there lived at Shang a saintly lama called Chyabtam lama; the purity of his life and his vast learning had made him an object of worship for all classes of people in Tsang. The jeweller Lhagpa, believing that if he made offering to so holy a personage his profits in trade would increase a hundred-fold, went to Shang and offered the lama Rs 1,250, besides numerous objects of value. The saint refused them all, telling him that they represented dishonest earnings, and were the property of a dishonest man. 'In a previous existence you were a great sinner, and in your next you will be a crocodile.'

On the following morning Lhagpa, filled with horror at his impending fate, came and begged the sage to tell him how he might avert the horrible punishment—what acts of charity, what good deeds would save him; but the lama made no reply. Again the next day he came, and the saint looked in his magic mirror, and said, 'If henceforth you give alms to the poor and helpless, of whatever station, creed, or country they may be, on every new moon throughout the year till your death, you will surely get immense wealth, as well as escape from rebirth as a crocodile. There are no other means to save you;' and he sent Lhagpa away without accepting his gifts. Since then he has been in the habit of distributing alms on the first day of the moon. His example has produced a wholesome influence on the merchants of Khams, who now show some hesitation in cheating. A trader, when he cheats others, thinks, as a general rule, if he is a Buddhist that the amount thus gained was due to him in a previous existence. This is a dangerous principle.

Close to the cemetery of Shigatse, called Kega tsal, is the Chinese graveyard, where there are about 300 tombs of varying size and very rude construction. At a short distance from this is the parade-ground, about half a mile square, called Jah-hu-tang, and touching it a walled enclosure, used for target practice with bow and gun, in the centre of which is a large house used by the Ambans. On the sides are high towers for the drum-beaters and trumpet-blowers. The headmen of the whole country had assembled here to-day to muster the porters and pack-ponies required by the junior Amban and the Tibetan officials returning to Lhasa. Three hundred ponies were ready, and it was decided that one man should accompany each horse. Orders had been given by the Amban to requisition all the ponies in the province, no matter whether they belonged to subjects, traders, or pilgrims.

December 22—To-day, at 9 a.m., the junior Amban, with a retinue of 300 men on horseback, left for Lhasa. The owners of the relay ponies followed them on foot, keeping pace with the ponies, or if they lagged behind they were whipped by the men on horseback; so that some dropped out and disappeared, abandoning their property to the Chinese rather than undergo their ill treatment. Of the six village headmen exiled to Re and Khamba *djong* for their share in the recent trouble, I learnt to-day that one had died on the road, and another is hanging between life and death.

December 23—To-day the Shape Lhalu and 100 followers, all on horseback, left for Lhasa. The ponies and the men who have to accompany them on the *ula* are treated with great hardship. They have to carry their food with them, as well as provender for their beasts. In the present case they had received but short notice, and are ill prepared for the long journey. This forced service is, however, patiently borne by the people, as it is a recognized custom of the country.

The market to-day received a large supply of pottery from the village of Tanag and Lholing, on the Tsang-po, a few miles northwest of Shigatse. In these localities excellent potter's clay is obtainable, and the people carry on a profitable trade in earthenware with the surrounding districts. The Tanag pottery has not only an extensive sale in Tibet, but in the cis-Himalayan countries as well, where most utensils are of untinned copper, and the Sikkim and Darjiling people use them exclusively in preference to the earthenware made by the Nepalese inhabiting the Lower Himalayas. The Tanag earthenware is carried to the banks of the Tsang-po on donkeys, and there transferred to hide-boats (*kodru*), in which it is brought down to the Patama ferry, about 4 miles to the northeast of Shigatse. The Patama dealers, who, by the way, raise fine crops on the alluvial soil along the river banks, and make a good deal of money by fishing and ferrying, carry the earthenware to Shigatse on donkeys that jog slowly along the road to the jingle of big bells fastened around their necks. The Lholing pottery is brought to Shigatse via Tanag; this locality manufactures very large vessels for keeping wine or water in, and so heavy that two men can hardly lift them. The Tanag pottery is so highly glazed that it compares favourably with the Chinese and European earthenware sold in the Calcutta shops.

There were on the marketplace many wildly dressed Dokpas of the Chang province. The women wore such heavy and fantastic apparel that one who had not before seen them might well be taken aback. From a distance these savages looked as if they wished to imitate the peacock's gaudy plumes in their costume; they had so many beads of glass, coral, amber, and turquoise suspended from their headdress that one could hardly see their faces.

To-day the tailor finished our winter suits, consisting of a Chinese coat (*kwa-tse*) and trousers (*pishu*). The lambskin lining in all the suits was quite neatly sewed. I was also furnished with a foxskin (*wapa*) cap, made after the Lhasa fashion. Provided with these, I felt well equipped for my journey to Dongtse. To make the linings of the coat, I had bought about sixty fine lambskins at a cost of Rs 7.8. These skins appeared to have been obtained from very young lambs, which must have died shortly after birth, for the cost of a single piece of skin was not more than three or four annas, and as the live lambs would fetch at least double that price, it is not likely that they had been killed for their skins. It is, however, not unusual for the shepherds to kill ewes for the soft skin of their unborn lambs, for they fetch a high price. The demand from China for this kind of lambskin has, however, of late years much decreased, and the practice of killing ewes for the purpose of obtaining them is becoming rare.

In the evening Tsering-tashi brought us the passport from the Tondub Khangsar, to enable us to bring our things from Lachan to Tashilhunpo. Though it is customary to issue passports in open covers, this one was enclosed in a letter to the Djongpon of Khamba, and we were therefore unable to know its wording, but feared from this fact that some orders, probably to examine closely our packages, were contained in it. The Tung-chen, however, did not apprehend that any trouble would arise from this fact, but we could not share his confidence.

December 24—In the morning, after washing, I went upstairs to sit in the sun. The cook brought tea and placed the pot on the stove before me. I had emptied three or four cups, warming my numbed hands against the warm cup, when Dungyig Phurching, a copyist, arrived, and was shortly followed by the Khamba Dungyig. I received the first with '*chyag-pheb nang-chig*' ('Please come in'), extending my right hand towards him, and, as an additional mark of respect to the latter, I half raised myself from my seat and placed him on my left hand on the same rug on which I was sitting. After an exchange of the usual compliments, he opened a bundle of papers and showed me an almanac he was engaged in copying for the minister.

He said he was sorry that he was unable to copy the manuscript of the *Dsamling gyeshe*, but recommended Dungyig Phurching; and the latter agreed to do the copying at the rate of six leaves for a *tanka*, exclusive of ink and paper.

To-day news arrived of the death of the Tsopon Shanku, one of the six headmen, and the richest among them, punished on account of the late riot. I saw several monks and laymen carrying from the monastery to Shigatse three huge copper caldrons, about 5 feet in diameter, and I learnt that tea and *tugpa* (a soup of *tsamba*, minced meat, and radishes) were to be prepared in them for the entertainment of upwards of a thousand beggars in honour of the deceased. The caldrons belong to the lamasery, and were loaned for the occasion.

During market-time Ugyen visited a Nepalese (Balpo) friend in Shigatse, from whom he learnt that Nepalese trade was suffering greatly by the introduction of Calcutta goods on the Tibetan market. 'The Balpo traders,' he said, 'used to make a hundred per centum profit in former times, but nowadays the introduction of Calcutta goods by shorter routes than the Katmandu one we have to follow has caused a great falling off in our profits and the bulk of our trade.'

Later on in the day the Tung-chen's men came and told us of the arrangements made for our journey to Dongtse, and that we were to be ready to start on the following morning. As we would only remain at Dongtse a very short while—for the minister was expected to return in a few days to Tashilhunpo—we were told not to take many things with us, and were not to hire donkeys, as we had intended, to carry our luggage. I passed the evening writing letters to send home by Phurchung, who was to start at the same time as we did for the Sikkim frontier.

III

Journey to Dongtse

December 25—We were up early, finishing our letters and getting Phurchung ready for his journey to the Sikkim frontier. After tea I sent Ugyen to the market to buy provisions for our journey, and he brought back a large quantity of *ping*, a piece of mutton, and vegetables, and also purchased some fresh *gya-tug* (vermicelli), of which I had become very fond. Two strong ponies were waiting saddled for us in charge of a groom at the western gateway (*gyalgo*) of the monastery. Our traps and bags being made over to the charge of the Tung-chen's men, we left Tashilhunpo at 3 p.m., and rode off at a gentle trot towards the village of Tashi-gyantsa. The Tung-chen wore his church raiment, and a silk-lined *chosa* or clerical hat, covered his head; but as soon as we had reached this village he changed it for a fox-skin cap lined with brown satin. The view of Tashilhunpo from Tashi-gyantsa was most beautiful, and the four gilded tombs of the former Tashi lamas, situated in the middle of the lamasery, blazed in the rays of the sun.

One approaches Tashi-gyantsa by a lane cut through a hillock some 20 feet high, on top of which the village stands. The alleys are crooked and dirty, the houses of comfortable appearance, are painted with clay in bands of red, black, and blue colour, and surrounded by walls forming a courtyard in front of each. On the left of the road is a neatly constructed *mendong*. The whole village is inhabited by clerks, copyists, painters, and artisans from Tashilhunpo, most of whom get allowances (*pod*) from Labrang. Cattle (*jo*) are plentiful in the village, and as we passed, a few yaks with pack-saddles on their backs were being led off from the village by two tall, savage-looking men dressed in goatskin gowns (*bokhu*). The old people sat in their doorways, warming themselves in the sun, and a caravan of yaks and donkeys had halted at the *chorten* just outside the village.

We passed by Perong shavea, a group of hamlets, in the midst of which is a little garden and a willow grove; then by the village of Deki-rabdan; and when 2 miles from Tashi-gyantsa we reached the large village of Khara Tedong, the chief of which is a Dahpon (general), lately dismissed from a command at Gartok, near Rudok. Judging from the outward appearance of the houses, the village is prosperous. Passing the villages of Sunapara and Sarsha, and leaving Doring and Semaron on our right, we came, after 2 miles, to the Num chu, now a nearly dried-up stream, which comes down from the mountains to the northwest of Nartang, which border the plateau-like valley of Chyugpu shung. A little to the east of this stream is the large village of Gyatso-shar, composed of a dozen hamlets forming two or three groups.

At 5 p.m. we reached the village of Chyang chu, about a quarter of a mile from the Num chu, belonging to our friend, the minister. To the east of the hamlet is a little garden, and in it a small house called Lobding: here the minister spends a few days during the autumn holidays, and takes the baths. Chyang chu is the birthplace of the Tung-chen, and we put up in his house, at the gate of which were chained two big mastiffs. Two servants assisted us to alight from our ponies, and two held the dogs back while we walked in. The headman of the village, the Deba Shikha, received us, and recognized me as an old acquaintance. We were conducted to the central room of the upper story, where we found two stuffed seats (*bu-dan*) spread for us. The room, though spacious, was dark and dusty, and a heap of yak-hair bags, resembling Indian gunnies, filled a corner of the room. My servant, Lhagpa-sring, spread my khamba rug on the seats, and busied himself fetching our bags and traps from the courtyard. The Deba presently arrived, and begged us to refresh ourselves with tea and *chang*. Lhagpa, looking with peculiar eagerness at the maid-servant who was pouring *chang* in Ugyen's cup, winked at her to fill his cup from her bowl, but to his disappointment she turned away; but shortly after another maid appeared with a large bowl, and poured out wine to the servants. Then the Deba's wife, with a very pretty jug in her hand, came to serve me, but I declined. After a few minutes dinner was served in tin-lined copper dishes resembling salad-bowls, the first course consisting of minced mutton and *tsamba*. This was followed by minced mutton and vermicelli, the Deba waiting upon me himself, to show me the attention due to a guest from a distant country.

After dinner the Tung-chen, who had taken his meal in a separate room, led me to his mother's room, where old lady Angla and the Deba's son, Damdul, were sitting around a blazing fire in a stove (*jalang*). The old lady had seen upwards of eighty summers, and her hair was snowy white. I joined the party, which was shortly added to by the entrance of several other members of the household, and we sat drinking tea and talking of the sacred cities of India, of Vajrashena, Varanasi, and Kapilavastu, and the state of Buddhism in modern India. Angla sighed repeatedly when she heard that all their sacred places in India were now in ruins. I then gave her a short history of ancient India and Tibet, which delighted the whole party, and the Tung-chen expressed himself highly pleased with my narrative. Before taking leave for the night of my kind host, I presented the Tung-chen with a couple of rupees, and his mother with one. They very reluctantly accepted them, saying, however, that as it was their duty to please me, they would not deny me the pleasure of making them presents. Lhagpa led me to my bed, which was spread in a corner of the room where we had dined; and the Deba, coming in to see if I was comfortable, found my wraps rather light, and brought me two thick blankets, in which my servant wrapped me up.

December 26—The Deba has a dozen *jomo* and cows yielding plenty of milk. A *jomo* yields four times the quantity of milk which a cow or female yak gives. The *di* yak cow, which pastures on mountain-tops, yields ordinarily two seers of milk a day, is not much prized, though yak milk is both sweet and wholesome; but the Tibetans value very highly the *jo*, which is, besides a good milker, most useful in husbandry.

The women of the house were up by four and busy milking and churning. The village looked from afar like one big house, but it is in reality composed of a number of houses, each with a courtyard in front. The place is vulgarly called the 'Anthill' (*Dog tsang*), on account of the great number of serfs inhabiting it. After breakfast, which consisted of boiled mutton, minced radish, and *pa-tug*, or balls of flour cooked in mutton broth, we mounted our ponies and started off.

To the southwest of Gyatso-shar is the plateau of Chyugpu Shung, dotted with numerous hamlets, chief of which is Lhena *djong*. About 2 miles from Chyang chu is Norgya Nangpa, with numerous hamlets surrounding it, and one mile and a half to the east of Norgya, where the valley approaches the edge of the mountains to the south, is Kena, composed of a dozen hamlets. The houses of Kena are well-built and prosperous looking, the doorframes and windows showing considerable taste, and the walls of most of them painted with long blue and red stripes, the favourite colours of the Tibetans. From Kena the mountains of Pankor-shornub, notorious as a lair of brigands, were clearly discernible, and far to the east, across the Nyang chu, we could just discern the village of Sanga-ling. At Kena we crossed, by a culvert some 15 feet long, an irrigation canal which comes down from Nyang chu. From this point our way lay over a barren plateau more than 2 miles broad; in the upper part of it are several villages, in the largest of which is the Shalu monastery. A little above the junction of the Shalu with the Nyang chu stands the hamlet of Chuta Chyangma, three or four dilapidated mud hovels, the ground everywhere overgrown with thistles and briars. Here, we were told, the Grand Lama's camels are pastured in winter. The Nyang chu flows here in several channels, and some cranes were seeking for food in the ice along the banks.

Going south-eastward for nearly two miles and a half, we reached a fertile tract of land, in which stand the villages of Panam-gang, Jorgya, Pishi, Penagangdo, and Natog, which, we were told, belonged to Hamdang Kam-tsan of Tashilhunpo. At Jorgya, which belongs to the Djongpon of Pagri, the same who stopped Sir Richard Temple near Chumbi, there is an irrigation canal running from the Nyang chu, and on its bank is a beautiful garden bordered with poplars, willows, and other fine trees. Its walks are tastefully laid out, and the two-storied building in its centre is the finest one this side of Tashilhunpo. In the principal lane of this village is a deep well about 4 or 5 feet in circumference at the mouth, and a number of women were drawing water from it in sheep's paunches.

A short distance beyond Jorgya we came to Pishi Mani Lha-khang in a grove of poplars and willows, with a large orchard and several hamlets close by. This place, which belongs to the Pishi Deba, is famous for its manufacture of a superior quality of serge and broadcloth called *unam*. At the entrance to the Mani Lha-khang, a *chorten*-shaped edifice, are rows of drum-shaped prayer-wheels. Five furlongs farther on we passed through Panam-doi and 2 miles beyond this place we came to the village of Taugang (or Tagong). The trail—for there is no regular road—then led by Patsal, Belling, to Penjang, from which village we could see, on the hillside beyond the Nyang chu, the large monastery of Kadong. We were now in the district of Panam, said to be very fertile, and to this the numerous hamlets scattered about give testimony. A mile to the south of Tagong we came to Tashigang, around which there is no vegetation, not a blade of grass nor a tree, nothing but sand and gravel. Here we were to spend the night. We were kindly received by an old lady, Angputi by name, and shown by the servant up a flight of stone steps to the top floor, where rugs were spread for us. Angputi had a headdress (*patug*) studded with flawed turquoises and faded coral; she had worn it, she said, for nearly twenty years, and purposed leaving it as a legacy to her second son. Shortly after we were seated, her daughter, a nun who had lately arrived on leave from her convent, brought us a kettle of tea and two wooden bowls of *tsamba*. The Tung-chen was given the room the minister uses when travelling along this road. It was provided with curtains, silk-covered ceiling, some nice tables, and had in it several volumes of *Yum* scriptures, a small chapel, two dozen bells, oblation cups, a sofa-like altar, and a number of pictures. The rugs in this room were made of the finest Panam wool, and were the best articles of furniture in the house. After drinking tea, the hostess brought me some boiled and dried mutton, *tsamba*, and tea. This kind of present is usually offered to guests on their arrival in a house, and is called *solichi*, or 'first show'.

December 27—Leaving the Tashigang valley, we came to the foot of the range which here borders the left bank of the Nyang. Two and a half miles to the southwest there is a precipice called Ritong, where some twenty years ago two generals of Lhasa were murdered by the usurper Gadan Gyahu. At this point we obtained a fine view of the fort of Panam, of Gontai, of Takar, Palri, and various other monasteries. Up to this point the river banks are overgrown with furze, brambles, and various thorny plants of which it is said camels are very fond.

Two miles to the west of this place we came to a large village, called Tsog-chi, with an imposing castle, formerly the residence of several noted generals, but now the property of one of the chief civil officers (Dung-khor) of Lhasa. Close by is Dukpa-nagpa, formerly a town of sorcerers or *nagpa*, but now mostly in ruins, and inhabited by only a half-dozen families.

A mile and a half farther on we came to Norpa khyung-djin ('Eagle's Gem'), where there was once an important lamasery of the Karmapa sect. Its ruins crown the hilltop, and the village, of a hundred houses, is scattered along the slope and the base of the hills. Near this place is Nembotong and Pangang.

In the upland near Taimen, a hamlet of three huts, where the wind that sweeps the broad plateau on which this place is built has drifted the sand in long waves, are the villages of Phola and Wangdan. The former place is the birthplace of King Miwang, and the latter is noted for the excellence of its rugs. Due south from Taimen, and at the head of the broad valley which opens between that place and Norpa khyung-djin, is the Gingu la, over which a trail runs to Retoi, or Upper Re, near Iago, and also the fort of Darchung *djong*.

A little more than a mile in a southerly direction from Taimen brought us to Shar-chyog Aniung, also called Isa. The poplar and willow groves around it give it a most prosperous appearance. Here we overtook a monk of the Dongtse monastery, sent by the minister to fetch him some books from the Kahdong gomba, near Panam *djong*. His tall, lithe frame, but poorly covered with torn raiment, his curious boots and headdress, and the bundle of incense sticks slung like a quiver across his back, evoked smiles from our party as he walked swiftly along, keeping pace with our ponies. Across numerous frozen irrigation ditches, and through various little hamlets of three and four houses, the road led us by Taling, Dao-targe, and Pangri, to the village of Nesar, where live some twenty families. Just before reaching this place a mad dog ran by, and though it bit an old man and several donkeys, the Tung-chen would not let me shoot it. Nesar has, on the hillside above it, a neatly built temple and a number of small towers, the latter sacred to the sylvan goddesses or Mamos. The images of Shenrezig and Padma Sambhava are painted on the walls of its *mani lha-khang* and on the towers on the hill. A little beyond this village we fell in with four Khambas, each armed with a long, straight sword, who were unquestionably highwaymen. Their dress and features showed them to be natives of Gyarong, in Markham, in the eastern part of Tibet.

At 5 o'clock we arrived at Dongtse. The monastery where the minister was residing was on a rocky eminence some 300 feet above the village. After walking up several flights of stone steps, we reached the gateway in the now partly ruined wall of the monastery. Near this I was welcomed by the minister's page, and led to the eastern room of his master's apartments, which had been set apart for my use. Before we had finished drinking tea a message came calling me to the minister's presence. With two scarves and a couple of rupees in our hands, we proceeded to the drawing-room, and approached his holiness with profound salutations. He touched our heads with his hand, and returned us the scarves we had in the first place presented him, tying them around our necks. His holiness graciously inquired after our health, and asked if we had not suffered great privations and hardships on the way. We gave a brief account of our troubles in the snows and of our miraculous escape at Tashi-rabka. 'By the grace of the Three Holies,' I added, 'we have overcome all difficulties, and now our delight is boundless in being able to present ourselves at last at your Holiness's feet.' The minister expressed his regrets at our sufferings and his pleasure on our safe arrival after an absence of three years. He had to go to prayers, but before leaving he gave orders that all proper attentions be shown us. Large dishes of biscuits, bread, fruit, and meat were then placed before us, and tea was poured into our cups from the minister's own pot, as a mark of his special favour.

December 28—After we had finished taking tea the page Ka-chan Gopa called us to the minister's presence, to whom we gave a detailed account of our journey. After listening with attention, he observed, 'Pundib la, I fail to see why you chose such a dangerous route as that by the Kangla chen and Tashi-rabka, for you had the passport issued to you three years ago by which you were permitted to return to Tsang by way of Khamba *djong*. Did not the officials at that place treat you well when you passed there on your way back to India?' I replied saying that I had feared that difficulties might have been raised by the Sikkim Durbar at the instance of the Phodang lama, who had of late been making trouble in Sikkim. The minister again remarked that there had been no necessity for our undertaking such a difficult and perilous journey through the Tingri *djong* country, when we had the Grand Lama's (Panchen rinpoche's) passport authorizing us to cross the Lachan pass, which was very easy and free from snow. After a short conversation he retired to his contemplation room (oratory).

December 29—We had an interview with the minister in the *Nihog* on the roof of the Tsug-la khang, over which a canopy had been spread. His holiness said that since last I had been to Tibet he had composed two large volumes on the history of the philosophical schools of Tibet, and that they were now being stereotyped at the Namring monastery. He showed us the manuscript of the second volume, and read us extracts from it.

December 30—After breakfast Ugyen-gyatso and I went to make obeisance to the deities (*choi jal*), carrying with us a bundle of incense sticks, two *tankas*' worth of clarified butter, and about a dozen *khatag*, to present as offerings to the gods. Descending a steep ladder we came to the lobby of the congregation hall (*dukhang*) of the Tsug-la khang. The portico faced eastward;

its painted wooden pillars had capitals most fantastically and picturesquely carved, the walls painted in fresco, with relief images of the sixteen Staviras (*Naten chudug*) gorgeously coloured, but of a much lower style of work than what is seen in India, though the thick coat of varnish which covered them hid their defects, when not examined too closely.

The most remarkable part of the building was the floor made of pebbles, nicely set and smoothly beaten to make a glossy surface. The *dukhang* is about 25 feet long and 20 broad; the images of the gods were arranged on a beautifully carved wooden and metal altar along the north and southwest sides of the building, the principal ones occupying niches. Most of the images were very old, and of gilt-copper, called *ser-zang* (gilt-copper), and had been made with much skill. The image of the Lord (*Jovo*) Buddha had been made, the Tung-chen told me, by a great Indian Buddhist in imitation of the great image of Shakya tuba at Lhasa. The founder of the monastery, Je Lha-tsun, once prayed that the gods might send him a skilful artist to make images for the newly built lamasery; and shortly afterwards an Indian visited Dongtse, made this image, and then returned to India. The Tung-chen, when he had told me this, smilingly asked me if I was not a reincarnation of this Indian Buddhist, and I felt proud to hear of my countrymen being so highly admired and venerated. Ugyen-gyatso prostrated himself before every one of the images, and touched with his head their feet or body, and I showed my veneration for these sacred shrines by touching with my head their right hand, thus to receive their *chyag wang* (blessing). My companions muttered mantras and made prayers to them, while I felt reverential gratitude to the Supreme Ruler alone, whose merciful providence had brought me safe thus far.

The roof of the *dukhang* is supported by two rows of pillars of wood, on the artistically constructed capitals of which hang shields and quivers full of arrows, the arms of the Dharmaplas, with which they protect Buddhism against demons and heretics. From the ceiling of the hall hang rich China brocades, with dragons magnificently embroidered on them in gold and silver. Among the various pictures seen here, the most interesting is that of the first Dalai lama, Lobzang-gyatso, in which he is portrayed receiving the kingdom of Tibet from the Mongol conqueror, Gushi Khan. His prime minister, the celebrated Desi Sangye, is seated on his left, and is thanking the magnanimous and liberal prince for his munificent gift on behalf of his thrice holy master. I was also shown the dais reserved for the minister. Opposite it, and at the top of the second row of seats reserved for the monks, is a chair 3 feet high, on which the head lama of the monastery sits during service. There is accommodation for about eighty monks in this hall, and I was told that service is held in it daily, at which most of the monks are present. They receive a monthly allowance of 60 pounds of barley from the church endowment fund (*labrang gzi*). This they parch and grind themselves, and bring a little supply of it daily with them to the hall in a small bag, to eat with the tea, which is given them three times during each service, and is furnished from the church stores (*labrang djo*). On returning from the *choi jal*, I was called to the minister's, whom I found seated on a satin-covered cushion in the shade of a *nyi-hok* on the roof of the third story of the chief temple of the Tsug-la khang.

His page (*shabdung*), Ka-chan Gopa, placed a cup of tea before me together with some *tsamba*, meat, and twisted sugar-biscuits. The minister raised his cup to his lips, and graciously said, 'Drink, Pundit, please' (*Pundib la, sol ja nang*). I at once drank a third of my cup, as etiquette requires, and every time he drank I also took a sip. He made inquiries respecting the lithographic press and the various other articles which I had brought to present to him, and which were now on the way to Tashilhunpo. After dinner he showed me a work he was writing on history, rhetoric, astrology and photography. The latter section he had composed from notes I had furnished him, in 1879, from Tassinder's *Manual of Photography*, and I was delighted to see the diagrams he had drawn to represent the various photographic apparatus I had then left with him. He afterwards read to me an account of the ancient controversies between the Brahmans and Buddhists of India.

While we were thus engaged the page informed him that the Dahpon Phala and Kung Chyang-chan were approaching Dongtse, so we went to the top of the fourth story of the Dongtse *choide* to see them arrive. The Dahpon being the chief of Dongtse, the monks had to show him due respect. When the party got near the foot of the hill on which the *choide* stands, two monks in full canonicals blew two long copper hautboys, two others played on a clarionet-like instrument called *gya-ling*; and when the party came to the grove, or *linga*, in front of the castle, the Chya-dso-pa received them with his band—a gong and two tambourines. The Dahpon and his friend rode spirited mules gaudily caparisoned with brocades and tinsel. They were preceded by five sowars, and followed by an equal number, all carrying lances with pennants at their points. The minister told me that of the four Dahpons, or commanders of forces in Tsang, two are ordinarily stationed at Shigatse, one at Gyantse, and one at Tingri.

December 31—I was anxious to take a trip to Gyantse, which Ugyen said was only 8 miles distant, and could be reached in two hours. He dissuaded me, however, saying it would not be prudent, as that place is frequented by Bhutia traders from Darjiling and Phagri. At nine I was called in to the minister's, and read a few sentences of English from the *Royal Reader No. 1* with him. After this I asked to be allowed to visit the great temple of Gyantse, called the 'Palkhor *choide*'. 'If you wish to visit Gyantse,' he replied, 'I will arrange it for you; but you must bear in mind that the people of that town are not good. They speak much, and are given to spinning a great deal out of a little. I will have the

Tung-chen take you there.' Ugyen-gyatso then asked if he might go there, as he wanted to buy me some blankets; and having obtained the minister's authorization, he left at noon.

January 1, 1882—For about half an hour the minister practised writing the Roman characters on a wooden slate (*chyang-shing*) about 2 feet long and 10 inches broad. A little bag of powdered chalk was tied to it; and when the slate had been washed and dried, the minister rubbed the chalk-bag lightly over the board, and thus covered it with a thin white film. In this he scratched letters with a steel style about a foot long. I told him of the slates we had in India—how much more convenient and neat they were than his rude contrivance. He smiled and said, 'My *chyang-shing* is a very nice one; even the great ministers of China use the like; but they are not clean. And if you can get me a couple of your Indian slates from Calcutta, I shall be much obliged.'

January 2—In the morning preparations were made for a grand reception of the Dahpon Phala and Kung Chyang-chan, the Tsipon. All the furniture of the room we occupied was replaced by choice articles from the minister's storeroom. Silk drapings and curtains were hung in the waiting-room and lobby, beautiful silk cushions were spread in the minister's drawing-room, and its ceiling made resplendent with a covering of orange-coloured Chinese brocade. Artistically worked dragons appeared everywhere—on the ceiling draperies, on the curtains, and even in the carpets. Handsome dining-tables, 3 feet by 18 inches, and 2 feet high, were placed before each cushioned seat. The minister's seat was placed as usual before a gilt chapel (niche), and 3 feet above the floor, on his right hand, were seats, 2 feet high, for his two guests, and to his left two other cushioned seats, about 18 inches high, for their sons. Pretty china cups, painted wooden and gilt metal bowls, were set on the tables, and all the curiosities and ornamental objects the minister had here with him were conspicuously displayed. On the corner of his table was the beautiful stereoscope I had given him in 1879, with some two hundred slides, and in the middle of the table a calendar-watch and some toys I had recently presented him. Different kinds of Tibetan and Chinese dainties were arranged by the head cook, under the Tung-chen's directions, and the minister personally supervised the arrangement of the seats and the decorating of the room. When all was ready I went on to the roof to see the procession arrive. On both the roads leading to the monastery from Dongtse the monks were waiting, bearing a dozen or so flags and musical instruments—two flageolets, a pair of brass hautboys, or *dungchen*, two tambourine-like drums, the same number of bells, and a gong.

At 1 o'clock the Dahpon and his friend, the Tsipon, together with their sons, arrived at the Dongtse *choide*, escorted by the Chya-dso-pa. They were very simply dressed in silk robes, Chinese jackets, soft yellow woollen hats, velvet boots, and silk trousers; from their right ear hung long earrings. The Dahpon appeared to be about thirty years old, the Tsipon a little older.

Arriving before the minister, they thrice prostrated themselves, each time touching their foreheads with their joined palms. The minister touched their heads with the palm of his hand and blessed them, and then they presented him with two pieces of red English broadcloth and a handful of silver coins each.

I was surprised to see such powerful and wealthy chiefs kotow before the minister; but great is the triumph in this country of the Church over the laity, and the greatest ministers of state fall down at the feet of the incarnate lamas!

Dinner was served with great ceremony. As soon as the minister had said grace, all fell to with chopsticks and spoon, and partook of each succeeding course in profound silence. After dinner, tea was served, when at last the silence was broken, conversation began, and the guests were shown the minister's curios, the watches and the stereoscopic views especially interesting them.

In the evening there was a review in the pleasure grove, or *linga*, by the commander of the militia, when exercise in musketry, running, archery, etc., took place in the presence of the two dignitaries.

January 3—After tea I was asked to read English with the minister. He transliterated the English words phonetically, but did not take the trouble of spelling them, observing that his ordinary duties left him hardly any time to devote to study. He intended asking the Grand Lama to relieve him for a time from his numerous duties in connection with the Church, when he hoped to be able to apply himself assiduously to the study of English.

Breakfast was now brought in, and consisted of a kind of pot-herb, called *pa-tsal*, cured in the cold draught, potatoes, and radishes, which had been kept in sand underground. I asked the minister if I might go to visit the Palkhor *choide* of Gyantse with the Tung-chen on the morrow; and having obtained his consent, two ponies were ordered to be ready for an early start.

January 4—The ponies were ready at an early hour, and after receiving from the minister a few *khatag* to present to the deities of the Palkhor *choide*, the Tung-chen and I rode off.

Our way lay across fields watered by the Nyang chu. The Nyang chu valley is one of the richest in Tibet, and extends from Shigatse to about 15 miles beyond Gyantse, a distance of from 60 to 70 miles, and has an average breadth of ten, every inch of which is cultivated. Its great natural fertility, and its being so very favourable for the growth of different kinds of millet and pulses, has given the whole district the name of *Nyang*, or 'land of delicacies', and the river which fertilizes it has been called Nyang chu, or 'the river of delicious water'.

Flocks of wild geese and ducks were swimming on the river, near the bank of which our road now and then led us, and long-billed cranes were stalking along searching for food. From the bushes of furze and other thorny plants with which the river banks were overgrown, hares leaped out and made off towards the mountain recesses, and beautiful little birds, probably a variety of kingfisher, were seen fishing in the stream—but the Tung-chen said that though the bird was pretty to look at, it emitted a most offensive odour from its body.

Passing a few villages, we came to a stream flowing into the Nyang chu from the south. Here were two flour-mills, of which we had seen at least a dozen since leaving Shigatse. They were very large, and the stones four times the size of our ordinary millstones in India. In the village of Gyabshi the people seemed very industrious, the women engaged with their looms or spinning, the men tending sheep or collecting fuel from the fields.

When we came within 2 miles of Gyantse, our attention was attracted by the Tse-chan monastery, the entire northeastern slope of a hill being closely covered by its whitewashed houses, so that it looked like a great castle of towering height. The Tung-chen told me that this lamasery was nearly eight hundred years old, and that the great reformer Tsong-khapa had spent several years here in the study of metaphysics *(tsan-nyid)*. I was also shown the Tinkar la, by which herdsmen travel to the foot of the Lachan pass of Sikkim, this being the shortest route between Gyantse and the latter country.

A few minutes' ride brought us to the bridge over the Nyang chu, a light temporary wooden structure, about 20 feet long and 6 feet broad, built on the ice which covered the stream.

We entered the town of Gyantse, passing beside a long *mendong*, on either side of which were dwellings, and by a narrow lane reached the gate of the Gandan Chakhang on the left side of the main street, and facing the great *chorten* of the Palkhor *choide*.

The *Kunyer*, or priest, of the Gandan Chakhang, an acquaintance of the Tung-chen, greeted him, and, showing him to a seat, had tea served us. We sent the groom, Lhagpa-rida, to the market to buy arrack, and he there met Ugyen, and told him of our arrival.

As we were eating our meal several pilgrims chanting sacred hymns entered the chapel of the Lha-khang, and added some spoonfuls of butter to the lamps. Some of them stared at Ugyen and me, observing to one another that we were strangers from beyond the Himalayas, taking Ugyen for a Sikkimese, but not being able to decide whether I was from Ladak or Besahir.

Ugyen told me of his movements since leaving me at Dongtse on December 31.

He had left Dongtse at noon on December 31, riding one of the Tung-chen's ponies. On the road he met some of the muleteers of the Dongtse Dahpon Phala, who were proceeding to Lhasa with barley, butter, and meat for the use of Bangye-shag, Phala's residence.

Ugyen inquired of them about the state of the road to Lhasa, and the best time to make the journey there. They told him that winter was the best season to travel to Lhasa, for then there was no rain, and one could easily ford the streams and get across the Tsang-po; moreover, feed was cheap, and meat, barley, and wine obtainable everywhere.

The following day (January 1, 1882) Ugyen visited the Gyantse *tom*. This market and the town generally are inferior to Shigatse in importance and in the variety of articles for sale. There were people selling Calcutta and Chinese goods of very inferior quality. He saw fifteen or twenty Nepalese shops and half a dozen pastry shops kept by Chinese. The *tom* (or marketplace) is the property of the Palkhor *choide*, the great monastery of Gyantse, and contributes largely to its maintenance. The monastic authorities also collect rents from the shops in the vicinity of the *tom*, which do not belong to either the Government or landholders (*gerpas*). The barley for sale was inferior to that of Shigatse, as was also the *chang*, which was, however, cheaper than there; and butter and mutton were in larger quantities than at the latter place.

The market only lasts for three hours daily, opening at 10 a.m. Ugyen here saw, for the first time, women selling fresh meat and dried carcasses of sheep and yaks. At Shigatse they never take part with the men in this business. Some of these women have amassed much wealth by this profession, and wear rich headdresses (*patug*) thickly studded with pearls, amber, and turquoises.

Returning to his lodgings, Ugyen made the acquaintance of a lieutenant, or Dingpon, named Nyima tsering, who was putting up in the same house. Ugyen plied him with *chang*, and when he had become very jolly over it, he questioned him about the military arrangements of Gyantse. The Dingpon stated that there were ordinarily 500 Tibetan soldiers stationed here. This force was divided into two battalions under two Rupon. Under each Rupon were two captains (Gyapon) and four lieutenants, or Dingpon. The commander, or Dahpon, of the Gyantse troops was Tedingpa. Besides these troops there are 50 Chinese soldiers under a Chinese official called *Da-loye* and the native militia. The troops both at Gyantse and Shigatse are under the inspection of the Chinese paymaster (*Pogpon*) of Shigatse. Nyima tsering told Ugyen that the Tibetan soldiers were very poorly paid by the Government. The Emperor of China contributes towards their maintenance five rupees per man a year, and the Government of Tibet gives them 40 pounds of barley per man a month, but no pay in money, on the ground that they are furnished by the landholders at the rate of one soldier for every *kang* of land.

The Dingpon and Gyapon receive pay at the rate of thirteen *srang* and twenty-five *srang* a year from the imperial treasury, but no more rations from the Tibetan Government than the soldiers.

The Emperor allows Chinese soldiers serving in Tibet a family allowance of six *srang* a month and 60 pounds of rice per head as subsistence allowance, in addition to their monthly pay of six *srang*. On the next day (January 2) Ugyen surveyed the town and its great monastery, the Palkhor *choide*. A stone wall nearly 2 miles and a half long surrounds the town. He estimated its length, by means of his prayer-beads, to be 4,500 paces. At each pace he dropped a bead and muttered '*Om mani padme hum*,' and the good people of Gyantse who accompanied him in his circumambulation (*lingkor*) little suspected the nature of the work he was doing. When he reached the foot of a *mendong* called Gojogs, and situated to the north of the *Djong*, he took the bearing of the Tse-chan monastery, one of the most ancient religious establishments of Tibet. It bore south-west, and was nearly 3 miles from him. To the north of Gyantse he saw Ritoi gomba, a cloistered lamasery with five or six long houses, each with a large number of cells. To the south-southeast of Gyantse *djong* is the road to Pagri, in the direction of the Nia-ni monastery and the Niru chu, one of the principal feeders of the Nyang chu, which drains the northern glacier of the Chumo-lha ri mountain. To the northeast of Gyantse the Nyang chu is visible for a great distance, and Ugyen conjectured from its course that it came from the snow-clad Noi-jin kang-zang mountains, which stretch out to the north and northeast. On the uplands to the north of Gyantse, and some 3 miles away, is the Choilung gomba.

The Chinese cemetery Ugyen found situated at the foot of the hill on which the *Djong* stands, a little above the high-road to Lhasa, and some 3 miles from the town. He counted three hundred tombs, some of which appeared very old and dilapidated, but a few quite new.

The castle or *Djong* of Gyantse stands on the top of a hill nearly 500 feet above the town. It is very strong, and was built by the famous Choigyal rabtan who ruled in the fourteenth century over the province of Nyang, of which Gyantse was the capital. This province was a part of the domain of the Sakya hierarchs. He had built a long stone-covered way running from the *Djong* to the foot of the hill, by which he meant to secure a supply of water in time of siege from the three deep wells at the foot of the hill. Ugyen visited these wells, where water-carriers were drawing water in hide buckets attached to a rope about 150 feet long passing over a pulley.

The landlord of the Litophug sub-division of Gyantse told Ugyen that about eighteen years ago the ex-Dewan of Sikkim had come here on some State business, and had put up in the same house in which he was now stopping. One night about fifty sinister-looking Khamba traders suddenly broke into the house, beat him with clubs, tore his earring out of his ear, stripped him of his clothing, carried off all his property, and thrashed his servants and forced them to run for their lives. Some of the robbers ran away from Gyantse, taking the Dewan's property, his mules and ponies; but on the following morning, when the matter was brought to the notice of the Djongpon, the chief of the robbers, who had stayed behind, was apprehended. He said that a year previously the Dewan had treated him and his accomplices most harshly during their stay at Chumbi on their way to Darjiling, exacting from them the last pice they had in their purses, besides depriving them of all their property to the value of upwards of Rs 500. The Dewan lost, in his turn, over Rs 1,000 in cash, besides jewellery, clothes, etc.

A well-informed Nyingma lama, the manager of Palri kusho's (an incarnate lama) estate near Panam Jong, came and put up at the house where Ugyen was stopping. He was on his way back from Lhasa, where he had stayed for two or three months after a pilgrimage to the Tsari country. His master was studying sacred literature at Lhasa. He promised to let Ugyen see the books of the Palri library, and to lend them to him on the surety of the minister or his Chyag dso-pa. He told him, furthermore, that there existed two printed volumes about Choigyal rabtan, the famous king who had founded the Palkhor *choide* of Gyantse, but that these works and the history of Gyantse were now kept as sealed works (*terchoi*) by the Lhasa government. Ugyen also learnt from the lama that in the recluses' monastery of Lhari-zim-phug, situated on a wild mountain to the east of Panam *djong*, there was a complete account of the life and writings of Lama Lha-tsun chenpo, who had introduced Buddhism into Sikkim.

At this season of the year the climate of Gyantse is very bad, high winds blowing daily, raising dense clouds of dust. The inhabitants spend this time of the year in idleness, having but little to do besides weaving and spinning.

Such was the information that Ugyen gave me to-day.

When we had finished our breakfast we went with the *Kunyer* of Gandan Lha-khang to perform *choi-jal* at the different shrines of Gyantse. The *chorten* is a splendid edifice of a unique style of architecture. Hitherto I had been under the impression that *chorten* were nothing more than tombs intended solely to contain the remains of departed saints, but now my views became entirely changed. This *chorten* is a lofty temple nine stories high. Ugyen, I, the *Kunyer*, Lhapa-rida, and our servant, Lhagpa-sring, went into the enclosure and entered the shrine with a number of pilgrims and travellers, most of whom seemed to be from Ladak or the Changtang. In the service hall, where the priests were assembled for religious service, hundreds of lamps were burning, and incense-sticks were smoking so as to nearly darken the room. We ascended at once to the top story, but the other visitors began their circumambulation from the bottom upwards—the usual practice, though many become so wearied going round and round that they do not reach the uppermost story. The chorten is about 100 to 120 feet high, the top covered by a gilt dome, the gilded copper plates of which are so thick that they have withstood centuries of exposure to the weather. The base of this sacred edifice is, we found by actual count, 50 paces square. From the cupola (*pumpa*), immediately under the gilt dome, I had a magnificent view of the town and monasteries and the surrounding hills and distant mountains; their black surface, broken here and there by some white-walled monastery, offered a singularly wild aspect.

There were inside the *chorten* innumerable niches filled with images of Buddhas and saints, and in visiting the various chapels we were required to do so walking from left to right, for this is the Buddhist usage.

On the first floor we were shown the statue of Choigyal rabtan, under whose benign rule Gyantse became famous, and who gave a fresh impulse to Buddhism and literature. The *Kunyer* of the *chorten* touched our heads with the sword of this illustrious monarch, and said that by his blessing (*jin-lab*) we could triumph over our enemies and enjoy longevity and prosperity in this world.

We were also shown two images of Dorje chang, the supreme Buddha of the Gelugpa sect, one of which was very old and of small size, the other large and very highly burnished. Once, the Grand Lama of Tashilhunpo, visiting the *chorten*, touched the breast of the former image to see if it was warm and full of life, as was popularly said. He soon repented him of his sacrilegious act, confessed his sin, and, to atone for his wrongdoing, had made the large gilt image, which was placed beside the old one.

Returning to the Gandan Lha-khang, we were refreshing ourselves with copious draughts of tea, when the abbot of the Palkhor *choide*, with half a dozen disciples, came to make reverence to the great image of the Buddha in the shrine, on whose right and left were images of Tsong-khapa and Maitreya.

The *Kunyer* remarked to me that I was peculiarly fortunate in having come to Gyantse to-day, as it was the full moon, a sacred day with Buddhists, on which day, and on the day of the new moon, the doors of all the shrines and of the great *chorten* were thrown open to the public.

After an hour's rest I went with the Tung-chen and Ugyen to visit the Palkhor *choide*. Its grand 'temple of learning' (tsug-la khang) is a splendid and lofty edifice, the hall lighted by one thousand lamps. On three sides—the north, east, and west—are high niches, in which are huge images of the Buddha and

Bodhisattvas. The image of the Buddha is made of copper, heavily gilt. Five hundred monks were engaged in divine service, and some two hundred more were occupied reading the sacred scriptures. No one lifted his eyes to look at us, so strict is the discipline observed here. We were conducted to the great library, the very sight of which filled my mind with feelings of awe and reverence. The books were all old, broad-leaved, and some 2 to 4 feet long. I was shown the sacred scriptures, all written in letters of gold.

With what assiduity and devotion the Buddhists perform the sacred duties of their religion, the deep interest they take in the collecting of sacred books and images, and their zealous care in preserving them, can only be realized by visiting such places as this. I was shown some sculptures executed by Indian Buddhists, and some stone images similar to what I had seen at Buddhagaya. The gilt, Indian-made images of the Sravakas, of Saripu, Mudgalputra, Ananda, Kashyapa, and other arhats were of exceeding interest. On each side of the image of Sakya Buddha were four rows of monks, of twenty each, and in front of them burned hundreds of butter-fed lamps. Behind the seats of the monks were drums, each with a long handle; these the monks beat at intervals, and to the accompaniment also of cymbals, brass hautboys (*dung chen*), and clarionets (*gyaling*), they chanted hymns in deep sonorous voices.

When exhausted by continual repetitions of mantras, they refreshed themselves with tea. Wine is not brought within the precincts of these Gelugpa monasteries; and, in fact, all drinkers of wine among the monks are expelled from the Gelugpa Church.

In the lobby of the monastery I found a grand collection of stuffed animals, such as the snow leopard, wild sheep, goat, yak, stag, mastiff, etc., and a Bengal tiger.

Returning to the Gandan Lha-khang, we visited the second and third floors of that building, where several recluses were reading the sacred books. I was told that when the Tashi lama visited the Palkhor *choide*, he puts up in this building, and I was shown the raised seat he occupies when here. I also learnt that successful students among the monks of Tashilhunpo are sent here to complete their course of study for the degree of *tom-rampa* (bachelor of sacred literature), which this lamasery alone has the right to confer.

In the portico of the building and underneath its eaves I noticed several sorts of flowering plants in bloom.

At 3 p.m. we left for Dongtse, where we arrived before dusk. The minister's page met me at the foot of the hill, and led me to his master, who made many kind inquiries about my trip. I told him how greatly I had enjoyed it, and that, as it was a holiday, all the buildings, the great *chorten* and the temples, had been open to me. 'I rejoice at it,' he replied; 'and I must say the gods have shown you the way (*lha lam tan song*), for it did not strike me at the time that to-day was a holiday. If you should have put it off till to-morrow, you would have seen but very little.'

January 5—I called on the minister, and talked to him of my visit to Gyantse. He told me that there were half a dozen *chorten* in Tibet like the one I had seen there. There were now, he said, about 600 monks in the Palkhor *choide*, and an equal number in the adjacent lamaseries, but in former times there were 3,000 monks on the register of the college.

Ugyen-gyatso returned to-day from Gyantse, and told the minister of his experiences there. He had been lodged in Litophug in a priest's house, whore the master (*nabo*) and mistress (*namo*) showed him great courtesy. Ugyen presented the minister a dozen oranges he had bought in the Gyantse market for one anna each. I told the minister that these oranges came from Sikkim. 'Oh, indeed!' he said. 'It must be a happy land. In Tibet no oranges mature; at Lhasa there are orange trees producing small fruit, which do not, however, ripen.'

In the evening Ugyen told me a tale he had heard from the Chyag-dso-pa of the Palri monastery.

Once Dugpa-kunleg, a famous but eccentric saint of the red-hat school, was staying at Khang-toi shikha, in Lhasa. He saw the wife of his host stealing a piece of amber from the bag of a beggar who was stopping in the house, and putting an apple in its stead into his wallet. The saint told her it was both sinful and criminal to act thus, and related to her the following tale by way of instruction.

In ancient India there lived two friends. One, a highlander, was a dishonest man; the other, a lowlander, was upright and honest. One day the two, while walking in a valley, found a bowl of gold. The lowlander said, 'Well, now that fortune has favoured us with a treasure, let us first return thanks to the local divinities, and then divide the gold between us.' The other rejoined, 'Friend, the day is far advanced; we can do all this to-morrow; let us rather take the bowl home now.'

To this the lowlander agreed. The next morning when he called at his friend's house, he found him in a corner wailing and shedding tears. 'Ah, friend,' he exclaimed, 'my heart is filled with grief and shame. How can I tell you! The bowl of gold has been miraculously changed, for this morning I found but sawdust in it. The gods alone know what has become of the treasure! This, I am grieved to say, will put an end to our friendship, for it will create in your mind a suspicion against me.' So saying he began weeping afresh.

The other, perceiving his design, said, with wonderful calmness, 'Friend, you need not cry. The loss of the treasure is not the greatest mishap which might befall us. If we two continue to be friends we should hold ourselves very happy. Chance brought the treasure; chance has taken it away; crying will not bring it back.'

The false friend, thinking he had gained his end, soon dried his tears. Before leaving for his home, the lowlander said, 'Friend,

I have not mentioned something to you. In my orchard most delicious mangoes and other fruits are now ripe. I have no children to eat them; let your two sons come home with me that I may regale them with the luscious fruits.'

To this the other assented, and the two boys accompanied the lowlander home. On his return to his home he bought two monkeys, to which he gave the same names as the boys, and trained them to come when called by their names.

After a while the false friend came to take his boys home, when the other came out crying in a loud and pitiful voice, 'Friend, my heart bleeds to have to tell you of the misfortune which has befallen you. Your two darlings have been changed into monkeys!'

'How can I believe such a story?' the other replied. 'If you doubt it, call your sons, and you will see.'

So the father called his older son by name, and a monkey came leaping forth, and sat upon his lap, fondling him and chattering to him as if he were an old friend. Filled with surprise, he called his second son, when out came the other monkey, and climbed into his lap also.

After a while the lowlander asked his friend, 'How can this have come about? Tell me how it was that the gold was changed into sawdust; it may help to explain this new wonder.' The other, fearing lest his sons had been transformed into monkeys by the incantations of the friend he had deceived, replied, 'Friend, I deceived you when I said the gold had been turned into sawdust. I have got it with me; we will divide it equally between us. Is it true, my much injured friend, that my sons have been transformed into monkeys?' 'Oh no. How could men become monkeys? Your sons are in excellent health, and are now in one of my distant orchards.' So the two returned to their houses with their respective treasures—the one with his children, the other with his gold.

Years passed by, and the two friends were finally summoned to the court of the Lord of death, there to have their good and bad acts weighed. Their moral merits and their prayers were also weighed, and the balance turned in their favour. A game of chess was then played by the gods and the demon, in which, by means of casting dice, the merits and demerits of gods and men are determined. In the mirror of karma (mundane actions) the two friends saw and blushed for the evil deeds they had done—the gold turned into sawdust, and the boys into monkeys. The Lord of death decreed that the uplander should pass 500 years in hell, and that the other should for 500 existences be born a monkey. The punishment of the latter was the severer in that he had stolen human beings, and said that they had been transformed into monkeys; but because he had desired to make offerings to the gods when the treasure had been found, the gods had pleaded for him.

Having finished his tale, Dugpa kunleg exhorted the woman to keep from stealing, and threatened her with such-like dire punishment if she did not desist. The woman put the amber back in the beggar's bag, and the saint left her house and returned to Lhobrag.

Ugyen also heard at Gyantse that much was to be learnt concerning the ancient history of that place in a work called *Nyang choi jung Nyimai odser*. He furthermore told me that he had heard that last year a mendicant from Gyantse visiting Sikkim gave out there that he was one of the discoverers of sacred books of which the Nyingma history of Sikkim makes mention. He showed what he claimed was a very ancient manuscript volume on the propitiatory ritual of Guru Thag-mar, a fearful deity of the Nyingma pantheon. The Sikkam rajah gave him a very warm welcome, and, in consultation with the chief lama of his Durbar, arranged to have block prints made of the text. Recently this impostor had returned to Gyantse, bringing with him many valuable copper and brass articles, silk gowns, and coined money.

January 6—The minister's mother, accompanied by a maid-servant, came to pay reverence to her saintly son while I was seated with him. I could not believe that she was his mother when I saw her make three profound salutations before the minister, touching the ground with her forehead and receiving his blessing. She then presented him with a few balls of butter and a *khatag*; and when his holiness said he would leave for Tashilhunpo in three days, she wept bitterly.

January 7—Early in the morning we received a message from the minister asking us to postpone our departure for Tashilhunpo, as the Chyag-dso-pa much wished me to accompany the minister to his house at Kye-pa Khangsar, where he proposed staying three days.

The parents of the minister, accompanied by their youngest boy, came again to pay their respects. The father, a quiet, respectable-looking, elderly man, saluted me by taking off his yellow felt turban and inquiring after my health. They kotowed before the minister, who gave them his blessing by touching the crowns of their heads with his hand.

At 2 o'clock the minister, dressed like a Buddhist cardinal, and accompanied by the Tung-chen, ourselves, and his domestics, entered the grand hall of worship (*dukhang*), the Tung-chen carrying a bundle of incense-sticks and some *khatag*. The head lama threw some grains of barley towards the images of the deities, and recited some mantras; then the minister, standing, recited a short prayer, and approaching the image of the Buddha, took off his mitre and placed a *khatag* on it. Then the head lama took the other *khatag* which the Tung-chen had brought with him, and flung them one by one at the other images, while the monks who accompanied him scattered flowers before them.

After this we circumambulated the monastery, and descended to the foot of the hill, where the son of the Chyag-dso-pa, dressed in a rich Mongol costume, was awaiting us with two spirited and richly caparisoned ponies held by grooms, one of which the minister mounted, while we walked the short distance which separated us from the gateway of Kye-pa Khangsar. A band of drums, hautboys, bells, gongs, and fifes marched before us, playing as we went through the lay town (*sho*) and along a broad road lined with poplars to the gate of the Khangsar, where the Chyag-dso-pa was standing to receive the minister. He was dressed in a rich scarlet satin robe girded by a yellow scarf, a yellow woollen turban, and a pair of Tartar velvet boots. His tall stature, graceful looks, broad forehead, and uncommonly well-shaped nose, gave him a commanding appearance. He greeted the minister with a profound bow, and presented him a *khatag*, and received a blessing (*chyag wang*) from the latter, who afterwards dismounted, putting his foot on a velvet-covered stool placed here for the purpose.

The Chyag-dso-pa salaamed to Ugyen, whom he took for me; and the latter, not taking off his hat to return his salutation (or pay his *chyam-bu*, as it is called), was reminded of it in a whisper by the Tung-chen.

We then ascended a flight of steps and entered the building. The minister was conducted by the host to his drawing-room, while we were led by his third son, Phuntso Yu-gyal, in company of the Tung-chen, to the chapel, the central room on the first floor. The house was very neatly built, with solid rubble walls and beautifully carved beams of old poplar. There was a skylight in the centre of the roof: thick cushions covered with Khamba rugs were placed around, and on these we took our seats. A collation was served on little tables consisting of Chinese cakes, buckwheat cakes, twisted sweet biscuits, and *tsamba* and tea was given us by the Chyag-dso-pa's page Pinu. After a little while we were led into the Chyag-dso-pa's presence, when we presented him *khatag* and a few rupees, also a *khatag* to his wife, Ama Tung-la, and his daughter-in-law, Rinpoche. After dinner we were conducted to a dormitory on the south side of the chapel, where we found three bedsteads, and after a cup of tea we retired to rest.

January 8—Early in the morning we asked our host's leave to start for Tashilhunpo, but he was most reluctant to let us go, and, having obtained the minister's sanction to our remaining here two days more, we postponed our departure.

Breakfast was served by a maidservant (*shetama*) and our host's daughter-in-law (*patsa*), Rinpoche, the only wife of his two sons. She is entitled to be addressed as *Chyam Kusho*, though it is seldom used in speaking to her. She is a young lady of about twenty, of modest manners and intelligent looks. She lingered about until the servants and other guests had left, with the evident intention of conversing with us.

Ugyen-gyatso opened the conversation by asking her to what family of Tibet she belonged. She replied by asking him if he had ever heard of Kusho Mankipa of Tanag. 'Yes,' replied he, 'if you speak of Manki, who is the maternal uncle of the Rajah of Sikkim.' ''Tis he,' she said; 'and he died last year without my seeing him. Are you a subject of my cousin Den Jong gyalpo (the chief of Sikkim)? Oh, how I long to see my aunt!' And she began to weep. 'It is now full three years since I came here, and never in that time have I been allowed to visit my fatherland. Oh, I am miserable! I have to work continuously at the loom, supervise the workwomen, attend to the kitchen, and serve the meals. My mother-in-law is without mercy. She thinks my frame is made of iron. Though this family is rich, they work like ploughmen.'

She then begged Ugyen to inform the Sikkim rajah's mother, Lha-yum Kusho, of her trouble, and to persuade her, if possible, to take her to Chumbi for a couple of months. I told her, by way of consoling her, that she was a most accomplished person, married into one of the richest families of Tsang, and might hope to soon be a mother, so she must not consider herself miserable. 'Do you know palmistry,' she suddenly asked; and placing her right hand on the table, she desired me to tell her fortune by the lines on her hand (*lag-ri*). I was much embarrassed, and told her that I understood very little of this art. Fortunately just then a servant came and called us to the presence of the Chyag-dso-pa.

I took a seat on his right hand, and his wife, Ama Tung-la, occupied one on his left, while Ugyen, seated a little distance off, acted as my interpreter. The Chyag-dso Kusho began with: 'In the sacred books we find mention of Indian Punditas who laboured for the diffusion of the enlightened religion. If you be a Pundita, as I hear from the minister that you are, we are most fortunate to have you among us. I also learn that you know about medicines, and I will later on avail myself of your knowledge.' Then, calling his son, Phunsho Yugyal, he desired me, to my great embarrassment, to foretell his fortune by the lines on his hand. Being considered a Pundit, it was impossible for me to say that I did not know such an essential science as palmistry. After mature reflection I told him that although I had studied a little palmistry, I never attached much importance to explanations it afforded of men's fortunes. The science was very little understood, anyhow, and, in my opinion, it did not deserve any more attention than it had received: nothing could be more unpleasant than a foreknowledge of one's misery. Human life was, albeit, full of trouble; it was for deliverance from its recurrence that the Buddha has expounded the doctrine of nirvana.

He listened attentively to me, and seemed to think very highly of me. He said that if he but knew how long he and his son would live, he could devise means of preventing accidents in consultation with the minister, for in the sacred books one is told of religious remedies by the use of which calamities caused by devils (*de*) can be averted. He pressed me to examine his palm, and stretched it out toward me. How could I refuse, and how could I predict falsely? So I told him that there are certain figures and lines in the palm of the hand from which experts in palmistry can draw indications of a long or short life. In his palm the line of life was very long; and as to fortune, it was well known that he was favoured by the gods.

Ama Tung-la then showed me her hand, and I said, 'Ama-la, you are very fortunate. The mother of three sons, all of them grown up and accomplished men; the wife of a great man. What more can you want of the gods?' She smiled at this, and said that for some days past she had been suffering from a cough; could I give her some medicine that would relieve her? I asked for some black pepper and rock-candy, and prepared a powder for her.

At noon we dined with the minister and the Chyag-dso Kusho. The dishes were prepared and served in the Chinese fashion. Chopsticks and spoons were used. The first course was *gya-tug*, a tape-like preparation of wheat-flour and eggs, cooked with minced mutton, and soup. The minister did not eat it, as he had, in common with all lamas, taken the vow of abstaining from eggs. The second course was rice and half a dozen preparations of mutton curry, rice, mutton with preserved vegetables, white and black mushrooms, Chinese green grass, vermicelli, potatoes, and fresh shoots of peas. The third course (*leu*, literally, 'chapter') was buttered and sweetened rice; the fourth, and last, boiled mutton, *tsamba*, and tea. The Tung-chen told me that at sumptuous entertainments thirteen courses are usually served.

About an hour after dinner we visited Jerung la, the second son of the Chyag-dso Kusho, who is a monk in the castle of Diba Dongtse. This building, about 600 years old, is built of stone of the best quality; it faces south, and has balconies (*rabsal*) provided with shutters along each of its five stories. It is of a partly Indian, partly Tibetan style of architecture, with a central courtyard about 100 feet broad and 200 long. Around this, on the sides, the building is 40 feet high, and has three stories, along the outer edge of which, on the courtyard side, are rows of drum-shaped prayer-wheels 2 feet high, and as much in diameter, that take the place of railings. There are some 300 of these prayer-barrels on the stories of the three sides. The main building is on the north side of the court, and is some 60 to 70 feet high. We ascended to the top story by a steep ladder, and were there shown the *gonkhang*, the shrine of the guardian deities—terrible figures, among which I noticed three of *Mamos*, resembling Jaganath, Balavendra, and Subhadra, of the Hindus.

There were several chapels, in each of which was a resident priest called *am-choi*. On the balconies of the wings three or four old women were weaving blankets, and at the entrance to the building a huge mastiff was chained, who made furious attempts to rush at us as we passed.

One hundred yards south of the castle is a garden (*linga*) with tall poplars—some 80 to 100 feet high, and four other kinds of trees planted in rows along its four walks, in the middle of which is a tastefully built summer-house, its cornice and external decorations remarkably pretty. One hundred yards away from it is a target for musket and bow practice.

While we visited the *linga* a greyhound was running about it, but he paid no attention to us. On our way homeward we passed through the village where, under some tall poplars, tradesmen were displaying pottery for sale. We also saw four yellow-turbaned men, who, we were told, were the tax-collector's understrappers.

January 9—While we were breakfasting Rinpoche came in, and again spoke of her hard work and of the merciless treatment of her mother-in-law. I asked her if her husband was not fond of her. 'Oh, sir,' she said, 'we two are like one soul and body; but he is most of the time at Shigatse, where he is the Dahpon's steward (*Nyerpa*).' She told me that she had just heard that her cousin, the Rajah of Sikkim, was coming to Tibet to get married. If his mother came with him, she could surely persuade her to take her with her to Chumbi for a couple of months. She also said to me that her mother-in-law ought not to have given her such a high sounding name as Rinpoche ('the Jewel'), for it is a name given to incarnate lamas and chiefs; but I answered, to her evident pleasure, that Rinpoche was a most appropriate name for handsome and accomplished women.

After this I went to the minister's apartment for dinner. Before it was served we washed our hands. A large copper bowl, or katora, was placed for the purpose before the minister, who, in washing his hands, rubbed them with a kind of wood dust called *sugpa* obtained from a plant growing in Tibet, and used instead of soap.

After dinner the Chyag-dso-pa made presents to the minister, consisting of blankets, Tibetan serge (*pulo*), three pieces of red, scarlet, and yellow English broadcloth, Gyantse rugs of superior quality, Khamba rugs, Chinese brocaded satin, spotted woollen chintz, about two bushels of *tsamba*, a large quantity of buckwheat cakes, twisted sugar cakes, loaves of bread, and 300 *tankas*. The presentation of these gifts he accompanied by profound salutations, and the minister gave him his blessing, when he begged him to pray to the gods to make him prosperous and happy. After this he gave presents of about half the value to the Tung-chen, and so on, less and less, according to each one's rank; to me he gave two Gyantse rugs, two pieces of spotted *pulo*, and a *khatag*. Alms were also distributed among the monks and the minister's menials.

When the Chyag-dso Kusho had finished making all these presents he returned to the minister's room, where we were with him. In course of conversation he suggested the propriety of my presenting the Tashi lama with an elephant. He said that two had recently been sent by the Rajah of Sikkim to Lhasa, to be presented to the Dalai lama, one of which had died on the way. He also spoke of the superiority of Indian metal images over those made in Tibet, and said that those made in Magadha, and called *jai-khim*, were very rare in this country. 'If you had brought some of these, or of *shar-li* (Bengal bell-metal), or *nub-li* (lower Indus valley) and presented them to the minister, he would have been infinitely more pleased than with glass and other fragile and useless toys.'

In the evening it was settled that the minister should start for Tashilhunpo on the morrow, and that Kusho Jambala, the Chyagdso-pa's elder brother, who was suffering from ophthalmia, should accompany him, to submit there to my medical treatment.

January 10—We were up early, and got ready to leave for Tashilhunpo. The Tung-chen advised me to start ahead of the minister, who would overtake me on the road, as he travelled very rapidly, and he furthermore let me pick out for my use the quietest pony in the stable. We had not gone four miles when the minister and four attendants caught up with us. We rode on together some six miles, and when we reached the bed of the stream, now dry, which empties into the Nyang chu, we all alighted. The minister ordered his page to bring him a basketful of earth from a spot he pointed out. This was placed before him as he sat cross-legged on a rug, when he muttered some mantras and made an oblation of *tsamba* and water. The Tung-chen informed me that on the last journey the minister had made this way he had at this spot fallen from his pony, and it was supposed that some evil spirit haunting this spot was desirous of hurting him, and so this ceremony was performed to drive it away.

When it was over we had a light collation, the minister giving me some dried dates and Cabul fruits, while the Tung-chen gave the others treacle, biscuits, and *tsamba*.

At 4 o'clock we reached Tashi-gang. After partaking of refreshments the minister took his seat on the roof of Ang-putta's second story. He called me and Ugyen up, and asked us to teach him the foreign system of land surveying. Ugyen showed him his prismatic compass with attached clinometer. We explained the use of these instruments, and expressed regrets that we had no tape-measure or chain with which we could take measurements, carefully abstaining from mentioning measuring distances by pacing, lest he might suspect us of being surveyors, and withdraw his protection.

He then spoke of his desire to have a sextant, various mathematical instruments, a chest of medicines, and an illustrated work on astronomy. Ugyen expressed his willingness to go to Calcutta to purchase them, were it not that he could not leave me here alone, and with my desire to see Lhasa unfulfilled. The minister replied, 'That is easily provided for. I will look after the Pundit; and as to his going to Lhasa, why, there is every probability that the Tashi lama will go there to ordain the Dalai lama in the fourth month (June), when it will be possible to arrange for the Pundit's going there also. The Shape Rampa, and Phala are my friends; they will help him. However, we will think of all this later on at Tashilhunpo.

He then said there were five persons in Tsang who took interest in science and study—the Shape Porapa, the Chief Secretary (*Dung-yig chenpo*), Ka-chan Dao, the Donyer, and himself. 'There are,' he added, 'many other learned men at Tashilhunpo and in various other monasteries in Tsang, but they only interest themselves in sacred literature; they do not care to know of the science and civilization of other great countries such as that of the *Phyling* (foreigners) and India.'

The minister finally informed me that to-morrow he would visit the Kyi-phug nunnery, about 3 miles off in the hills behind Tashi-gang. The Lady Superior and her nuns (*tsun-mo*) had repeatedly begged him to visit their convent, but he had been so pressed for time that he had only been able to do so once in the last six years.

January 11—The minister and his party left for the Kyi-phug convent at 7 a.m., and we set off for Tashilhunpo after breakfast. Old Kusho Jambala was unable to keep up with us. As he followed slowly the minister's muleteers, his yellow-satin mitre, his spectacles, his manner of sitting on his pony, and his tall lank figure recalled to my mind the renowned knight of La Mancha. With his leave we rode ahead. We saw on the way a woman sweeping the ground, and on inquiry she told us that she was removing the thick grime which covered the ground so that her cattle might the more easily pick up the grass. Many sheep, we were told, die in winter on account of the ice crust which covers the grass. At 4 p.m. we arrived at Chyang chu, where we were most kindly received by the Deba Shikha, and lodged in the same quarters we had previously occupied.

January 12—After breakfast we strolled about the *linga* in front of the minister's bathing-house (*cham chu*). It is surrounded by a wall of sun-dried bricks, stones, and turf 7 feet high. In the southeast corner is the snug little two-storied house where the minister passes a few days in October. The cooking and bathing is done under yak-hair tents pitched in the western avenue of the grove.

At 9 o'clock we set out, and were at Tashilhunpo by noon, and there found Phurchung, who had arrived the day before from Khamba *djong*. The Djongpon, who knew him, had told him that unless he came bearing a passport from the Tashi lama or the Commander of Shigatse, he could not let him pass the frontier. There were formal orders from the Lhasa Government not to let any one cross the frontier, even if bearing letters from the high officials of Labrang, who are not, however, in charge of frontier affairs. So Rinzing Namgyal had to leave our luggage with the Pipon of Lachan, and had gone back to Darjiling.

IV

Residence at Tashilhunpo, and Preparations for Journey to Lhasa

January 13—The money we had brought from Darjiling being almost expended, we were now in the necessity of selling the pearls and gold we had brought with us. I therefore sent Ugyen to the market to inquire of Lupa gyaltsan, with whom we had left some tolas of pearls for sale, if he had been able to dispose of them. Lupa gyaltsan told him that he had shown the pearls to a Lhasa merchant, who had not offered more than cost price for them. The market for pearls, he added, was very poor, and we must not expect to realize much profit out of ours for some months to come.

He also told Ugyen that great preparations were being made for the Grand Lama's visit to Lhasa in May, for the ordination of the Dalai lama. On that occasion the Tashi would have to make return presents and give rewards in money to the various officials and chiefs of Tibet, for which robes, boots, etc., were now being made in great numbers.

January 14—On the way to the market to-day Ugyen met Lupa gyaltsan, who informed him that some traders from Phagri, Chumbi, and Rin-chen-gang had just arrived, and that, to judge from their conversation, they were not well disposed towards us. He therefore cautioned Ugyen, so that he might not meet them unprepared. Ugyen, in consequence, first went to the police station and learnt from his friend, the Chinese havildar of Shigatse, who the newcomers were; then he looked them up, and questioned them about the passes to India. They told him they had been able to get here through the Lhasa Government having declared the Phagri pass open. As to the Sikkim rajah coming here, they could give no definite information, though they said there was much talk about his marrying the daughter of a great man of Lhasa.

In the afternoon the minister sent for me, and told me that the boxes containing the lithographic press sent him some months ago had not been opened for fear of smallpox. 'I thought the cases contained some miraculous remedies which could neutralize smallpox. One night I smelt some gaseous emanations coming out from the boxes, which I thought contained the germs of smallpox; so I could not sleep that night, so troubled was my mind lest smallpox should attack us.' We laughed heartily at his holiness's fancies, and I told him that the vaccine he had asked for was among the things still at the Lachan pass. At last he was convinced of the groundlessness of his fears, and joined with us in laughing at them.

January 15—After breakfast we unpacked in the minister's library the lithographic press, and set it up, the minister taking great interest in the work and assisting me himself.

January 16—After breakfast, which we took with the minister in the west drawing-room of the Phuntso Khangsar, he told me that he was most anxious to get the things I had at Lachan. Phurchung was not intelligent enough to get around the Djongpon of Khamba, even if he were provided with the best of passports. He thought it indispensable for Ugyen to undertake the journey to Lachan, especially as he had relatives there, a circumstance which would greatly facilitate the accomplishment of his mission.

Ugyen objected to start on such a difficult journey at a season of the year when the cold would be intense and the Kangra lamo pass would be blocked with snow; but he felt, nevertheless, called upon to comply with the minister's request, if he provided him with a proper passport. Not only did the minister promise to give him an excellent passport, but he also said that he would propitiate the gods to the end that they would protect him from dangers from man, beast, or disease, till the first of the third Tibetan moon (end of April, 1882).

When this was settled Ugyen begged the minister to look after me in his absence, and not to allow any injury to be done me on the ground that I was a foreigner. He asked him to give him a letter stating, first, that he (the minister) would see to my welfare, and that I would be in no way molested; second, that on Ugyen-gyatso's return he and I might go on a pilgrimage to Central Tibet; third, that we should be protected in any difficulty which might arise on the score of our being foreigners.

Besides the great importance of obtaining these written assurances from the minister, the production of such a letter by Ugyen, in case of my death during his absence, would relieve him of all responsibility towards our Government.

The minister promised to keep me in his house as a member of his family, to defray all my expenses, and to send me to Lhasa in May with the Tashi lama's party. Should, however, neither the Grand Lama nor himself go to Lhasa, he would make other arrangements for our pilgrimage there. As to the third point mentioned in the above agreement, he said that he was fully aware when he invited us to come to Tashilhunpo of the responsibility he assumed towards us, and that he would not allow us to be molested by any one during our stay in Tibet.

January 17—The minister went in the morning to Shigatse, to grant absolution to the departed soul of Shang-po, one of the six Tsopon who had been so severely punished by the Chinese authorities on the 13th of December last, and who had died from the effects of the flogging then received. We devoted the whole day to the setting up of the lithographic press.

January 18—The minister told Ugyen that Kusho Badur-la, the head of the transportation department, wished to see the pearls we had brought with us. Ugyen did not find him at home, but conversed with his wife, whom he at once recognized, having seen her at Tumlung and Chumbi, she being the elder sister of the present Rajah of Sikkim. She gave him a very kind reception, and talked to him for nearly an hour, treating him to tea and *gya-tug* (vermicelli).

January 19—To-day being the day of the new moon, nearly a thousand beggars lined the road leading from Tashilhunpo to Shigatse, where Lhagpa tsering was distributing alms to them.

At noon Ugyen visited the marketplace, where he witnessed a quarrel between a woman and a Khamba over a *tanka*'s worth of *tsamba*, in the course of which the woman challenged the man to take an oath very common in Tibet, namely, that if he told an untruth, he might never see the Grand Lama's face. The people of Khams are a fierce race who infest the solitudes of Tibet, and generally carry on depredations on the isolated villages north of Lhasa. They are a dangerous class.

January 20—Early in the morning we received an invitation to dine with our acquaintance, Lupa gyaltsan. We were told that to-day was the New Year's Day of the working class, and was so observed by all the people of Tibet, with the exception of the clergy.

After breakfast we went to the minister's, and told him the press was ready for working. I asked him to print a very auspicious hymn, that the first fruit of our labour might be a sacred composition. He at once ran to his study and brought a stanza, or *stotra*, composed by the present Grand Lama in honour and praise of the minister. This he copied himself on the transfer paper, and we obtained excellent impressions of it, much to his delight. The 'stone press' (*do par*) was forthwith given the name of the 'miraculous press' (*tul par*).

At three in the afternoon we asked leave to go to Lupa gyaltsan's house, where I had a most hearty reception, he and his wife coming to help me dismount from my pony. We were ushered into a newly finished room on the first floor, where was also his chapel. First *chang* was served, then tea was brought by his daughter, a girl of ten, and the wife placed a wooden bowl filled with *tsamba* and some pieces of boiled mutton on a little table before us. Then Lupa gyaltsan, taking off his turban, asked me to take *sol ja* and consider that I was dining in my own house. Shortly after, Ugyen, in accordance with Tibetan custom, made a short speech exhorting Lupa to always inquire after my health during his absence from Tashilhunpo, and to get for me all such articles of food, etc., that I might want. He thanked him for his kindness, and added that, as Lupa and I were old acquaintances, we should behave to each other as brothers born of the same mother. So saying, he presented him and his wife with a rupee and a *khatag* each, putting the coins in their hands and the scarves round their necks. Ugyen then put a *khatag* around my servant Lhagpa's neck, telling him to serve me ever faithfully. Lupa's daughter, having dressed herself in her gala dress, danced for us and sang a song, first in the Tibetan way, then in the Chinese; she sang also a Chinese song, Lupa accompanying her on the flute (*ling-bu*). After this Lupa's wife sang a song, and then wished us a happy new year. We then took leave of our hosts, wishing them also a happy new year.

Having inquired if the observance of this day was a purely Tibetan custom, I gathered from their reply that this was the New Year's Day according to the Tibetan custom of the pre-Buddhist period. It is the only remnant of ancient Tibetan custom, as far as I know, which has not been displaced by Buddhism.

January 21—This day was also observed as a holiday by the laity. There were so few persons in the marketplace that Ugyen could buy no provisions. The minister graciously insisted that I should take up my quarters in his residence, Phuntso Khangsar, where he offered me the library with an attached waiting room and bathroom.

In the evening Nyima-dorje, the oldest son of the Chyag-dso-pa of Dongtse, came and consulted me about his eyes. On the right one I found that a cataract had formed. I told him I was exceedingly sorry I had no medicines with me to suit his case, but that Ugyen was going to Calcutta as soon as he had obtained a passport, and that he would bring back some drugs with him. He then said that it was this passport that had brought him here to speak to the minister about, and that he believed it would be ready in a day or two.

January 22—I resumed reading English and working sums in arithmetic with the minister. After reading a few lines he turned over the pages of Ganot's *Physics*, and asked me to explain the diagrams on telegraphy and the camera obscura. He wanted everything explained to him; but, unfortunately for me, I was not myself acquainted with most of the subjects which excited his curiosity. Not prepared to expose my ignorance, I dwelt longer on such questions as I could best explain, and with which I was most familiar; but in spite of all my attempts to evade his inquisitiveness, the shrewd minister gauged me well, and expressed his earnest desire to meet such men as I had described to him, Dr Sircar and my brother, Navin Chandra, to be.

In the afternoon Nyima-dorje brought the *lam-yig* (passport), and presented it to the minister. We were called in and shown it; but Ugyen disapproved of it, as nothing was said in it of his return journey here, so it was sent back for correction.

January 23—Crowds of visitors came to receive the minister's blessing (*chyag-wang*); among them were many Khalkhas and other Mongols from remote sections of that country. The Khalkhas were introduced by Lobzang Arya, my cook during my first sojourn at Tashilhunpo in 1879, and now a man of standing and elder (*gyer-gyan*) of the Khalkha in Khamtsan. The minister talked with him in Mongolian, after receiving the pilgrims with much kindness.

January 24—Early in the morning I was called by the minister, and found a young monk of the Nyagpa Ta-tsang (a Tantrik school) sitting with him. The minister asked me to examine his eyes, which were a little swollen, telling me at the same time that this young man had served him devotedly during his residence at the Nyag-khang, and was deserving of my care. I gave him a few doses of alum lotion to wash his eyes with, and made him promise to walk round the monastery several times a day whenever it was fair weather.

In the afternoon I lunched with the Tung-chen, and we conversed about the high winds which at this season blow every afternoon. He spoke also of the Phagri pass, and told me that the collector of customs (Serpon) there was a friend of his, and that if Ugyen went to Darjiling by the Phagri pass, he could give him a letter of introduction to that officer. I thanked him for his kindness, adding that Ugyen preferred the Lachan pass, as he had a passport from the commander of Shigatse which did not extend to Phagri *djong*.

January 25—The minister told me that in certain stellar maps he had examined he saw that figures were given the different constellations, and that he understood these figures really existed in the sky; so, wishing to see them, he had bought a large telescope at much cost. He did not know, however, how to use it, and was most anxious to have a well-illustrated work on astronomy, that he might know what to look for and where to look for it. He also remembered my saying that the regions of the moon, Saturn, and even of the sun, were visible through the telescope, and he was curious to know what these luminaries contained, for he had hitherto been under the impression that these celestial bodies were angelic luminaries who, for the excellence of their moral merits, had been promoted to celestial mansions of different heights, thence to shed on us their radiant lustre, and thereby guide all living beings of the earth in the path of dharma.

While we were thus talking Nyima-dorje arrived, and presented the passport to his holiness. After perusing it he handed it to me, and I passed it to Ugyen. We found that the commanders of Shigatse (*Dahpon*), in order to prevent the introduction of smallpox, had instructed in it the Djongpon of Khamba to examine the contents of our boxes, to prevent contagion being brought into the country in them. This would put the Djongpon in a position to exact from Ugyen any amount of money he might choose; but as it would be inconvenient to wait longer for a corrected *lam-yig*, the minister advised Ugyen to be satisfied with the present one, and to do the best he could with it.

January 26—Ugyen declared that Phurchung's services were absolutely necessary to him, and asked that he be lent to him for six months, adding that without him he would not start on the journey. After breakfast the minister consulted with the Tungchen and Gopa about keeping me with him. Arrangements were soon made; but they all objected to my keeping Lhagpa as my servant, telling me that a Shigatse man could not be trusted, as they were cunning, deceitful, and faithless. He added that, as he had undertaken to look to my wants and comforts, there was not the least necessity for my keeping a servant at my own expense. Fearing lest he should suspect me of ulterior designs, I at once accepted his decision, though I had hoped, by means of Lhagpa, to keep myself informed of what was going on in the monastery and the town, I myself being practically confined within the walls of the minister's residence, as I was required, according to custom, to wait upon his holiness.

January 27—Ugyen and Phurchung busied themselves in preparing for the journey. The former took a pair of Gyantse blankets and a suit of lambskin clothes, and I gave Phurchung a pair of my own blankets for his use during the journey. They purchased a large quantity of sheep's fat to distribute among the Sikkimese on the way. Dried mutton, *tsamba*, and sheep's fat are the dainties the Sikkimese esteem above all others. They hired four ponies to ride and carry their luggage.

In the evening we were invited to take tea with the minister, when Ugyen took formal leave, making three profound bows to his holiness, and praying that his blessing might always be on him, and that, by the mercy of the sacred Buddhas, he might reach his destination safely.

January 28—To-day, the 10th of the 12th moon, was considered a highly auspicious day on which to start for India. At 6 o'clock Ugyen, Phurchung, and I went to the minister's apartment, when his holiness, after a short prayer, wished them a safe and pleasant journey, and placed *khatag* on their necks. At Ugyen's special request I desired Phurchung in a short speech to serve Ugyen as he would serve me, to which he answered, '*La laso, laso*' (yes, sir, yes). Then we returned to the Torgod chyi-khang, our lodging, where, after breakfast, I presented parting *khatag* to my faithful companions. The scene was extremely touching, and they shed tears at leaving me alone. I, too, could not suppress my feelings as I exhorted them to take care of themselves in the snows, and to be prepared for heavy snowfalls. They both rode off in high spirits towards Delel.

Shortly after I sent Wang-chyug gyalpo and the minister's page to fetch my clothes, utensils, etc., to my new quarters. They brought some, and told me that my trusted servant, Lhagpa, was quietly carrying off my kettles and plates. I immediately went to the Torgod chyi-khang, and asked him to give up the missing articles, but he denied any knowledge of them, though we could see the breast of his gown stuffed out with them, and he insisted the devils (*de*) must have carried them off. I at once sent for the Nyerpa and the Tung-chen. It was impossible, however, to search Lhagpa, so we had to confine ourselves to drawing up a list of the things missing and of the things I had with me; and then, locking the door of my lodgings, the Tung-chen told Lhagpa to return quietly to his house. The Tung-chen smiled at the roguery of my trusted servant, and made me understand that I knew very little about Tibetans, and that I should not have trusted Shigatse people.

January 29—The minister came to my rooms, and insisted on nailing up a curtain, so as to divide the room in two, the books in the northern part, and my seat and bedstead in the southern half of it. He said that such an arrangement was necessary, as the books were of arsenical paper, and I would fall ill if I continually breathed the air of this place. Underneath my room was the cook-room (*sol-tab*), the heat from which kept the library dry and warm. There was but one window, about 4 feet square, in my room, through which I could see the Nartang hills.

At 9 o'clock breakfast was announced, when the Nyerpa conducted me to the minister's presence. Tea was served me in a pretty china cup, and Kachan gopa brought me a bowl of *tsamba* and a few slices of boiled mutton, and, noticing my difficulty in making dough of the *tsamba* and tea after the Tibetan fashion, took it from me and mixed it himself, twirling the cup on the palm of his hand, and mixing the flour and tea with his forefinger.

In the dining-room there was a parrot lately presented to the minister by the Chyan-dso shar of Tashilhunpo, and a small saffron plant raised from some seed brought from Kashmir. This plant throve well, I was told, but yielded no saffron.

After breakfast I returned to my studies, and, with the permission of the minister, commenced a search for Sanskrit books in his library. At noon the cook placed on an earthenware stove near me a pot of steaming tea, and in the afternoon he filled it again. I was told it was injurious to drink cold water; Tibetans very seldom drink it; the laymen quench their thirst with draughts of cold fermented barley liquor (*chang*), and lamas with hot tea.

As the minister, on account of his vows, was debarred from eating in the afternoon, evening, or night, he desired me to take my supper with the secretary; so when the lamp was lighted I went downstairs, and sat gossiping in the kitchen with him.

January 30—To-day I discovered three Sanskrit works written in the Tibetan character. They were the *Kavyadarsha* by Acharya Sri Dandi; the *Chandra Vyakarana* by Chandra Gomi; and the *Svarasvat Vyakarana* by Acharya Ami. I was transported with joy when I saw that they contained explanations in Tibetan.

In the afternoon I showed Sri Dandi's work to the minister, who, to my surprise, was able to give me more information concerning him than I had expected, and he had committed the entire work to memory. 'Dandi,' he said, 'must have lived a thousand and more years ago, for his work was translated into Tibetan by one of the Sakya hierarchs who lived about six hundred years ago, and it is probable that the work was not very new when it came to be known in this country.'

January 31—Preparations for the New Year's ceremonies now occupy the attention of all classes. Large numbers of men are coming to take the first vows of monkhood, and Kachan Shabdung introduced to-day a number of them to his holiness. The minister's time was largely taken up with these religious duties, and I could not see him for more than ten or twelve minutes. When I withdrew to my room, the astrologer, Lobzang, came to see me; he was busy with the almanac for the new year, and kept turning over its pages to see if there were any mistakes. The minister also had to examine it before submitting it to the Grand Lama.

Lobzang, seeing the lithographic press, was curious to know what 'those stones and wheeled apparatus,' as he put it, were meant for. He begged me to explain the process of printing, but I evaded his questions, as I had been told not to talk of the press to outsiders.

In the evening the Deba Shika arrived with a large supply of butter and *tsamba*, evidently to be used in the New Year's ceremonies.

From this time on I devoted myself to the study of the sacred books and histories of Tibet, and ceased to keep a regular diary, noting only such things concerning the customs and manners of the country as seemed interesting. When I felt tired of Tibetan I refreshed my mind with the melodious verses of Dandi's *Kavyadarsha*, both in the original and the Tibetan translation, and during my leisure hours I conversed with the Tung-chen, the Nyerpa, and other well-informed men.

The first part of February was very cold; the north wind blew daily, raising clouds of dust in the plain to the west and south of the city. People, however, were busily engaged out-of-doors, gathering fuel and tending cattle; in fact, this is the busiest season of the year, a period of universal merry-making, and also of great activity in trade.

The Tibetans, whether monks or laymen, are very early risers. In the monastery the great trumpet (*dung chen*) summoned the monks to the congregation hall for prayers at three in the morning, and those who failed to be present were punished at the Tsog-chen; for, though there is no roll call, yet the absence of a single monk is surely remarked by the provost.

The minister, who frequently peeped into my room to see whether I was studying or no, excused me from early rising on the ground that he often found me up with my books at midnight.

On the 16th I was asked by the Deba Shika to go with him the following day to see the Grand Lama dance, or *cham*. On my observing that I feared the whips of the stage guards (*djim-gag-pa*) if I mixed with the crowd, he promised to have seats reserved for our party.

Early the next morning men and women dressed in their best began streaming into the monastery to see the *cham*. Accompanied by the Tung-chen, the Deba Shika, and a lama friend, we went our way towards the Nyag-khang, in the courtyard of the Tsug-la khang, in which the dances were to begin. On the way we stopped to visit an old chapel containing several inscriptions relating to Gedun-dub, the founder of Tashilhunpo, and the mark of a horse's hoof impressed on a rock, which passers-by touch with their heads.

Then we took our seats on the balcony of the second floor of the Nyag-khang building, and watched the preparations for the dance. Twenty-four sacred flags of satin, with embroidered figures of dragons and other monsters worked in threads of gold, were first unfurled at the top of long and slender poplar poles, and square parti-coloured flags were also hung all around the Tsug-la khang. About a dozen monks wearing coats of mail had masks which, for the most part, represented eagles' heads. The dancers entered one after the other, and then followed the abbot of the Nyag-pa Ta-tsan, Kusho Yondjin Lhopa by name, holding a *dorje* in his right hand, and a bell in his left. He wore a yellow mitre-shaped cap, with lappets covering his ears and hanging down to his breast. He was tall and fair; he looked intelligent, his manners were most dignified, and he performed his part most cleverly.

After a while the flag-bearers, the masked monks, and all the cortege repaired to the great Tsug-la khang of Tashilhunpo, which is about 300 yards long and 150 feet broad. Round this courtyard are four-storied buildings with handsome pillared balconies, the Grand Lama's seat being on the western side. The long balconies on the east and south were occupied by the nobility of Tsang, and those on the north by Mongol pilgrims and a number of

Shigatse merchants. The abbots of the four Ta-tsan had seats just above the Nyag-pa, who, to the number of fifty-odd, and assisted by their Om-dse and the Dorje Lopon, these holding in their hands cymbals and tambourines, went through a short religious service under the direction of the Kusho Yondjin Lhopa. This latter made during this service peculiar motions with his hands, in which he held, as I have said, a *dorje* and a bell.

When this was over a figure with a dark-coloured mask, and representing the Hoshang Dharma-tala, advanced, and the spectators flung him *khatags*, which his two yellow-faced wives picked up. When these three had left the scene, the four kings of the four cardinal points appeared, dressed in all the wild and barbaric splendour in which such monarchs could indulge. Then came the sons of the gods, some sixty in number, dressed in beautiful silk robes glittering with gold embroideries and precious stones. These were followed by Indian *atsaras*, whose black and bearded faces and uncouth dress excited loud laughter among the crowd. Then appeared four guardians of the graves, whose skeleton-like appearance was meant to remind the spectators of the terrors of death. After this the devil was burnt in effigy on a pile of dry sedge, and with this the *cham* came to an end. While it was in progress incense was burnt on Mount Dolma (Dolmai-ri), behind the monastery, and on all the other neighbouring mountain-tops. I learnt from the Tung-chen that there were several books on the subject of these religious dances and music.

The following day (February 18) I went with the Tung-chen for a walk. Proceeding about 300 paces, we came to a flight of stone steps below the western gateway. This latter, which is some 12 feet high and 8 wide, has massive doors, which are closed between sunset and sunrise; it is the principal entrance of the monastery. About 50 feet beyond this gate, and on a line with the gilt mausolea of the grand lamas (*gya-phig*), we came to another flight of steps, some of them cut in the rock, which led us to the northwestern corner of the monastery and well up the slope of the Dolmai-ri, whence we obtained a good view of the whole of Tashilhunpo monastery, the adjacent villages and mountains.

We now turned to the northeast along a narrow rocky path, which brought us behind the Nyag-khang. I was surprised to notice among the rocks some willows (*chyang-ma*) in flower, and we saw also the impress of hoofs on the rocks, left there, the Tung-chen said, by the chargers of some Bodhisattvas; *rang chyung*, or 'naturally produced', the Tibetans say of such marvels. There were several half-starved pariah dogs lying about, who looked at us with sleepy eyes, and the Tung-chen remarked that in all probability they had been sinful *gelong* (monks) in some former existence, and were now expiating their evil deeds. He much regretted that we had not brought some balls of *tsamba* for them.

Some 200 paces farther on in the same direction we came to a huge stone building called Kiku-tamsa. It is about 60 paces in length and 30 in breadth, and I counted nine stories in it. Though it is upwards of 200 years old, it is still in excellent repair. Captain Turner made a sketch of it in 1783, but he mistook it for 'a religious edifice'. It is at present used as a godown for dried carcasses of yaks, sheep and goats. Every year, in the latter part of November, all the sacred pictures of the Labrang are hung up on this building for the benefit of the people, who, by touching these paintings with their foreheads, receive the blessings of the gods they represent.

On our way down to the eastern gateway of Tashilhunpo we met two Ladaki Tibetans, who told us that they had just come from the Chang-tang, or the desert in the northwestern part of Tibet.

The Tung-chen showed me the Dongtse Khamtsan, where the people of Dongtse and neighbourhood put up. We also saw a juniper bush planted by Gedun dub, the founder of Tashilhunpo, in which that saintly lama's hair is said to still exist. I had pointed out to me, as we walked along the spacious buildings of the Taisamling college, the Kyil khang Ta-tsan and the Shartse college.

The descent to the foot of the hill proved very steep, but all along it we found rows of prayer-wheels, which we put in motion as we passed; near the gateway, and beside a *mendong*, there were two dozen of them together.

Passing by the main Mani lha-khang, we reached the eastern gateway of Tashilhunpo. Over it is a notice forbidding smoking within the monastery, for both the red- and yellow-hat schools of lamaism strongly denounce tobacco-smoking by monks.

From this gateway a road leads south to the Kiki-naga, where the Grand Lama's mother resides, while another runs westward to the court of the Tashi lama, or Labrang gyal-tsan tonpo.

It was dusk when we had finished our walk around the monastery, and lamps were already burning in many of the houses to bid farewell to the old year.

February 19, New Year's Day—The preparations for the day's celebration commenced before dawn, and the noise of the blowing of the kitchen fires never ceased, as there were many dishes and dainties to be got ready for the dinner the minister was to give to a large party of nobles and incarnate lamas.

When the minister came back from visiting the Grand Lama, he told me that the latter had inquired about me, as he had some translation into Sanskrit which he desired I should make for him. 'His holiness,' the minister said, 'has given me a hundred and twenty titles of chapters of a work he has written, and wishes you to put them into Sanskrit for him.' The minister further said that when I had finished this work he would present me to the Grand Lama.

The next day the minister was called to Dongtse by the illness of the Dahpon Phala's wife; his prayers, it was hoped, would restore her to health. About a week after his departure he was suddenly recalled by the Grand Lama, with whom he had, on March 3, a long conference. The Dalai lama's Government had protested against the Tashi lama having taken the vows of monkhood from the Sakya Pan-chen, a red-hat lama, the hierarch of the Sakya school. The Dalai lama charged him with encouraging heresy, if not with being a heretic himself. It was for this reason that the Tashi lama had not been invited to ordain the supreme ruler of Tibet, for, belonging to the Gelugpa or yellow-hat school, the Dalai lama could have no connection with the school of which the Sakya Pan-chen was the chief.

On March 4 the minister ordained some forty monks (*gelong*). Formerly the Grand Lama used to perform this ceremony himself, but he has now delegated a large portion of his religious duties, including ordination, to the minister.

Two days after this the minister was again asked to go to Dongtse, as the wife of the Dahpon was still ill, and he (the Dahpon) had orders to proceed at once to Lhasa. The minister asked me if I would accompany him, and I readily assented, as it would enable me to make arrangements for my journey to Lhasa during the next summer.

On March 7 we started, and reached Tashigang the same day. Some of the people we passed were already ploughing, and the trees showed signs of budding.

The next day we reached Dongtse by 4 o'clock in the afternoon. We found the Dahpon's wife, a lady of about thirty, and his sister, Je-tsun Kusho, in the central room of the fifth floor of the castle (*phodrang*).

The Lhacham was dressed in a Mongol robe; on her head was a crown-shaped ornament studded with precious stones and pearls of every size. Pearl necklaces, strings of amber and coral hung over her breast, and her clothes were of the richest Chinese satin brocades and the finest native cloth. The Je-tsun Kusho, an elderly woman and a nun, was dressed very plainly; but, though nuns all shave their heads, she wore all her hair. She belonged, it appears, to the Nyingma school, which allows nuns certain privileges, this one among others.

The following day I prescribed some medicines for Je-tsun Kusho, who was suffering from bronchitis, and four days later I administered some to the Dahpon's wife, who had had until then a lama from the Tse-chan monastery attending her. My medicines did her no good, and at this the minister appeared much concerned. I tried a second dose, but with like absence of effect. In fact, the Lhacham felt worse, and said that evil stars were in the ascendant in her quarter of the sky (*khams*), and would work her ruin. Some people, she said, insisted she was being persecuted by evil spirits who had followed her here from Tingri (*Djong*), but she did not believe it; it was the stars which were against her. The minister looked at me and asked me how it was that my medicines were unavailing in the Lhacham's case. In the midst of a dead silence I told him that all the medicines which different persons had administered to the patient were affecting her nervous system, each in a different way. I had heard her say that she had first taken those of a Chinese quack, then those of a Nepalese physician, and lastly the medicines of several learned lama doctors. Under the circumstances I should not have prescribed for her at all, but that as every one had expected me to do something for her, I had ceded to their wishes. It was, however, my opinion that if the Lhacham would be cured, the only medicine she required was no medicine at all.

Under this new treatment, which she promptly adopted, there was a marked improvement in the Lhacham's health within the next ten days. I used frequently to talk with her, and she seemed to entertain a kind regard for me. One day the minister suggested in her presence that it would be a good thing if I could be sent to Lhasa to see the Lord Buddha, the incarnate Shenrezig, the Dalai lama. The Lhacham approved the suggestion, and promised to have me lodged in her residence at Lhasa, and to take me under her protection while there.

On March 23 I left Dongtse for Tashilhunpo. On the way to Tashigang we saw lambs picking the young shoots of grass, and the country folk were busy in the fields with their yaks, which were decorated with red, yellow, blue, and green hair tassels, and collars of coloured wool, and cowries. The farmers hold certain religious ceremonies on beginning ploughing and on first putting the yokes (*nya-shing*) on their yaks. They also have at this time most amusing ploughing races.

Beyond Norbu khyung-djin we saw, as we rode along, afar off on a slope of rock, incised in gigantic characters, the sacred formulae, *Om vajra pani hum, om wagishvari hum, om ah hum*, etc.

The next day, at 3 p.m., just as we reached the house of the Deba Shika, there was quite a heavy fall of snow. On the 25th we arrived at Tashilhunpo, and I once more took up my interrupted historical studies.

V

From Tashilhunpo to Yamdo Samding, and Thence to Lhasa

On Wednesday, April 26, 1882, being the eighth day of the third moon of the water-horse year of the Tibetan cycle, I left Tashilhunpo for Dongtse, there to make my final arrangements for the journey to Lhasa.

The cook, Dao-sring, nicknamed Aku chya-rog, or 'Uncle Daw', on account of the dirt and soot which always covered his face, now turned out with well-washed face and hands, in new leather boots and fur cap, and helped me to mount my pony.

Tsering-tashi, who had been designated to accompany me, had procured all that was necessary for a long journey—butter, meat, pounded dry mutton, spices, rice, a copper kettle, an iron pan, flint stones, tinder, and a bellows, and the Tung-chen had presented me with *tsamba*, *chura*, and pea-flour for the use of the servants, and peas for the ponies. Of all the articles Tsering-tashi had brought, the one which he valued the most was a bamboo tea-churn, which he thought the most beautiful and useful of all our belongings.

I tied up my medicine-case in one of my saddle-bags, and in the other I put my clothes, and at 2 o'clock we started. There were five of us in the party, all mounted, and riding in single file: first came the Tung-chen, then I, then came Tsering-tashi, and the cook and a groom brought up the rear. We followed the same road I had already gone over on several occasions, and stopped the first night at Chyang-chu, where we put up in the house of our friend the Deba Shika.

April 27—About 2 inches of snow had fallen in the night, and there was a slight fog when we got up in the morning. In front of the house I noticed some men and women digged a kind of root called *rampa*. This underground grass acquires, in some places, a length of 5 or 6 feet, and in the early spring, when vegetables and forage are scarce, it is dug up. The people know where to dig for it by the little shoots which rise above the ground.

We were detained at Chyang-chu all day, waiting for Tsering-tashi, who had been obliged to stop over at Tashi-gyantse to make some purchases.

In the evening tea was served by Po-ka-chan, a grey-haired monk who works on the estates of the minister at Tanag. He had travelled much in Kongpo, Naga, and among the Mishmis, and in Tsari. He related how the savage Lhokabra harassed the Tibetan pilgrims, and how the Tsang-po river entered the country of defiles in Eastern Bhutan, rushing in a tremendous waterfall over the top of a gigantic precipice called the 'Lion's Face', or Sing-dong.

April 28—The villagers had all assembled to bid us farewell, and the Tung-chen's sister presented me with a 'scarf for good luck' (*tashi khatag*). We saw as we rode along numerous flocks of cranes (*tontong*), and brown ducks with red necks were swimming in the river and the irrigation ditches. We stopped for the night at Pishi Mani lha-khang, where Angputti received us with the same kindness she had shown us on my former visits. Snow fell during the night, but our hostess's servants watched over our ponies, and stabled them under the roof of the *okhang*, or godown, on the ground floor.

We reached Dongtse at 4 p.m. on the 29th, and took up our lodgings in the *Choide*; but in the evening the Deba Chola came and invited us to put up at the castle, where the minister was still staying.

The Tung-chen took an early opportunity to inform the minister that his presence was anxiously expected at Tashilhunpo, where hundreds of lamas were awaiting his return to be ordained *gelong* (priests). He also told him that the Mirkan Pandita, a Mongol Kutuketu who had come to Tibet for the sole purpose of studying under the minister, now intended coming to Dongtse, and had begged that arrangements might be made for his accommodation in the minister's residence. While the minister recognized the necessity for his returning to Tashilhunpo, he said he could not leave until the services for the propitiation of the Lord of Death, Dorje jig-je, to be undertaken for the recovery of the Dahpon's wife, were finished.

May 2—The monks of Dongtse, headed by a learned old lama named Punlo, arrived at the castle to commence reading the Kahgyur. Arrangements were made in the *nyihok* for the worship of Dorje jig-je. *Torma* offerings were placed on the terrace on the top of the castle, and rugs were spread on the floor of the little glazed room (*nyihok*) on it for the accommodation of the lamas. In the house was a raised seat for the minister, and in a corner of the room a little chapel, with all the necessary church furniture, among which the *tsegi bumba*, or 'bowl of life', of Tsepamed was conspicuous. This propitiatory ceremony occupied three days.

May 8—News arrived to-day that smallpox was raging at Lhasa and other places of Central Tibet. Several persons had also died of it at Gyantse, and three or four localities between that town and Lhasa were infected. The Lhacham was in so great dread of the disease that she confined herself to her sitting-room, refusing to see any one.

On May 9 the Lhacham left for Lhasa, after confiding to the minister's care Ane, her third son, a boy of ten, who was destined for the Church. The Lhacham and her two other sons, Lhasre and Kundi, made their devotions at the different chapels of the castle, which it took them nearly an hour to accomplish, and then returned to the fifth story of the building to receive the minister's blessing, after which they took their leave.

At the foot of the ladder in the courtyard a white pony, with handsome housings of embroidered cloth and a Tartar saddle, awaited the Lhacham. With her pearl-studded headdress, her gold and ruby charm-boxes, her necklaces of coral and amber, and her clothes of satin and *kinkab*, she looked like a heroine of romance or a goddess.

On the following day I went with the minister and the Kusho Ane, and took up my residence in the Dongtse *Choide*. Here I witnessed the opening ceremonies connected with the Kalachakra mandala worship. The Om-dse, or high priest of the *Choide*, with the help of two assistants, had described with coloured *tsamba* a circle about 20 feet in diameter on the floor of the northern room on the third floor of the Tsug-la khang. Within this mandala were drawn the entrance, spires, doors, and domes of the Kalachakra mansion. The presiding deity was tall, many-armed, and had several heads; his attendants were of the tantrik order of deities, and all these paintings were made in coloured powders and *tsamba*. The minister highly praised the work, and gave as a gratuity to each of the eighty monks of the monastery half a *tanka*, and an entertainment of tea and *tsamba*.

May 11—A messenger arrived to-day to inform us that the Lhacham would leave Gyantse the next morning, and that we would do well to see her at Gyankhar before she started; so, though I was feeling very poorly, I made up my mind to start at once.

My ponies were brought inside the monastery by Pador, a stalwart young fellow who had been several times to Lhasa, and who had been chosen by the Chyag-dso-pa to accompany me, and I got ready to leave early on the morrow.

At an early hour the next day I went with Tsering-tashi to see the minister, ask his protection (*kyab ju*), and beg to be favoured with his advice as to the conduct of our journey, or *sung-ta*, as it is called.

As is usual on such occasions, each of us presented him with a *khatag*, in the corner of which were tied up a few *tankas* in a bit of paper, on which was written our request.

After a hurried breakfast, while the servants were engaged in saddling the ponies and packing, I went and kotowed to the Buddha in the temple, placed *khatag* on the sacred images, and distributed alms to the monks assembled in the courtyard to offer prayers for my safe journey. Then I returned to my room, picked out the handsomest *khatag* I possessed, and presented it to the minister. His holiness graciously touched my head with his palms, and in solemn tones said, 'Sarat Chandra, Lhasa is not a good place. The people there are not like those you meet here. The Lhasa people are suspicious and insincere. You do not know, and, in fact, you cannot read their character. I advise you not to stay long in one place there. The Lhacham Kusho is a powerful personage in Lhasa; she will protect you, but you should so behave as rarely to require her protection. Stay not long in the vicinity of the Dabung or Sera monasteries. If you intend to make a long stay at Lhasa, choose your residence in a garden or village in the suburbs. You have chosen a very bad time for your pilgrimage, as smallpox is raging all over Central Tibet; but you will return safely, though the journey will be trying and fraught with immense difficulties.' Then, turning to Tsering-tashi, around whose neck the minister's page put a *khatag*, he said to him, 'Tsing-ta, I believe you know whom you are accompanying. You should serve him as you would serve me; your relations with him must be those of a son with his parents.'

After saying goodbye to the members of the minister's household, presenting and receiving *khatag* and various other little presents, and drinking tea, I mounted my pony and set out for Gyantse. Thus did I start on a journey to a hostile, inhospitable, and unknown country with only two men as my companions, and they strangers to me.

At a huge willow stump I waited a while for Tsering-tashi to join me, for Pador, with the pack-pony, had gone to his home to get his lance. As Tsering-tashi came up, he was delighted to see water flowing from a pool in the direction we were to follow; this he took for a most auspicious sign. On reaching the *chorten*, about a mile from the town, we alighted and waited for Pador, who shortly after made his appearance with a lance full 12 feet long in his hand.

By noon we reached Gyantse, and, passing rapidly through the marketplace, where I feared to be recognized, we entered the Gyankhar, or castle of Gyantse.

At 1 p.m. the Lhacham and her sons started for Lhasa, and as she passed by me she told me to meet her at Gobshi that evening.

I was now surrounded by the Chyag-dso-pa and his family, all curious to see the Indian physician of whom they had heard so much of late. From what the Chyag-dso-pa told me, I concluded he had chronic bronchitis, which might end in consumption. I gave him a few grains of quinine and some doses of elixir of paregoric, and directed him also as to his diet.

After partaking of some *gyatug*, rice, and boiled mutton with the family, I asked permission to leave, and was escorted to the gate, where, mounting my pony, I bade them farewell.

The Lhasa high-road I found very similar to a rough Indian cross-road; in some places it is more than 20 feet wide, in others a mere trail, while in many places, where it runs between fields, it is also made to serve the purpose of an irrigation ditch. The Tibetan Government pays very little, if any, attention to road-making, though, in such a dry climate, it would be easy to construct good ones, and it would be little trouble to keep them in repair. Thus far on my travels in Tibet I had seen no wheeled conveyances, and I now learnt that such things are unknown throughout the country.

Shortly after starting it began snowing heavily. As we rode on along the bank of the Nyang chu, Tsering-tashi pointed out to me the road to Phagri, the monastery of Na-ning, the ruins of Gyang-to, both formerly places of importance. Then we entered the *rong*, or defiles, where used to live three tribes of herdsmen, the Gyang-ro, Ning-ro, and Gang-ro, who carried on a thriving trade in yak-tails (*chowries*), felt hats, felt, and blankets.

Crossing the river at Kudung zampa, we reached by dusk the village of Gobshi, where the Lhacham had only preceded us a little. I found her very gloomy, for she had just learnt that there were in the house where she was now stopping five smallpox patients. I was asked to vaccinate her and her whole party; but, unfortunately, the lymph which I had asked for in India had not reached me before leaving Tashilhunpo; it was still at the Lachan barrier with Ugyen-gyatso.

May 13—Gobshi, or 'four gates', is a large village of about fifty houses, half of it belonging to the Lhacham's father-in-law. There are a few poplar and pollard willow trees growing in front of the village, and terraced fields planted with barley extend along the riverbanks. A little to the east of the village, in the hills beyond the confluence of the Nyang and Niro chu, there is a very ancient Bonbo lamasery, called Khyung-nag, or 'Black Eagle' monastery, which in the fifteenth century was a place of pilgrimage famous throughout Tibet.

After leaving Gobshi, we passed by Kavo gomba, a Ningma religious establishment, and Tsering-tashi called my attention to the blue and red bands painted on the walls of the temple and dwellings of the lamas, telling me that these coloured stripes are characteristic of this sect.

Pushing on through a number of small villages, the road in some places extremely difficult and even dangerous, we forded the Nyang chu at Shetoi, took a shortcut to the Ralung zamba, and by 3 p.m. reached the village of Ralung chong-doi, crossing once more the river by a wooden bridge before entering it.

Ralung is one of the most sacred places in Tibet, for it is here that the great Dugpa school of red-hat monks originated, a school still influential with numerous adherents in Southern, Northern, and Eastern Tibet, and in Bhutan, which latter country is, in fact, called Dugpa owing to the preponderance of this sect. The Ralung-til, the head monastery of the Dugpa, is to the southeast of this village. This monastery owes its name to the fact that it is surrounded by mountains as the heart (*mt'il*) of a lotus is by the corolla.

May 14—We left without even waiting for a cup of tea, as the Lhacham was desirous of reaching Nangartse the same day, and, in spite of my enfeebled condition, I was anxious to keep up with her party, for the country we had to traverse is infested by brigands.

After following up the river for a while, we ascended the Karo la, a lofty plateau from which we could distinguish to the northeast the snow-covered slopes of the Noijin kang-zang (or Noijin norpa zang-po and Kang zang-po). The plateau of the Karo la is called Oma tang, or 'milky plain', as is also the little hamlet near the summit of the pass. On this plateau, which is about 5 miles broad where we traversed it, there is fine grazing, and we saw numerous herds of yaks by the sides of the little streamlets which meander over its surface, the one flowing westward becoming the Nyang chu; the other flows to the east, and is called the Kharnang-phu chu, and along this the road led. On the summit of the pass I noticed a species of thorny shrub, the like of which I had not seen in any other part of Tibet; the thorns were quite long, and the stem and leaves of the plant of an ash-grey colour.

A short way down the other side of the pass we came to a little hut made of loose stones, where we rested and partook of some refreshments. In conversation with the Lhacham, I mentioned the superiority of sedan chairs (*shing-chyam*) over saddle-horses, especially for women when travelling. But she held that it was degrading men to make them serve as beasts of burden, and that if it should be tried in Tibet the people would certainly resent it as an indignity. 'There are only the two Great Lamas, the Amban and the Regent, who are allowed to use sedan chairs in Tibet,' she went on to say; no other persons, however great they may be, can make use of them.

About 6 miles down the valley we came to the hamlet of Ringla, where the Kharnang-phu chu turns north to empty into the Yamdo-yum-tso. At this village the Nangartse plain begins, and the monastery of Samding becomes faintly visible.

The road now became good, and the ponies quickened their pace, and by 5 o'clock we came in view of the town of Nangartse.

The houses of the fishermen and common people (*misser*) are perched on the hillside overlooking the prefect's house (*djong*), and the broad blue expanse of Lake Palti's waters spreads out beyond. The party stopped, and the Lhacham changed her garments for finer ones, and put on her jewelled headdress (*patug*). On arriving at the gate of the house where we were to stop, there was a raised platform covered with soft blankets; here the Lhacham alighted, while her sons and the rest of the party got down near by.

The brother and nephew of the host were laid up with smallpox (*lhan-dum*), and in a corner of the house some lamas were reading the holy books to bring about their speedy recovery. In the courtyard lay another man lately arrived from Lhasa, and suffering from the same disease, and near him were two lamas chanting mantras to the discordant accompaniment of a bell and a damaru (hand drum).

I passed a miserable night, with a raging fever and violent cough racking my whole frame. My two companions sat beside me and did what they could, but concluded that it was impossible in my present state for me to keep up with the Lhacham's party all the way to Lhasa.

The next morning I was no better, the fits of coughing were more violent. The sons of the Lhacham and her attendants came to see me, and expressed their sorrow at having to leave me. The host said that the best thing for me to do was to go to the Samding monastery, where there were two skilful physicians who had recently successfully treated a case similar to mine. Hearing this, one of the Lhacham's maids suggested that her mistress might give me a letter of introduction to the lady abbess of this convent, the Dorje Phagmo, with whom she was related and on the most friendly terms; the only danger was that she might not allow me to enter her convent, as, on account of the epidemic of smallpox, she had closed it to pilgrims.

I followed the advice of those around me, and the Lhacham kindly wrote to the Dorje Phagmo to take care of me and look to my wants; and after taking an affectionate farewell, and telling me to come straight to her house at Lhasa as soon as I recovered, she recommended me to the people of the house and rode off.

After taking a little breakfast, I made up my mind to go at once to the Samding gomba, which I learnt could be reached in two hours' ride.

My companions wrapped me in woollens and blankets, and with a turban round my head they set me on my horse. About two miles from town we came to the river (the same we had followed since crossing the Karo la), and found it teeming with a small variety of fish. After crossing several rivulets we came to the foot of the hill, on the top of which stands Samding lamasery. A flight of stone steps led up to the monastery, and I looked at the long steep ascent with dismay, for I did not see how I would ever be able to climb it in my present condition. Taking a rest at every turn in the steps, I managed finally to reach the top, some 300 feet above the plain. We had not, however, arrived at the convent; a narrow pathway led up to the gateway, near which were chained two fierce watch-dogs (*do khyi*), who barked furiously and strained at their chains as we passed. The Yamdo dogs, I had heard, were famous throughout Tibet for their size and fierceness, and these certainly justified the reputation given them.

I sat down on a stone near the gateway to wait until Tsering-tashi had looked up the physicians. After an hour he returned and informed me that one of the *Amchi* (physicians) was in the lamasery, and he led me to his house, at the top of which I waited his coming. After a little while the doctor made his appearance. He was a man of about seventy years of age, but still sturdy, of middle stature, with an agreeable face, broad forehead, and dignified appearance. He asked me a few questions, examined my eyes and tongue, and then led the way into his house. We ascended two ladders, and thus reached the portico of his apartment. The old man sat for a while turning his prayer-wheel, and taking frequent pinches of snuff while he scrutinized me closely. Then he gave me a powder to be taken in a little warm water, and ordered his cook to give me some weak tea (*cha t'ang*), after which, bearing the Lhacham's letter in his hand, he went with Tsering-tashi to present it to the Khyabgong Dorje Phagmo.

In the evening I was led to a house in the western end of the lamasery belonging to a monk called Gelegs namgyal, where I had to accommodate myself as best I could under the portico.

Tsing-ta, as Tsering-tashi was usually called, told me that he had asked the Dorje Phagmo to tell my fortune, and that she had made out that my illness would prove very severe but not fatal, but the performance of certain religious ceremonies was most urgently needed to hasten my recovery. She sent me word that, in view of the letter of introduction from the Lhacham I had brought with me, she would shortly be pleased to see me, and that we might have all we required while stopping in Samding.

The next day my companions asked me to give a 'general tea' (*mang ja*) to the eighty-odd monks of the convent, and to distribute alms to them at the rate of a *karma* (two annas) a head. I gave my consent, and at the same time my companions made, in my name, presents to the Dorje Phagmo and to the deities that were pointed out to them as best able to drive away the fiends of disease which surrounded me.

The Dorje Phagmo gave Tsing-ta a sacred pill (*rinsel*) containing a particle of Kashyapa Buddha's relics, and the latter hastened to bring it to me, and insisted on my swallowing it forthwith.

The *Amchi* advised me to carefully abstain from drinking cold water, especially as the water of the lake was injurious to many persons even when in good health. He also forbade me drinking buttered tea.

By agreeing to pay my host a daily sum of four annas, I managed to rent his two miserable rooms. They were about 6 feet by 8, and 6 feet high. In the bedroom were a couple of little tables, half a dozen books, and a couple of boxes; in a corner there was a little altar and two images of gods.

The next day there was a new moon, and the monks assembled early in the congregation hall to perform religious services, as on the morrow began the fourth month (*saga dao*), the holiest of the year.

At the conclusion of the ceremonies Tsing-ta again saw the Dorje Phagmo, and, presenting her with a *khatag* and a couple of *tanka*, obtained another sacred pill. The doctor and his assistant impressed upon me the importance of only taking such medicines as experience had shown were efficacious in the Yamdo country. They also insisted that it was essential to my recovery that I should not sleep in the daytime. I felt so weak and ill that towards midnight I called my companions to my side, and wrote my will in my notebook. Later on some medicine given me by the doctor's assistant, Jerung, brought me some relief.

May 18—Tsing-ta again gave the lamas a *mang ja*, and money to read the sacred books to my intent, and got still another sacred pill from the Dorje Phagmo. On his way back to our quarters he saw the ex-incarnate lama of the Tse-chog ling of Lhasa. He had been degraded for having committed adultery.

Seeing no pronounced improvement in my condition, my faithful follower went again in the afternoon to see the Dorje Phagmo, presented her a *khatag* and ten *tanka*, and got her to perform the ceremony known as 'propitiating the gods of life' (*tse dub*). She also gave him a long list of religious rites, which, according to her, it was imperative that I should immediately get learned lamas to perform to insure my speedy recovery.

These rites were the following:

1. Reading the Pradjna paramita in 8,000 shlokas, together with its supplements—twelve monks could do this in two days.
2. Making the three portion (*cha gsum*) offerings, these consisting in painted wafers of *tsamba* and butter. One-third is offered to the ten guardians, Gya-ljin (Indra), the god of fire, the ruler of Hades, the god of wind, etc.; another portion is offered to the spirits, and the third to the demigods.
3. *Gyal-gsol*, or propitiating certain genii to the end that the patient's mind may be at rest and he enjoy peaceful dreams.
4. Libations to the gods or *Gser-skyems*. This is held to be one of the most efficacious ways of propitiating the gods.
5. 'To deceive death' (*hchi-slu*), by offering an image of the sick person, together with some of his clothes, and food to the Lord of Death, and beseeching him to accept it instead of the person it represents. This means is resorted to after all others have failed.
6. 'To deceive life' (*srog-slu*), by saving from death animals about to be killed. This is also known as 'life-saving

charity'. The saving of the lives of men, beasts, and particularly fishes, is calculated to insure life. When Tsing-ta proposed this to me, I at once agreed to save 500 fish. The old doctor said he would go to the fishermen's village, some 3 miles away, buy the fish, and set them free for me, if I would but lend him a pony. He came back in the evening, and reported that he had successfully accomplished this most important mission, by which much merit would come to me.

In spite of all these rites and observances, for some days my illness showed no signs of improvement, and so at last, on May 22, Tsing-ta went once more to the Dorje Phagmo, and, making her a present of five *tanka* and a *khatag*, asked her to find out by her divine knowledge if the old *Amchi* was the right man to attend to me. She threw dice (*sho-mon*), and then said that the two physicians could be depended on.

Accordingly, I sent for the physicians, gave them each a present, and begged them to prepare some new and energetic remedy for me. In the evening Jerung brought me some pills, which smelt strongly of musk, and some powders, probably those known as *gurkum chusum*. After having taken some of each I felt somewhat better.

By the following morning there was a marked improvement in my condition, and I was able to sit propped up on my blankets. The news of the favourable change was at once reported to the Dorje Phagmo, who advised Tsing-ta to have performed the ceremony for propitiating Tamdrin, Dorje Phagmo, and Khyung-mo (the Garuda); especially of the first-named. Tsing-ta made her a further present of seven *tanka* and a *khatag*, and she agreed to perform these ceremonies herself.

May 24—Early this morning the old doctor visited me. 'The danger is over,' he said; 'the fatal stage is passed; you can take a little food, some *tsamba*, a little soup and meat.' In truth, I felt so much better to-day that I took some exercise, and the fresh, bracing air did me a world of good.

May 25—The next day I was able to visit the shrines of Samding, on which tour my two companions accompanied me, carrying a bowl of butter, a bundle of incense-sticks, and about fifty *khatag*.

We first went to visit the kind old physician and his assistant, and I was much struck by the neat appearance of the floors of his rooms, made of pebbles very evenly laid in mortar, and beautifully polished. In the doctor's sitting-room the walls were frescoed with Buddhist symbols, trees, and hideous figures of guardian deities. The furniture comprised of four painted chests of drawers, half a dozen small low tables, some painted bowls for *tsamba*, two little wooden altars covered with images of gods, and some rugs spread on the top of large mattresses. On the walls hung some religious pictures covered with silk curtains, and in a corner there were a sword and shield.

On leaving the physician's house I entered the courtyard of the monastery, which I found more than 150 feet long, and 100 broad. There were buildings on three sides, and broad ladders, each step covered with brass and iron plates, leading to the main floor; the middle ladder is used by the Dorje Phagmo alone. On inquiring for her holiness, we learnt that she was engaged in certain religious duties, and would see me later.

In the meanwhile I visited various chapels and shrines. In the *gong-khang* (upper rooms) are lodged the most terrifying of the demons and genii; their appearance is so awful that they are usually kept veiled. Almost all the images were dressed in armour, and held various weapons in their hands. To each of the images Tsing-ta presented a *khatag* and a stick of incense, and Pador poured a little butter in the brass or silver lamps kept continually burning before them.

It is due, by the way, to the Dorje Phagmo's spiritual influence that the waters of the inner lake or Dumo tso ('Demons' Lake'), of the Yamdo tso, are held in bounds, for otherwise they would overflow and inundate the whole of Tibet. 'Twas for this that the Samding lamasery was originally built.

In the largest room on the same floor are the mausolea of the former incarnations of Dorje Phagmo. The first is made of silver gilt, and was built in honour of Je-tsun Tinlas-tsomo, the founder of the monastery. The whole surface of the monument is studded over with large turquoises, coral beads, rubies, emeralds, and pearls. In shape it resembles a *chorten*, 6 to 7 feet square at the base. Inside of it, on a slab of stone, is an impress of the foot of the illustrious deceased. The second monument is also of silver, and in shape like the preceding, but I could not ascertain the name of the incarnation in whose honour it had been erected. The third, also of silver, is that of Nag-wang kunzang, the predecessor last but one of the present incarnation, and has around it, placed there as great curios, some pieces of European chinaware and some toys. The upper part of the monument is most tastefully decorated with gold and precious stones. This work, I believe, has been done by Nepalese, though some persons said it is of native workmanship.

In another room, not open to the public, however, are the mortal remains of the former incarnations of Dorje Phagmo. I was told that each incarnation of this goddess visits this hall once in her life to make obeisance to the remains of her predecessors.

After visiting all the shrines we returned to the Dorje Phagmo's apartments, where I was most kindly received. She occupied a raised seat, and I was given a place on her left, while the ex-incarnate lama, of whom I have previously spoken, occupied one a little behind her, but his seat was higher than mine. The ceremony of propitiating Tamdrin (Hayagriva) was proceeding, and twelve lamas in full canonicals were acting as assistants. A number of respectably dressed men and women who had come to be blessed were also seated about on rugs.

The service lasted about two hours. Every now and then the Dorje Phagmo used an aspergill, with an end of peacock feathers and kusha grass, to sprinkle saffron water taken from a 'bowl of life', most of it, much to my annoyance, for I feared catching cold, falling on me, but it was a much envied token of her special favour. I could not catch the words of the charms (mantras) she uttered, as she spoke very rapidly, so as to get through the services as quickly as she could.

At the termination of the service sugared *tsamba* balls, about the size of bullets, most of them painted red, were distributed among those present. Before each person received any he prostrated himself before her holiness, who then gave them to him.

When all the spectators had left, the Dorje Phagmo told me that she took great interest in my recovery on account of the Lhacham, who was not only her friend, but her half-sister. I besought her to allow me to proceed on my journey to Lhasa, as I was most desirous of reaching the sacred city by the 15th of the present moon (June 1), the birthday of the Buddha, and she graciously gave me leave to start as soon as I was strong enough to bear the fatigue of travelling.

On taking leave, she gave me three more sacred pills, and directed her valet (*gzim-dpon*) to show me through her residence, where there was great store of handsomely carved and painted furniture, images of gold, silver, and copper neatly arranged on little altars. There was also a library with about 3,000 volumes of printed and manuscript books. One work, in 118 volumes, was by Podong-chogleg namgyal, the founder of the sect to which the Dorje Phagmo belongs.

The present incarnation of the divine Dorje Phagmo is a lady of twenty-six, Nag-wang rinchen kunzang wangmo by name. She wears her hair long; her face is agreeable, her manners dignified, and somewhat resembling those of the Lhacham, though she is much less prepossessing than she. It is required of her that she never take her rest lying down; in the daytime she may recline on cushions or in a chair, but during the night she sits in the position prescribed for meditation.

I learnt that the Dorje Phagmo, or the 'Diamond Sow', is an incarnation of Dolma (Tara), the divine consort of Shenrezig. In days of old, before the time when the Buddha Gautama appeared, there was a hideous monster called Matrankaru, who spread ruin and terror over all the world, he was the chief of all the legions of demons, goblins and other evil spirits; even the devils (*raksha*) of Ceylon had to become his subjects. He subdued to his rule not only this world, but the eight planets, the twenty-four constellations, the eight Nagas, and the gods. By his miraculous power he could lift Mount Rirab (Sumeru) on the end of his thumb.

Finally the Buddha and gods held council to compass about Matrankaru's destruction, and it was decided that Shenrezig should take the form of Tamdrin ('Horse-neck'), and his consort, Dolma, that of Dorje Phagmo ('the Diamond Sow'). When the two had assumed these forms they went to the summit of the Malaya mountains, and Tamdrin neighed three times, to fill the demon with terror, and Dorje Phagmo grunted five times, to strike terror into the heart of Matrankaru's wife, and soon both were lying prostrate at the feet of the two divinities. But their lives were spared them, and Matrankaru became a devout follower of the Buddha, a defender of the faith (*chos gyong*), and was given the name of Mahakala.

In 1716, when the Jungar invaders of Tibet came to Nangartse, their chief sent word to Samding for the Dorje Phagmo to appear before him, that he might see if she really had, as reported, a pig's head. A mild answer was returned him; but, incensed at her refusing to obey his summons, he tore down the walls of the monastery of Samding, and broke into the sanctuary. He found it deserted, not a human being in it, only eighty pigs and as many sows grunting in the congregation hall under the lead of a big sow, and he dared not sack a place belonging to pigs.

When the Jungars had given up all idea of sacking Samding, suddenly the pigs disappeared to become venerable-looking lamas and nuns, with the saintly Dorje Phagmo at their head. Filled with astonishment and veneration for the sacred character of the lady abbess, the chief made immense presents to her lamasery.

May 26—To-day we made our preparations for the journey to Lhasa, and as food of all kinds was very scarce at Samding, the Dorje Phagmo was so kind as to supply us with all the necessary provisions. The old doctor presented me with a basket of dried apricots and some rice, and our landlord brought us some wild goose eggs.

May 27—We left to-day for Lhasa. From a little hillock behind our lodgings I cast a last glance towards the lake and the dark hills around it, behind which rose the snow-covered mountains. My eyes fell on the Dumo tso, and on the place where the dead are thrown into the lake, and I shuddered as I thought that this had come near being my fate. Dead bodies throughout Tibet are cut up and fed to vultures and dogs, but on the shores of Lake Yamdo the people throw their dead into the lake. It is generally believed that a number of Lu (serpent demigods) live in Lake Yamdo, and that they keep the keys of heaven. In a palace of crystal in the deep recesses of the lake lives their king, and the people think that by throwing their dead into the lake there is a chance for them of reaching heaven by serving the king of the Lu during the period intervening between death and regeneration. *Bardo* this time is called.

Passing through cultivated fields, where the ponies sank up to their knees in mud, we came to a broad steppe where wild goats and sheep and a few musk deer were grazing. Dorje Phagmo is their special patron, and no wild animals may be killed in the Yamdo district.

At about 2 o'clock we reached Nangartse, and, passing by the town, proceeded northward along the bank of the far-famed Yamdo (Palti) lake, also called Yum tso, or 'turquoise lake'—a name which the green-blue waters of the lake amply justify.

Travelling along the lakeside by the villages of Hailo, Dablung, and Dephu, where the fishermen's hide boats (*kudru*) were drying against the houses, and near which are a few fields where a little barley is raised, we came to the Kal-zang zamba, where we rested a while and drank some tea. Though this place is called 'bridge' (*zamba*), it is in reality an embankment about 300 to 400 feet long dividing a narrow arm of the lake into two parts.

A little beyond the Kal-zang zamba, at a place where a string of coloured rags, inscribed with prayers, stretched between two crags on either side of the narrow path, Tsing-ta made me dismount. He climbed on to a large rock, and scattered a few pinches of *tsamba*, and, striking a light, lit an incense-stick, which he fixed in a cleft in the rocks. This place is called Sharui teng, and is the haunt of evil spirits; should any traveller neglect to make these offerings, he would incur their anger.

On reaching Palti *djong*, we put up at a house where the Lhacham had stopped when on her way to Lhasa, and were most hospitably received. We bought some milk, a few eggs, and some *chang* from the hostess, who supplied us also with water, firewood, and two earthen cooking-pots. I was offered some fish, but I forbore buying any, as it would have been incompatible with my character of a pious pilgrim, such indulgence being forbidden by the Dalai lama. The Grand Lama, I must mention, having lately taken the vows of monkhood, had issued an edict prohibiting his subjects killing or eating fish for the space of one year.

From ancient times the town of Palti has been a famous seat of the Nyingma sect, and the lake was popularly known by its name. The name of the town as applied to the lake by foreigners probably originated with the Catholic missionaries who visited Tibet in the eighteenth century.

When, in the eighteenth century, the Jungars invaded Tibet, their wrath was especially turned against the lamaseries and monks of the Nyingma sect. There then lived in Palti *djong* a learned and saintly lama, called Palti Shabdung, well versed in all the sacred literature, and proficient in magic arts. Hearing that the invaders had crossed the Nabso la and were marching on Palti, he, by his art, propitiated the deities of the lake who caused the waters of the lake to appear to the Jungar troops like a plain of verdure, so that they marched into the lake and were drowned, to the number of several thousands. Another corps which had advanced by the Khamba la, not finding the troops which had gone by the Nabso la, retraced their steps, and so the town of Palti was saved.

May 28—We left by daylight, and followed along the shore of the lake till we reached the foot of the Khamba la. The ascent was comparatively easy; on the rocks by the wayside were painted in many places images of Buddhas and Bodhisattvas. From Tamalung, a small village halfway up the, mountain, a trail led eastward along the cliffs overhanging the lake, and the sinuosities of the shore could be followed with the eye to the remote horizon.

On the summit of the pass are two large cairns, to which each of my companions added a stone; they also tied a rag to the brush sticking out above the heaps, and already covered with such offerings. Then they made an offering of a little *tsamba* and some dust, instead of wine, to the mountain god, reciting a prayer the while, which they brought to an end by shouting—

> '*Lha sol-lo, Lha sol-lo!*
> *Lha gyal lo, Lha gyal lo!*
> *Kei-kei—ho, hooo!*'

From this point I enjoyed one of the grandest views I have ever had in Tibet—the valley of the Tsang-po was before me, the great river flowing in a deep gorge at the foot of forest-clad mountains. Here and there was to be seen a little hamlet, most of the white-walled houses surrounded by a cluster of tall trees.

By 3 o'clock we had reached the foot of the pass, the way down being over a tedious zigzag for over 5 miles. Along the wayside grew brambles and wild roses, a few evergreens and rhododendrons, and some flocks of sheep were grazing on the hillsides.

Then we came to a sluggish stream, and shortly after reached the straggling village of Khamba partshi, with some forty wretched stone hovels. Passing through a patch of barley surrounded by pollard willows, we reached the sandy banks of the Tsang-po, and followed along it to Tongbu, the surrounding plain being known as Khamba chyang tang.

Two women weeding their barley patch approached me as I rode by, and offered me a bunch of the young sprouts, in the hope, as Tsing-ta explained, that I would give them some money. This is a custom obtaining throughout Tibet, and is called *lubul.*

Further on, near Toi-tsi, we saw women making bricks, and some donkeys and yaks were carrying away those which had become sufficiently dry to be used. Two miles beyond this point we came to the famous Palchen chuvori monastery and the chain bridge (*chag-zam*) over the Tsang-po. This bridge, built, tradition says, by Tang-tong gyalpo in the fifteenth century, consists of two heavy cables attached at each end to huge logs, around which have been built large *chorten.*

The bed of the river here is about 400 feet broad, but at this season of the year it spreads out several hundred feet beyond the extremities of the bridge, and travellers are taken across in boats.

The monastery of Palchen chuvori was also built by Tang-tong gyalpo, who is likewise credited with having constructed eight chain bridges over the Tsang-po, 108 temples, and 108 *chorten* on the hills of Chung Rivoche, in Ulterior Tibet, and of Palchen chuvori, in Central Tibet, or U. The Palchen chuvori monastery, where there are upwards of one hundred monks, is supported by the toll collected at the ferry.

We and our ponies crossed the river in a roughly made boat about 20 feet long, but a number of skin coracles were also carrying travellers and freight from one side to the other. It was sunset when we reached the village of Jim-khar, belonging to the Namgyal Ta-tsan, the great monastic establishment of Potala at Lhasa. Here we obtained lodgings for the night in the sheepfold attached to the house of the headman, or *gyan-po*. All the members of the *gyan-po*'s family were ill with smallpox, and he himself had but recently recovered from it. It began to rain shortly after our arrival, and what with the leaks in the roof and the noise made by nine ponies tied up near us, we passed a miserable night, and were glad to resume our journey at the first streak of dawn. After proceeding some distance we came in sight of the ruins of Chu-shul *djong*, on a ledge of rocks about a mile from where the Tsang-po is joined by the Kyi chu, the river of Lhasa. Some 200 years ago Chu-shul was a place of importance, but now it is but a village of about sixty houses, surrounded by wide fields, where barley, rape, buckwheat, and wheat are grown.

Passing near the hamlets of Tsa-kang and Semu, the road in many places so boggy that the ponies sank in the mire up to their knees, we came, after about 4 miles, to the ruins of Tsal-pa-nang, where we overtook some of the attendants of the Lhacham on their way to Lhasa. After conversing with them for upwards of an hour, they rode on ahead, as they were desirous of reaching Netang by sunset; and they advised us to put up in the Jya-khang (or Chinese post station) of the same place, where we would find good accommodation.

Beyond Tsal-pa-nang the road led over a sandy plain, while crossing which we scared up several rabbits. Proceeding eastward for several miles, we came to the large village of Jang hog, or 'Lower Jang', then to Jang toi, or 'Upper Jang', where the beauty of the country so greatly charmed me, each cluster of houses surrounded by groves of willows and poplars, and the fields a mass of flowers, that I called a halt, and, spreading my rug under a willow tree, we made some tea, and my companions indulged in a good long drink of *chang*.

From Jang toi, following a narrow trail overhanging the Kyi chu, we came to Nam. Beyond this little hamlet the path leads over a confused mass of rocks and boulders along the riverbank; it is called *gag lam*, or 'narrow road', and a false step would throw one amidst the quicksands on the river's bank, or into its eddying waters. I was not surprised to be told that the two elephants sent to the Grand Lama by the Sikkim rajah had had great difficulty in getting by this place. After a tedious journey of about 3 miles through the sand and over the rocks, we got sight of the famous village of Netang, where the great saint and Buddhist reformer, Atisha, or Dipankara, died.

An old woman led us to the Jya khang, where we were most hospitably received, and though there were other travellers stopping in it, we were accommodated for the sum of a *tanka* in a well-ventilated outer room, the inner ones being reserved for officials, particularly Chinese. Netang has about forty or fifty houses, all built closely together, but many are only miserable hovels.

May 30—We were off at an early hour, as to-day we wanted to reach Lhasa. The hamlets of Norbu-gang and Chumig-gang, through which we passed, had a number of fine substantial houses belonging to civil officers (*Dung-khor*) of Lhasa, and around them were gardens and groves of trees. Leaving these places behind, we travelled for some miles over a gravelly plain, the river some distance on our right.

When near a gigantic image of the Buddha, cut in low relief on the face of a rock, Potala and Chagpori came in sight, their gilt domes shining in the sun's rays. My long-cherished wish was accomplished—Lhasa, the sacred city, was before me.

Four miles over a fairly good road now brought us to the Ti chu zamba, a large and handsome stone bridge about 120 paces long and eight broad, beneath which flowed a rivulet coming from the hills to the northwest, where stands the monastery of Tsorpu, founded by Karma Bagshi, one of the two celebrated lamas who resided at the Imperial court of China in the time of the Emperor Kublai.

The Ti chu zamba is in the lower part of the big village of Toilung, around which are numerous hamlets, each amid a little grove of pollard willows. The adjacent plain, watered as it is by the Kyi chu and the Ti (or Toilung) chu, is extraordinarily fertile. The country around was everywhere cultivated, and the barley, wheat, and buckwheat were in many places already a foot high.

The road now became alive with travellers, mostly grain-dealers or argol-carriers, on their way to the city with trains of yaks, ponies, mules, and donkeys with jingling bells.

We halted for breakfast in a small grove in front of the village of Shing donkar, belonging to Sa-wang Ragasha, one of the senior Shape of Lhasa. We could hear from where we sat the voices of lamas chanting prayers, and I learnt from an old woman who brought my men some *chang*, that there were some eighteen Dabung lamas reading prayers for the recovery from smallpox of the foreman (*shinyer*) of the farm.

About a mile from Shing donkar we came to Donkar, which is considered as the first stage for persons travelling officially from Lhasa. Then we passed by Cheri, where is the city slaughterhouse; and here, strange as it may seem, the Kashmiris come to buy meat, for most of those living at Lhasa are so lax in their observance of the Mohammedan laws about butchering that they will eat yaks killed by Tibetans, even though they have been put to death by wounds of arrows or knives in the stomach.

We stopped at Daru at the foot of the hill covered by Debung and its park, and Pador went to look up a friend whom he was desirous of attaching to my service. After an hour's delay he returned without having found him, and we pushed on, passing the far-famed temple of Nachung chos kyong, where resides the oracle by whom the Government is guided in all important affairs. The temple is a fine edifice of dark red colour, built after the Chinese style, and has a gilt spire surmounting it. At this point the road nears the river, and the whole city stood displayed before us at the end of an avenue of gnarled trees, the rays of the setting sun falling on its gilded domes. It was a superb sight, the like of which I have never seen. On our left was Potala with its lofty buildings and gilt roofs; before us, surrounded by a green meadow (maidan), lay the town with its tower-like, whitewashed houses and Chinese buildings with roofs of blue glazed tiles. Long festoons of inscribed and painted rags hung from one building to another, waving in the breeze.

Beyond Daru the road lay for a while through a marsh (*dam-tso*) overgrown with rank grass; numerous ditches drained the water into the river, and at the northeast end of the marsh we could distinguish the famous monastery of Sera. Beyond a high sand embankment on our left was the park and palace of Norbu linga, and the beautiful grove of Kemai tsal, in the midst of which stands the palace of Lhalu, the father of the last Dalai lama.

At 4 p.m. we passed Kunduling, the residence of the regent, and entered the city by the western gateway, called the Pargo kaling *chorten*, and my heart leaped with exultation as I now reached the goal of my journey—the far-famed city of Lhasa, the capital of Tibet.

VI

Residence at Lhasa

Preceded by Pador carrying his long lance and by Tsing-ta driving the pack-pony, we entered the city. The policemen (*korchagpa*) marked us as newcomers, but none of them questioned us. My head drooped with fatigue, my eyes were hidden by dark goggles, and the red pagri around my head made me look like a Ladaki. Some people standing in front of a Chinese pastry shop said, as I passed, 'Look, there comes another sick man; smallpox has affected his eyes. The city is full of them. What an awful time for Tibet!'

After a few minutes' ride we came to the Yu-tog zamba, a short stone bridge with a gate, where a guard commanded by a lama is stationed, which examines all passers-by to ascertain the object of their visit to the city. To the great delight of my companions, who had been most anxious about my getting over the bridge, we passed by without a question being asked us.

Near the bridge I noticed the *doring*, a monolith on which is an inscription in Tibetan and Chinese. Though a thousand years old, the stone has been but little affected by the weather, and the characters can be easily read. The monolith I took to be between 8 and 10 feet in height, and it stands on a low pedestal.

At the Yu-tog zamba the city proper begins. The street on both sides was lined with native and Chinese shops; in front of each was a pyramidal structure, where juniper spines and dried leaves obtained from Tsari are burnt as an offering to the gods.

Coming to the street to the south of Kyil-khording, we found on either side of it Nepalese shops several stories high, also Chinese ones, where silk fabrics, porcelain, and various kinds of brick-tea were exposed for sale.

A lama guided us from this street to the Bangye-shag, a castle-like building three stories high, the residence of Sawang Phala, the husband of my protectress, the Lhacham. Leaving me at the postern gate, my two companions went in and presented the lady with a *khatag*, and she directed them to take me to Paljor rabtan, a building belonging to the Tashi lama, where all officers and monks from Tashilhunpo find lodgings when in Lhasa, and where we would be given accommodation.

The gateway of Paljor rabtan was about 8 or 9 feet high and 5 feet broad, and from the lintels fluttered fringes about a foot and a half broad. Two stout flag-poles 20 to 25 feet high, carrying inscribed banners, stood on either side of it. Ascending a steep staircase, or rather a ladder, we came to a verandah, opposite which was a pretty glazed house, the dwelling of the *khang-nyer* (or 'housekeeper'), and were soon given by him a room to lodge in, and served with tea and *chang* by an old woman. From the window of our room we could see the *damra*, or grove of poplars and willows in a marshy bit of land adjacent to the Tangye-ling monastery, and further west shone the lofty gilt spires of Potala.

May 31—The heavy shower which had fallen last evening cleared up the atmosphere, and the gilt domes and spires glittering in the morning sun filled me with delight, and I had difficulty in subduing my impatience to visit all the monuments now before me, and of which I had dreamed for so many years. At 7 o'clock Pador brought me a pot of tea prepared in the house of the water-carrier; but, instead of butter, tallow had been used in its preparation, and I could not swallow it; but we managed, after a while, to make some in our own room. Shortly after Tsing-ta came in, bringing a pair of rugs, two cushions, and two little tables he had borrowed at the Bangye-shag. He had also an invitation from the Lhacham to visit her in the afternoon.

Having shaved and donned my lama costume and goggles, we started for Bangye-shag, which was about a mile from our lodgings. Most of the shops we saw were kept by Kashmiris, Nepalese, or Chinese; the Tibetan ones were few and poorly supplied.

Bangye-shag is a lofty, flat-roofed stone building with two large gateways. The ground floor is used as storerooms and quarters for the *amlas* or retainers of the Phala estates. The beams, the cornices, as also the window-frames, are painted red; a few of the windows have a little pane of glass in them, but most of them are covered with paper. On reaching the second floor, the Lhacham's maids (*shetama*) greeted me most kindly, and insisted on my taking a cup or two of tea, after which they led me to her ladyship's room, where, taking off my hat, I presented her a visiting scarf (*jadar*) and a piece of gold of about a *dzo* weight. Making motion to one of her maids to present me a scarf, she kindly wished me welcome ('*Chyag-peb nang chig, Pundib la*'), and bade me take a seat ('*Pundib la, shu dang shag, shu dang shag*'). After conversing with her a while about my recent illness, and telling her of the kindness of the Dorje Phagmo, that merciful Lady of the Lake to whom I owe my life, I took my leave and returned home.

June 1—June 1 is the holiest day of the year, *saga dawa*, the day of the Buddha's nirvana, and incense was burnt on every hilltop, in every shrine, chapel, lamasery, and house in or near Lhasa. Men, women, and children hastened to the sacred shrine of Kyil-khording (or Jo khang, as it is commonly called), to do puja to the Jo-vo (Lord Buddha) and obtain his blessing. All carried in their hands bundles of incense-sticks, bowls of butter, and *khatag* of all sizes and qualities. Our fellow-lodgers went with the rest, calling at my room on the way out, and in a short time we also joined the crowd.

A broad street runs in front of the Jo khang, and the road which comes from the Pargo kaling gate terminates on its western face, and here grows a tall poplar said to have sprung from the hair of the Buddha. Beside this is the ancient stone tablet erected by the Tibetans in the ninth century to commemorate their victory over the Chinese, and which gives the text of the treaty then concluded between the Emperor of China and King Ralpachan.

The magnificent temple engrossed, however, all my attention. In front of it is a tall flag-pole, at the base of which hang two yak-tails, some inscriptions, and a number of yak- and sheep-horns. In the propylon of the chief temple (*Tsang khang*), the heavy wooden pillars of which are 3 to 4 feet in circumference, and about 12 feet high, upwards of a hundred monks were making prostrations before the image of the Lord (Jo-vo) on a throne facing the west. This famous image of the Buddha, known as Jo-vo rinpoche, is said to have been made in Magadha during the lifetime of the great teacher. Visvakarma is supposed to have made it, under the guidance of the god Indra, of an alloy of the five precious substances, gold, silver, zinc, iron, and copper, and the 'five precious celestial substances', probably diamonds, rubies, lapis-lazuli, emeralds, and *indranila*.

The legend goes on to say that the image was in the first place sent from India to the capital of China in return for the assistance the Emperor had given the King of Magadha against the Yavanas from the west. When the Princess Konjo, daughter of the Emperor Tai-tsung, was given in marriage to the King of Tibet, she brought the image to Lhasa as a portion of her dowry.

The image is life-size and exquisitely modelled, and represents a handsome young prince. The crown on its head is said to be the gift of Tsong-khapa, the great reformer. The Kunyer said that the image represented the Buddha when at the age of twelve; hence the princely apparel in which he is clothed and the dissimilarity of the image to those seen elsewhere. On the four sides of it were gilt pillars with dragons twined around them, supporting a canopy. On one side of the image of the Buddha is that of Maitreya, and on the other that of Dipankara Buddha. Behind this, again, is the image of the Buddha Gang-chan wogyal, and to the right and left of the latter those of the twelve chief disciples of the Buddha.

We were also shown the image of the great reformer, Tsong-khapa, near which is the famous rock, called *Amolonkha*, discovered by Tsong-khapa. On this rock is placed a bell with a gem in the handle, supposed to have been used by Maudgalyayana, the chief disciple of the Buddha.

After the image of the Buddha, the most celebrated statue in this temple is that of Avalokiteswara with the eleven faces (Shenrezig chu-chig dzal). It is said that once King Srong-btsan gambo heard a voice saying that if he made a full-sized image of Shenrezig, all his wishes would be granted him; so he constructed this one, in the composition of which there entered a branch of the sacred Bo tree, some soil of an island in the great ocean, some sand from the River Nairanjana, some *gosirsha* sandalwood, some soil from the eight sacred places of India, and many other rare and valuable substances. All these were first powdered, then, having been moistened with the milk of a red cow and a goat, made into a paste and moulded into a statue. To give it additional sanctity, the king had a sandalwood image of the god brought from Ceylon put inside of it.

This statue is also known as the 'five self-created' (*nya rang chyung*); for the Nepalese sculptor who made it said that it had sprung into shape rather than had been moulded by him, and it is further said that the souls of King Srong-btsan gambo and his consorts were absorbed in it. It occupies the northern chapel in the temple, and is surrounded by the images of a number of gods and goddesses.

In the outer courtyard of the temple is a row of statues, among which is that of King Srong-btsan gambo and various saints and Pundits. On the porch of the Tsang-khang are images of the Buddhas of the past, present, and future. Innumerable other highly interesting images and votive offerings were shown us, among which I will mention 108 lamps made out of stone under Tsong-khapa's directions.

Among the other objects of interest shown us was a stone slab (*Padma pung-pa*) which King Srong-btsan gambo and his wives were wont to use as a seat when taking their baths, and a life-size statue of Tsong-khapa surrounded by images of gods, saints, and worthies. In the room where these statues are seen, and which is closed by a wire lattice, is also a famous image of the god Chyag-na dorje (Vajrapani). When the iconoclast King Langdarma began persecuting Buddhism, he ordered this image to be destroyed. A valet tied a rope around its neck to drag it from the temple, but he suddenly became insane, and died vomiting blood, and the image was left undisturbed.

In the outer court, or *khyamra* is the image of the god Tovo Metsig-pa, by whose power the invading armies of China were routed in the war which immediately followed the death of King Srong-btsan gambo. Near it are statues of the king and his two consorts, and some huge yak-horns, of which the following anecdote is told to inquisitive pilgrims by the temple servants (*kunyer*). Ra-chung-pa, a disciple of the great saint Milarapa, had been to India, and had there studied under the most learned masters all the mysteries of the faith, and had returned to Tibet filled with pride over his knowledge. Travelling to Lhasa with his master, they reached the middle of the desert called Palmoi-paltang, when Milarapa, who knew of the conceit of his disciple and wished to teach him a lesson, ordered him to fetch him a pair of yak-horns lying near by. But Ra-chung-pa said to himself, 'The master wants everything he sees. Sometimes he is as fretful as an old dog, at others as full of childish fancies as an old man in his dotage. Of what possible use can the horns be to him; he can neither use them for food, drink, nor clothing?' Then he asked the sage what he proposed doing with them. 'Though it is not possible to say what may occur,' replied Milarapa, 'they will certainly be of use some time or other'; and he picked them up himself and carried them along.

After a while a violent hailstorm overtook the travellers, and there was not so much as a rat-hole in which they could find shelter. Ra-chung-pa covered his head with his gown, and sat on the ground, till the storm had passed by. When he searched for the lama, he could see him nowhere; but he heard a voice, and, looking about, lo! there was Milarapa seated inside one of the horns. 'If the son is the equal of the father, then,' said the saint, 'let him seat himself inside the other horn;' but it was too small to even serve Ra-chung-pa for a hat. Then Milarapa came out of the horn, and Ra-chung-pa carried them to Lhasa, and presented them to the Jo-vo.

After visiting all the ground floor we climbed up to the second and third stories, where we were shown a number of other images, among which I noticed that of Paldan lhamo. By the time we had seen all the images we had exhausted our supply of butter, for Pador had put a little in every lamp lighted that day in the chapels. Those before the image of the Jo-vo were of gold, and each must have held 10 or 12 pounds of butter.

By the time we reached our lodgings I was completely worn out, and passed the rest of the day in my rooms or on the housetop, the view from which always charmed me, especially when the rays of the setting sun shone brightly on the gilded domes of the temples and palaces.

I was much troubled in my mind by hearing from Tsing-ta that smallpox was raging in town, even the keeper of our house, his wife and children, were down with the disease, and in every dwelling in the neighbourhood someone was ill with it.

On the following morning (June 2), after an early breakfast, I went to visit the famous shrine of Ramoche, carrying, as on the previous day, a bundle of incense-sticks, some butter and *khatags*. We took a horribly muddy lane, where heaps of filth emitted a most offensive odour; then, turning northward, we crossed the Potala road at the northwest corner of the Tomse-gang, as the Kyil-khording square is commonly called, and passed by the lofty Wangdu *chorten*, which was built to bring under the power (*wang*, 'power'; *du*, 'to subjugate') of Tibet all the neighbouring nations. This spot is also called Gya-bum gang, for it is said that once during the Ming dynasty of China 1,00,000 (*gya-bum*) Chinese troops camped (*gang*) on the plain to the north of this *chorten*. Other accounts explain this name by saying that in the war with China, after the death of King Srong-btsan gambo, 1,00,000 Chinamen were killed in a battle near this spot.

A few hundred paces beyond this place we reached the gate of Ramoche, the famous temple erected by the illustrious Konjo, daughter of the Emperor Tai-tsung, and wife of King Srong-btsan gambo. It is a flat-roofed edifice three stories high, and has a wide portico. At the front of the building there is to be seen a very ancient inscription in Chinese, giving probably the history of the building of the temple. The image of Mikyod dorje (Vajra Akshobhya), brought here by King Srong-btsan's second wife, a Nepalese princess, is of undoubted antiquity, even though the face of the statue is covered with gilding.

In the northern lobby are heaps of relics—shields, spears, drums, arrows, swords, and trumpets, and in a room to the left of the entrance, and shut in by an iron lattice, are a few very holy images. With the exception of a very small gilt dome built in Chinese style, I saw nothing strongly indicative of that description of architecture, and, taking it all together, Ramoche fell far short of the preconceived idea I had formed of it.

Lay monks, or Serkempa, usually perform the services held at Ramoche, and half a dozen of them and a *kunyer* (sexton) live in the upper stories of the temple.

As we left the temple we were met by a party of singing beggars, who followed us to our house clamouring for *solra*, or alms; finally we sent them off with a *karma*, or the value of two annas. Had we given more we would have been persecuted by numerous other parties of these pests.

June 3—A lama of Khams, whom I had met at Tashilhunpo, came to see me to-day. He told me that he was waiting for nine loads of silver from Tashilhunpo, on the arrival of which he would leave for Western China, coming back to Lhasa next March or April. I had heard at Tashilhunpo that he had a caravan of 700 mules, and carried on trade between Darchendo and Lhasa. This Pomda lama was a man of gigantic stature, something over 6 feet, well proportioned, and of great strength; he was well known to brigands, and none dared molest him. My further acquaintance with him confirmed me in the opinion I had formed of the Khambas. Though they are wild, they are devoted friends, and when once one becomes intimate with one of them, he will be faithful to the end.

I heard to-day the following story about the famous Regent Tsomoling and his social reforms. Once there came to Lhasa a lama pilgrim from Tsoni, in Amdo, and he was admitted into the Sera convent, where he studied under a learned Mongol lama. After a few years the Amdo lama's tutor returned to his home, and on parting he left his pupil a couple of earthen pots, a *khatag*, and a bag of barley, the most valuable things he possessed, as he told him. The pupil, disappointed with these gifts, carried the pots to the market and sold them for half a *tanka*, with which he bought butter that he put in the lamps burning before the great image of the lord (Jo-vo), praying that if he ever became Regent of Tibet, he might be able to reform the social customs of the country.

In the course of time he rose to the dignity of a teacher in his convent; then he became its abbot, or *khanpo*; and finally he rose to the rank of Regent. One of the first acts of his administration was to expel all public women from Lhasa, and to compel all women to cover their faces with a coating of catechu, so as to hide their comeliness from the public view. Women were also made to wear a bangle cut out of a conch-shell on their right wrist, by which they could be held when arrested. From his time also dates the use by women of aprons (*pang-den*) and of the present style of headdress, or *patug*. The old style of *patug* is now only worn by the wives (or Lhacham) of the Shape (ministers). He was the first of the Tsomoling lamas, and his reincarnations still inhabit the lamasery of that name behind Ramoche.

On June 4 I again visited the Jo khang. After paying reverence to the Jo-vo and circumambulating his sacred throne, the *kunyer* poured some holy water (*tu*) into my hand from a golden vessel. In a little *chorten* in one of the chapels on the south side of the temple is kept a statue of red bell-metal, or *li-mar*, made, so says tradition, in the days of King Kriki, when men lived 20,000 years. For many centuries it was kept by the kings of Nepal; but when a princess from that country married King Srong-btsan gambo, she brought it to Tibet, and placed it in this temple, where it is the object of constant worship.

But perhaps the most revered of all the images in the Jo khang, exclusive of that of the Jo, is that of Paldan lhamo (Srimati devi). The terrifying face of the goddess is kept veiled, but the *kunyer* uncovered it for us. This terrific goddess is regarded as the guardian of the Dalai and Tashi lamas. The chestnut-coloured mule she rides, the offspring of a red ass and a winged mare, was given her by the goddess of the sea. The saddle she sits on is the skin of an ogre, and the bridle and crupper are vipers. Kya dorje gave her dice with which to play for lives, and the ogres, or Srinpo, presented her a string of skulls, which she holds in her left hand, and the goblins that haunt graveyards gave her corpses, on which she feeds. In her right hand she holds a club given her by the god Chyagna-dorje. 'Twas in such fearful attire that she waged war against the foes of Buddhism, and became the greatest of all its guardian deities.

The chapel of Paldan lhamo is overrun by mice, so tame that they crawled up the *kunyer*'s body. They are supposed to have been lamas in former existences. On one of the walls we saw a painting made with the blood of King Srong-btsan.

As we were walking home I saw some men hawking books, and told them what works I would buy if they could but procure them for me. They promised to bring them to me shortly.

The excellent brick-tea (*du tang-nyipa*) which I had brought from Tashilhunpo was now exhausted, and I was reduced to drinking a miserable quality known as *gya-pa*. *Du tang*, or first-quality tea, is more highly flavoured than the quality I liked, but it was too strong for me.

Tea was introduced into Tibet earlier than the tenth century, but it only became of universal use from the time of the Sakya hierarchy and the Phagmodu kings. During the early part of the Dalai lama's rule the tea trade was a governmental monopoly, and since the beginning of the present century, though nominally open to every one, the trade is practically in the hands of the officials.

Some notes on the mode of selection of incarnate lamas may not be out of place here. It used to be customary when selecting incarnate lamas to either decide by throwing dice or by some other trial of luck, or by taking the opinion of the College of Cardinals; but that method not giving perfect satisfaction, it was decided that the candidates should undergo certain examinations, which, together with the hints thrown out from time to time by the defunct incarnation as to where and when his successor would be found, helped in the determination of the lawful reincarnation.

From the middle of the seventeenth century down to 1860, when the Dalai lama, Tinle-gyatso, was chosen, the rightful reincarnation of a defunct saint was found out by the use of the golden jar, or *ser-bum*.

Three years after the death of an incarnate lama the names of the different children, who it was claimed were his reincarnation, were taken down. These names, in the case of the Dalai or Tashi lamas, were sent to the Regent for examination, after which the president of the conclave, in the presence of the Regent and the ministers, enclosed in *tsamba* balls slips of paper, on each of which was written the name of a candidate. In other *tsamba* balls were slips on which was written 'yes' or 'no', as well as some blank slips. All these were put together in a golden jar, which was placed on the altar of the principal chapel of Lhasa, and for a week the gods were invoked. On the eighth day the jar was twirled round a certain number of times, and the name which fell out three times, together with a pellet in which was a slip inscribed 'yes', was declared the true reincarnation. Those who were sent to bring the reincarnated saint to Lhasa or Tashilhunpo submitted him to certain trials; as, for example, picking out from a number of similar objects the rosary, the rings, cup, and mitre of the deceased lama.

In 1875, a year after the death of the Dalai lama Tinle-gyatso, the Regent and the College of Cardinals consulted the celebrated Nachung Chos-gyong oracle about the Dalai's reappearance, and the oracle declared that the reincarnation could only be discovered by a monk of the purest morals. It required, again, the supernatural powers of the oracle to find the future discoverer of the Grand Lama; he was the Shar-tse Khanpo of Gadan, a lama of great saintliness and profound knowledge. The oracle further stated that he should go to Choskhor-gya, as the reincarnation was to be found somewhere near Kong-po. The Khanpo went there accordingly, and sat in deep meditation for seven days, when, on the night of the last day, he had a vision and heard a voice which directed him to repair to the Mu-li-ding-ki tso (lake) of Choskhor. Awakening from his sleep, the Khanpo went to the lake, where, on the crystal surface of the water, he saw the image of the incarnate Grand Lama seated in his mother's lap, and his father fondling him. The house, its furniture, all was shown him. Suddenly the image disappeared, and he set out at once for Kong-po. On the way he stopped in Tag-po at the house of a respectable and wealthy family, and at once he recognized the child and all the images seen in his dream. He promptly informed the Government at Lhasa, and the Regent and the cardinals came to Tag-po and took the child, then a year old, and its parents to the Rigyal palace, near Lhasa. This child, now aged ten, is called Nag-wang lo-zang tubdan gya-tso, 'the Lord of speech, the mighty ocean of wisdom.'

The reason why the golden jar was not used for finding this reincarnation was because of the apprehension that the Dayan Khanpo's spirit—he had but recently died, and had been violently opposed to the Dalai lamas and their form of government—might be able to cause a wrong name to be drawn from the jar.

June 5—Early this morning I was invited to dine with the Lhacham at Bangye-shag. I was received most graciously, and was led by the Lhacham to her drawing-room, a room about 16 feet by 12, facing the south and on the third story of the building. There were in it two Chinese chests of drawers, on top of which were a lot of porcelain cups; Chinese pictures—picnics and dancing most of them represented—covered the greater part of the walls; the ceiling was of Chinese satin, and thick rugs of Yarkand and Tibetan make covered the floor. Well-polished little tables, wooden bowls for *tsamba*, and some satin-covered cushions completed the furniture of the room.

After conversing for a while and drinking a few cups of tea, the Lhacham withdrew, and one of her maids showed me the rooms in the mansion. The furniture was much the same as that in the Lhacham's room, only of inferior quality and ruder make. The walls were painted green and blue, with here and there pictures of processions of gods and demons, and the beams of the ceiling were carved and painted. The doors were very roughly made and without panels; the windows were covered with paper, with a very small pane of glass fitted in the middle of each. There were no chimneys in any of the rooms, but earthenware stoves, or *jala*. In a few of the rooms flowers were growing in pots.

Returning to the Lhacham's room, dinner was served me at noon, and while I ate she asked me many questions concerning the marriage laws of India and Europe. When I told her that in India a husband had several wives, and that among the Phyling a man had but one wife, she stared at me with undisguised astonishment. 'One wife with one husband!' she exclaimed. 'Don't you think we Tibetan women are better off? The Indian wife has but a portion of her husband's affections and property, but in Tibet the housewife is the real lady of all the joint earnings and inheritance of all the brothers sprung from the same mother, who are all of the same flesh and blood. The brothers are but one, though their souls are several. In India a man marries well several women who are strangers to each other.' 'Am I to understand that your ladyship would like to see several sisters marry one husband?' I asked. 'That is not the point,' replied the Lhacham. 'What I contend is that Tibetan women are happier than Indian ones, for they enjoy the privileges conceded in the latter country to the men.'

June 7—My two men had heard from Gadan Tipa, a soothsayer, that they would be stricken with smallpox if they ventured to go to Samye, and they besought me to give up the idea; but I declared emphatically my resolve to visit that famous lamasery, and also that of Gaden.

On June 8th I again visited the Jo khang. The numerous wooden pillars supporting the second story are among the most remarkable things in this temple. The largest of these have capitals with sculptured foliage, and are called *ka-wa shing-lho chan*. At their base are buried, it is said, great treasures of gold and silver. Other pillars, with dragon-heads as capitals, have hidden under them charms against devils, for curing diseases, and for keeping off and thwarting the evil designs of the enemies of Buddhism and of the government of the church. Other pillars, again, called *seng go-chan*, 'having lions' heads as capitals,' have concealed under them many potent charms (*yang-yig*) to insure bounteous crops.

Under the floor of the Lu-khang are many charms and precious things wrapped in snow-fox or snake-skin. These, it is supposed, preserve the flocks and herds of Tibet. Beneath the image of Dsambhala is hidden in an onyx box some *tag-sha*, which preserves the precious stones, the wool, the grain, and the other riches of the country.

Among the other objects of special sanctity, I was shown in the passage for circumambulating the temple a cavity in the rock where neither moss nor grass grow; it is said to keep back the waters of the Kyi chu from invading the Jo khang.

June 9—I went out walking to-day in the direction of Ramoche. On the streets I met numerous bands of *ragyabas*, or scavengers, wandering from place to place, clamouring for alms from every newcomer or pilgrim they saw. If no attention is paid to them, they thrust their dirty hats in the stranger's face and lavish insults on him; and if he take offence, they reply, 'Why, my lord, this is not insolence; we are but saluting you!'

These *ragyabas* of Lhasa form a guild. Persons convicted of any crime, or vagabonds, are usually sent back to their native villages, there to work out their sentence; but when the authorities cannot learn whence they come, they are handed over to the chief of the *ragyabas*, who receives them into his guild. Besides begging, the *ragyabas* cut up the corpses which are brought to the two cemeteries of Lhasa, near which they live, and feed them to vultures and dogs. A *ragyaba* may not show his wealth, however great it be; the walls of their houses must be made with horns of sheep, goats, or yaks, the convex sides turned upwards.

At present the chief of the *ragyabas* is a man of about fifty years, called Abula; he wears a red serge gown and a yellow turban. Cursed is the lot of the *ragyabas*, and twice cursed is Abula, if a day passes without a corpse being brought to the cemetery; for people believe that if a day passes without a death it portends evil to Lhasa.

In connection with the erection of Ramoche, it is said that the princess who had it built discovered that the spot on which the temple was erected was in communication with hell, and that there was a crystal palace inhabited by the Nagas deep in the earth underneath this place.

Among the most remarkable relics preserved in this temple, and which I had not had time to examine on my first rather hurried visit, I now noticed one of Dolma made of turquoise, and which is said to render oracles, one of Tse-pa-med made of coral, and one of Rin-chen Khadoma in amber, and a number of others of jade, conch-shells and *mumen*, besides many jars and bowls of jade and gold.

In the afternoon I called on the Lhacham, and was sorry to learn that her second son had smallpox. I told her how disappointed I was at not having been able to get even a glimpse of the Kyabgong; the 'lord protector' of Tibet, the Dalai lama. 'Alas!' I added, 'I have not acquired a sufficient moral merit in former existences to be able to see Shenrezig in flesh and blood!'

'Do not be cast down, Pundib la; though it is not an easy matter for even the Shape and nobles of Tibet to see the Dalai lama, I will arrange an audience for you.'

Early the next day a gentleman (*ku-dag*), who was a Dungkhor of Potala, called on me, and said that the Kusho Lhacham of Phala had arranged with the Donyer chenpo of Potala for an audience for me with the Dalai lama, and that I must get ready as soon as possible.

Swallowing breakfast as quickly as possible, I put on my best clothes, and had hardly finished when the Dungkhor Chola Kusho, accompanied by a servant, arrived. Having provided myself with three bundles of incense-sticks and a roll of *khatag*, we mounted our ponies and sallied forth. As we crossed the doorway we saw a calf sucking, and several women carrying water. My companions smiled, and Chola Kusho remarked that I was a lucky man, as these were most auspicious signs.

Arriving at the eastern gateway of Potala, we dismounted and walked through a long hall, on either side of which were rows of prayer-wheels, which every passer-by put in motion. Then, ascending three long flights of stone steps, we left our ponies in care of a bystander—for no one may ride further—and proceeded towards the palace under the guidance of a young monk. We had to climb up five ladders before we reached the ground floor of Phodang marpo, or 'the Red Palace', thus called from the exterior walls being of a dark red colour. Then we had half a dozen more ladders to climb up, and we found ourselves at the top of Potala (there are nine stories to this building), where we saw a number of monks awaiting an audience. The view from here was beautiful beyond compare: the broad valley of the Kyi chu, in the centre of which stands the great city surrounded by green groves; the gilt spires of the Jo-khang and the other temples of Lhasa, and farther away the great monasteries of Sera and Dabung, behind which rose the dark blue mountains.

After a while three lamas appeared, and said that the Dalai lama would presently conduct a memorial service for the benefit of the late Mera Ta lama (great lama of Meru gomba), and that we were allowed to be present at it. Walking very softly, we came to the middle of the reception hall, the roof of which is supported by three rows of pillars, four in each row, and where light is admitted by a skylight. The furniture was that generally seen in lamaseries, but the hangings were of the richest brocades and cloths of gold; the church utensils were of gold, and the frescoing on the walls of exquisite fineness. Behind the throne were beautiful tapestries and satin hangings forming a great *gyal-tsan*, or canopy. The floor was beautifully smooth and glossy, but the doors and windows, which were painted red, were of the rough description common throughout the country.

A Donyer approached, who took our presentation *khatag*, but I held back, at the suggestion of Chola Kusho, the present I had for the Grand Lama; and when I approached him I placed in his lap, much to the surprise of all present, a piece of gold weighing a tola. We then took our seats on rugs, of which there were eight rows; ours were in the third, and about 10 feet from the Grand Lama's throne, and a little to his left.

The Grand Lama is a child of eight with a bright and fair complexion and rosy cheeks. His eyes are large and penetrating, the shape of his face remarkably Aryan, though somewhat marred by the obliquity of his eyes. The thinness of his person was probably due to the fatigue of the Court ceremonies and to the religious duties and ascetic observance of his estate. A yellow mitre covered his head, and its pendant lappets hid his ears; a yellow mantle draped his person, and he sat cross-legged with joined palms. The throne on which he sat was supported by carved lions, and covered with silk scarves. It was about 4 feet high, 6 feet long, and 4 feet broad. The State officers moved about with becoming gravity: there was the Kuchar Khanpo, with a bowl of holy water (*tu*), coloured yellow with saffron; the Censor-carrier, with a golden censor with three chains; the Solpon chenpo, with a golden teapot; and other household officials. Two gold lamps, made in the shape of flower vases, burnt on either side of the throne.

When all had been blessed and taken seats, the Solpon chenpo poured tea in his Holiness's golden cup, and four assistants served the people present. Then grace was said, beginning with *Om, Ah, Hum*, thrice repeated, and followed by, 'Never losing sight even for a moment of the Three Holies, making reverence ever to the Three Precious Ones. Let the blessing of the Three Konchog be upon us,' etc. Then we silently raised our cups and drank the tea, which was most deliciously perfumed. In this manner we drank three cupfuls, and then put our bowls back in the bosoms of our gowns.

After this the Solpon chenpo put a golden dish full of rice before the Dalai lama, and he touched it, and then it was divided among those present; then grace was again said, and his Holiness, in a low, indistinct tone, chanted a hymn, which was repeated by the assembled lamas in deep, grave tones. When this was over, a venerable man rose from the first row of seats and made a short address, reciting the many acts of mercy the Dalai lamas had vouchsafed Tibet, at the conclusion of which he presented to his Holiness a number of valuable things; then he made three prostrations and withdrew, followed by all of us.

As I was leaving, one of the Donyer chenpo's (or chamberlain) assistants gave me two packets of blessed pills, and another tied a scrap of red silk round my neck—these are the usual return presents the Grand Lama makes to pilgrims.

As we were going out of the hall, we were met by Chola Kusho's younger brother, a monk in Namgyal Ta-tsan, the monastery of the palace, and in his and his brother's company I visited the palace, and learnt from them much relating to the history and the traditions of the place.

We first visited a chapel where is an image of Shenrezig with eleven heads and a thousand arms, an eye in the palm of each of his hands. Near it is an image with four arms, also many small gold *chorten* and objects in bronze. Next I was led to a hall where there is an old throne, opposite which are images of King Srong-btsan, his two consorts, his minister Tonmi Sambhota, General Gar, and Prince Gungri gung-btsan. Leaving this room, we went to the great hall where Ngawang lobzang, the fifth Dalai lama, used to hold his court. Old paintings, supposed to be indestructible by fire, representing King Srong-btsan's family, Shenrezig, and the first Grand Lama, hung from the pillars, and several images, among which one of sandalwood representing Gon-po, may be seen here.

We were then led to the hall where the Desi Sangye-gyatso used to hold his councils. Here also is the tomb of the first Dalai lama. It is two-storied, and the dome is covered with thin plates of gold. The Dalai's remains are entombed with many precious things, and the sepulchre is ornamented with various objects of the richest designs and most costly materials brought hither by devotees. This tomb is called the Dsamling gyan, and is the prototype of the tombs we saw around it containing the remains of the other incarnations of the Dalai lama; but these are all smaller than it.

After visiting these halls we descended to the Namgyal Ta-tsan. The architecture of the Phodang marpo embarrassed me greatly, the halls and rooms being piled up story on story. The stonework was beautiful, but it is so poorly drained that in many places the odours are stifling.

Entering a small room, the cell of our guide, we were given seats and served with tea and a collation. Shortly after we started home, having expressed in the warmest terms our thanks to Chola Kusho and his brother for their kindness. We followed the *ling-khor*, as the road which encircles Lhasa is called. On the way we passed a small grove where is the elephant-shed, the solitary occupant of which—a present from the Rajah of Sikkim—was standing in a barley patch near by. Further on we came to a place where the corpses of the townspeople are fed to pigs, whose flesh, by the way, is said to be delicious. Near here are numerous huts of *ragyabas*.

In the evening a drove of donkeys loaded with *tsamba* and butter arrived from Gyantse, and I was distressed to learn that my friend the minister had smallpox. My men again began pestering me to return to Tsang, alleging as a pretext that I might be of assistance to the minister, and I finally prepared to go to him, especially as the donkey-men said he had expressed a desire to have me near him.

On June 11 I went to see the Lhacham, thanked her for having obtained for me an audience of the Kyab-gong Rinpoche, and spoke to her about my intention of setting out for Dongtse. She advised me to leave at once, as smallpox was raging at Lhasa; her two sons now had it, and from her appearance I feared that she was about to fall ill of the same disease.

Returning to our lodgings, I despatched Tsing-ta to her to ask a loan of 200 *tankas*. The sum was brought me in the evening by her maid Apela, and the Lhacham also sent me provisions for the journey and feed for the ponies.

VII

Government of Lhasa—Customs, Festivals, Etc.

The Dalai lama's position resembles that held until lately by the Pope in the Christian world. He is believed by the Northern Buddhists to be the Buddha's Vice-regent incarnate on earth, and the spiritual protector of Tibet. He is known as Tug-je chenpo Shenrezig, or the Most Merciful Avalokiteswara. He never dies, though at times, displeased with the sinfulness of the world, he retires to the paradise of Gadan, leaving his mortal body on earth. The ancient records of Tibet say that he has only appeared on earth fourteen times in the eighteen centuries from the time of the Buddha's death to the beginning of the fifteenth century.

In the year 1474 Gedun-gyatso was born, an embodiment of Gedun-dub, who was an incarnation of Shenrezig, and the founder of the famous lamasery of Tashilhunpo. Gedun-gyatso was elected head lama of Tashilhunpo in 1512, which office he resigned to fill the same position in Dabung, the chief lamasery of Lhasa. He had built at this latter place the Gadan phodang of Dabung, which since then has been famed as the principal seat of Buddhist learning. He was the first of the line of Dalai lamas.

His successor was Sonam-gyatso. He was invited to Mongolia by the famous conqueror Altan Khan, and on his arrival at the latter's camp the Khan addressed him in Mongol by the name of

Dalai lama, the Tibetan word *gyatso*, 'ocean', being the equivalent of *dalai* in Mongol. Altan, knowing that the lama's predecessor had also the word *gyatso* in his name, took it for a family name; and this mistake has been the origin of the name of Dalai lama since given to all the reincarnations of the Grand Lama.

In 1642 Kushi Khan conquered Tibet, and made over the sovereignty of the central portion of it to the fifth Dalai lama, Ngawang lobzang-gyatso, and that of Tsang, or Ulterior Tibet, to the Grand Lama of Tashilhunpo, though he continued himself to be the de facto sovereign, appointing Sonam chuphel as Desi, or Governor, of Central, and another as administrator of Ulterior Tibet. The spiritual government remained, however, in the Dalai lama's hands, and he conferred on Kushi Khan the title of Tandjin chos-gyi Gyalbo, 'the most Catholic king'.

In 1645 the Dalai lama erected the palace of Potala, Kushi Khan having his residence in the Gadan khangsar palace in Lhasa itself. Engrossed with extending and consolidating his newly acquired kingdom, he had, little by little, to transfer to the Dalai lama and the Desi most of his authority over Tibet. In 1654 Kushi Khan died, and the Desi Sonam chuphel followed him shortly to the grave. By this time so much of the temporal authority had devolved on the Dalai lama, that, from the time of the death of Kushi till his successor Dayan arrived in Lhasa in 1660—even though for a year (1658–1659) there was no Desi—the country enjoyed peace and prosperity under his rule.

During Dayan Khan's reign, which only lasted eight years, a Mongol chief, Jaisang Teba, was Desi of Tibet, and the Desi who succeeded him was appointed by the Dalai lama himself.

The successor of Dayan was Ratna-talai Khan, but by this time the management of State affairs had entirely passed into the hands of the Grand Lama. In 1680 he appointed Sangye-gyatso Desi, and conferred on him such authority that, under the title of Governor-Treasurer (*Sa-kyong-wai chyag-dso*), he was in reality

King of Tibet. He remodelled the Government, and introduced many useful reforms in every branch of the public service.

The Desi is commonly called 'regent' (*gyal-tsab*), or 'king' (*gyalbo*). The office is now elective, but no layman may hold it; it is filled by a lama from one of the four great *lings*, Tangye ling, Kundu ling, Tse-chog ling, and Tsomo ling; though there have been cases, as, for instance, that of the Desi Shata (or Shadra), where lamas from other places have been selected.

The council of ministers (*Kalon*) and the Prime Minister (*Chyikyab khanpo*) select the Regent, and their choice is confirmed by the oracles of Nachung chos-gyong and Lhamo sung chyongma; and, lastly, the nomination is ratified by the Emperor of China.

When the Dalai lama reaches his majority, fixed at eighteen years, the Regent, in the presence of the Kalon, the chiefs and nobles, presents him with the seals of office of both spiritual and temporal affairs. Since the beginning of the present century no Dalai lama has reached majority, and the regency has been without interruption.

The Regent is assisted by a Chasag, whose appointment is also subject to confirmation by the Emperor of China. He wields great power, and sometimes exercises the functions of the Regent himself. No petitions on any official business can reach the Regent without passing through his hands. He is entrusted with the great seal, and when a paper has been prepared by the chief secretary, or Kadung, the Chasag affixes the seal to it. The word *chasag* means 'a strainer for tea', the dignitary so designated being the test and model of merit.

The council of ministers, or *Kalon shag lengya*, is composed of four laymen and one monk, all of them appointed for life. Formerly there were only four Kalon, but of late the preponderating influence of the clergy has forced the Grand Lama to put in the council one of its members, and he takes the first seat in the council hall, or *kashag*, the Kalon kripa coming next to him. The council sits daily from nine to two, and transacts the political, judicial, and administrative work of the Government. It hears appeals from the Djongpon, or from the Court of the Timpon of Lhasa, known as 'the black court' (*Nagtsa-shar*). The ministers sit cross-legged on thick cushions placed on raised seats, with a bowl of tea on a little table in front of each of them, which is kept full by the Court Solpon. The secretaries and clerks occupy adjoining rooms. The ministers and all the officers of their court are provided with dinner at the expense of the State.

Estates (or *Lonshi*) are set apart for the maintenance of the ministers, who receive no other salary. They are not allowed the privilege of being carried on sedan chairs (*pheb-chyam*), the Amban, the Dalai, the Panchen lamas, and on certain occasions the Regent, being alone permitted to use this conveyance. The Kalon dress in yellow tunics, and wear Mongol hats with a coral button on top.

When the office of a Kalon becomes vacant, the Regent, in consultation with the other Kalon, selects two or three generals (*Dahpon*), and sends their names to the oracles of Nachung and Lhamo sung-chyong-ma of Potala for them to pronounce upon. The person approved of by the oracles is appointed.

In literary style the ministers are called *Chying-sang* or *Dunna-dun*, but colloquially they are known as *Kalon* or *Shape*, and the title of *Sa-wang* ('power of the land') is usually affixed to their names, as they are selected from among the wealthy and powerful nobles. 'When sitting in a judicial capacity they are known as *Shalchepa*, and *Shulenpa* when they perform the duties of advocate.

Formerly the wives of Gyalbo and Desi were addressed by the title of *Lhacham*, but nowadays it is only given to the wives of Kalon. Their sons are called *Lha-sre*, or 'prince'.

There are four secretaries, or *Kadung*, chosen from among the Dungkhor, and one chief clerk, or *Kabshopa*, attached to the Kalon's court. Under these secretaries are 175 Dungkhor, or civil officers, under the immediate supervision of the Tsipon, or accounting officer.

The Dungkhor are chosen from among the best scholars of the Yutog school, where the sons of nobles and the leading people are educated. They are taught accounting by serving five years in the Bureau of Accounts, or Tsi-khang, after which they are deputed to perform various duties, especially in connection with the treasury, and the most experienced among them are appointed Djongpon, or prefects.

The salaries of the Dungkhor are barely sufficient for their maintenance; but, as they belong for the most part to well-to-do families, this question is unimportant. The Dungkhor have a peculiar way of dressing their hair, which distinguishes them from all other officers.

Those among the sons of the wealthy and prominent people of Lhasa who, having become members of the Church, desire to enter public life, are trained at the Tse labdra of Potala, after which they become *Tse-dung*, or monk officials. The number of these Tse-dung cannot exceed 175. In all places of trust and responsibility there are two officers, and sometimes more, one at least of whom is a Tse-dung. Thus, in the office of the treasurer of Potala there are two Tse-dung and one Dungkhor; in the Labrang treasury there are two Tse-dung and one Dungkhor, etc. The Tse-dung are appointed to these offices for a term of three years.

The Djongpon, or prefects, are entrusted within their respective *Djong* with civil and military powers; they try civil and criminal cases, and levy taxes, the latter duty being performed under *Kargya*, or, as we would say, *Purwanas* from the Court of Kalon. There are 53 Djong and 123 Sub-prefectures under Djongnyer.

There are two Djongpon to every Djong, their authority being equal in all respects. In military matters they are subordinate to the generals and the Amban. They render yearly accounts to the

Amban of the military stores in their district, and have also to show their proficiency in shooting, riding, and other athletic sports at the annual inspection of the troops made by the Amban and the Dahpon; and the former confers on them blue or crystal buttons, to be worn on their official hats.

The establishment of a Djongpon comprises two Dungkhor and two storekeepers (*Djongnyer*)—administering sub-districts—and a number of under-strappers. The heads of villages (or *Tsopon*), the headmen (or *Mipon*), the elders (or *Gyanpo*), all of whom are elected for a term of years, are also under his orders.

In every Djong there are two store-houses—the *kar-gya*, or reserve store, and the *djong-dso*, or repository of the Djong. The keys of the former are kept by the Kalon, and it is opened only once or twice a year. The Government sends annually a revenue officer to check the accounts of the Djongpon and tax-collectors (*Khraldupa*), and to take over the revenue collected by them. The Djongpon have, like the Kalon, their jagirs or *djong-shi* for their maintenance, in lieu of salary.

The following citation, taken from a work entitled *Sherab dongbu*, or 'Bits of Wisdom', may prove of interest:

> Whenever petitions or requests are made, they should be carefully examined. Impartiality should be shown to all classes alike, to great and small, to lamas and to laymen. Uninfluenced by gratuities or the fear of criticism, the Djongpon should administer perfect justice. Questions of jurisdiction, of taxes due by the *misser*, and of forced labour, should be settled by the rules (*tsa-tsig*) of each *Djong*. The villages, houses, and inhabitants should be counted and inspected yearly, and the numbers compared with those of preceding years. He should have returned to their houses those who have left them, particularly *misser* who have been absent from their houses for not more than five years. Servants and labourers of the *Djong* should not be employed by him at his private work; the number of servants allowed him is fixed by

the *tsa-tsig*. He should be kind to the *misser*, and not without a good cause have disputes with neighbouring Djongpon, as the Government's interests would thereby suffer. He should not allow the public lands to be encroached upon, nor should tenants on them be taken away by landholders (*gerpas*).

No women should be allowed to loiter about the *Djong*, and the Djongpon should carefully refrain from any flirtation. He should see to facilitating the courier service, and he should see that no one receives supplies for their journey unless they are bearers of passports (*lam-yig*). Frontier or foreign traders who cannot show a passport should be held, and any information he may obtain of affairs in other quarters should be transmitted to Lhasa.

As previously mentioned, the Kalon and Djongpon exercise judicial functions. In the case of the Sera and Dabung lamaseries, the abbots decide all minor offences committed within the monastery limits, but the more serious charges are committed to the court of the Regent and the Kalon. In all other lamaseries only offences against the common law are tried by the convent authorities.

It is customary for both parties in a suit to make presents to the judge. When the case has been examined, the judge fixes the costs (*tim-teg*) to be borne in equal portions by the plaintiffs and defendants. As a general rule, disputes are settled by the village elders; but few lawsuits occur on the whole, for the Tibetans are a peaceful, kind-hearted, law-abiding people, and very amenable to reason.

The Amban, or Imperial Resident of China in Tibet, is the head of the Tibetan army. His Chinese staff consists of an Assistant Amban, two Laoyeh, and a paymaster (*pogpon*). There is also one Tibetan general, or Magpon, six Dahpon, or division commanders, six Rupon commanding regiments, and a number of subordinate officers.

The Amban is the medium of all communications between the Tibetan Government and China. He settles all political differences between the various states of Tibet and the Lhasa Government; he confers titles and honours on native military officials; but he has, theoretically, no authority in the internal administration of the country. He ordinarily resides at Lhasa, and annually makes an inspection of the Nepalese frontier as far as Tingri *djong*. Sometimes the Assistant Amban performs this duty, and he then inspects the military stores and forces at the different *Djong*.

The political relations between Tibet and China are now so intimate that the Imperial Residency established at Lhasa in the first quarter of the last century has converted Tibet from a protected state into a dependency of China. The two Ambans are commanders of the militia, and arrogate to themselves the supreme political authority of the country. The appointment of two Ambans to watch the political interests of the country is probably based on the principle that the one acts as a spy on the other. This has, as in China, become a custom in Tibet.

The Ambans are the terror of the Tibetans, who abhor them from the depth of their hearts. Whenever they leave the capital on pleasure excursions, or on inspection tours, provisions, conveyances, and all sorts of labour are forcibly exacted from the poor villagers, who are deprived of their ponies and yaks, which, owing to the merciless treatment of the Ambans' numerous retainers, die in numbers on the road. No compensation is given them for their losses, and no complaints are admitted by the courts of justice, presided over by the lamas, against this kind of oppression. *Tsamba* and sheep are also on these occasions taken away by force from the people, who, unable to bear the oppression, not unfrequently rise in a body against the Ambans' retainers, when matters are settled by the district Djongpon, who are generally the creatures of the Ambans. Nor is this all. Every Chinese or Manchu soldier or merchant who enters Tibet, whether in a public or private capacity, is provided with a pass from Peking, which facilitates his journey and brings him safe to his destination free of charge, The same is the case with those who leave Tibet for China, the Ambans being the only officials qualified to grant passports. The happy traveller, armed with the Ambans' authority, takes every advantage of his pass, and never fails to use his whip freely when the villagers delay in complying with his requisitions.

One of the Ambans at least is required to pay a visit to the Tashi lama once a year, to confer with him on State affairs, when, as the representative of the Emperor of China, he is received with the highest marks of distinction. The Amban is required to make a low salutation with joined palms, and as he approaches the throne he presents a *khatag* to the lama. The Tashi lama, on his side, blesses him by touching his head with his open hand, and seats him on his right on a State cushion. After a short interchange of compliments the conversation turns on the health of the Emperor, the happiness of the people, and the prospects of the year's crops. Interpreters who understand the Mongol, Manchu, and Chinese languages always accompany the Amban, and the Tashi lama has also his interpreters. When the Amban appears abroad he is carried in a yellow chair, and attended by a numerous retinue bearing the insignia of his high office.

Of the Dahpon, two are stationed at Lhasa, two at Shigatse, one at Gyantse, and one at Tingri *djong*. Three of the six Rupon belong to Central Tibet, and three to Ulterior.

The regular army consists of 6,000 men, 3,000 being under arms, and the other 3,000 at home on half-pay. Those in active service serve for three years at a monthly pay of 2 ounces of silver. After this they return to their homes, and enter the territorial army, or *yul-mag*, whence they may be at any moment recalled to active service. They are not usually uniformed, though some wear a black Chinese jacket. They are armed with matchlocks, bows and arrows, long spears, and slings (*ordo*).

Besides the regular army, the Government may, in case of need, call out all the forces of the country, when each family has to supply one man fully equipped and provisioned, and every landholder sends a man for every *kang* of land he owns, and a follower to carry his provisions. The Kalon, Djongpon, Dahpon, and chief men furnish quotas of cavalry (or *tamag*), all those who have ponies being incorporated in this arm.

Besides the expense of maintaining the army—each Chinese private being paid fourteen rupees a month and thirty *surs* of *tsamba*, and every Tibetan 2¼ rupees a month—the Tibetan Government has to contribute 50,000 rupees to the Residency establishment, exclusive of the Amban's salary. The Tibetan Government, as well as the whole nation, groan under this excessive and useless expenditure; but the maintenance of this order of things is declared to be essential for the protection of the holy lamas against the encroachments of the English, Nepalese, and Kashmir Governments. Both the latter states are allies of Tibet, while the very name of the first is dreaded by the Government officers, especially the monk officers, as an invincible power, and as being the incarnation of the Lhamayins (giants) who fought against the gods.

It is universally believed in Tibet that after 200 years the Tashi lama will retire to Shambala, the Utopian city of the Buddhists, and will not return to Tibet, and that in the meantime the whole world will succumb to the power of the Phylings (Russians and English). Neither the Emperor of China nor the combined legions of gods and demi-gods who reside round the golden mount of Birab (Sumeru) will be able to arrest the progress of their arms or the miracles of their superior intellect. It is the policy of the Tibetans to keep them at a distance, not by open hostilities, but by temporizing and diplomacy. They were initiated into this policy by the Ambans, who are always busy in devising fresh plans for guaranteeing the safety of the country against all sorts of imaginary foreign aggressions.

The Nepalese are not now so much the object of this terror as they were a century ago, but are regarded as peaceful allies under the rule of the Emperor of China. Tibet pays no tribute to Nepal, nor does it entertain any agent at Katmandu, while Nepal maintains an agent at Lhasa to promote friendly relations, as also to protect her commercial interests with Tibet. It is to be remembered that the richest merchants and bankers of Lhasa are Nepalese Palpas.

During the late disturbances between the monks of the Tosam ling College and the Nyer-chang chenpo, the late Tashi lama did not consult the Amban, or invite the aid of his soldiers to quell the rebellion among the 1,500 disaffected and unruly monks, but secretly apprised his subjects of the neighbouring villages of his intentions, and on the appointed day 10,000 armed men were assembled, carrying long spears, bucklers, matchlocks, and slings, who at once struck the rebel monks with terror. He has since that day been convinced of the sincere veneration and devoted loyalty of his people and of the perfect uselessness of the Amban's forces. This instance of tact in the Panchen rinpoche has raised him higher than ever in the estimation of the people, much to the discomfort of the jealous Amban. It is also pleasing to notice some signs of independence in the youthful Tashi, who is now the senior sovereign of Tibet, the Dalai lama being as yet an infant. The villagers and common folks, who suffer most from the Amban's tyranny, say that in course of time the present Tashi will prove a worthy successor of the great Tempai nyima in faith as well as in strength of mind.

The principal sources of revenue of the Lhasa Government are the family-tax and the land-tax, the first being usually paid in coin, and the latter in kind. The family-tax may be paid at any time of the year.

Apart from the lands held by chiefs and nobles, there are, as already stated, altogether fifty-three *Djong*, or districts, under Djongpon, and a hundred and twenty-three sub-districts under Djongnyer. These constitute what are called *shung shi*, or State lands. Each *djong* contains, on an average, 500 families of *misser*, or farmers. A *misser* family consists of one wife, with all her husbands, children, and servants. Each family, on an average, possesses two or three *kang* of arable soil. If one *khal* (50 lbs) yields nine or ten *khal*, it is considered a good harvest; six to eight is a tolerable crop, four to six a bad one. The Government revenue for each *kang* is, on an average, fifty *srang* (125 rupees), or about 150 *khal* of grain. The Crown revenue, if taken entirely in kind, would therefore amount to 2,625,000 *khal*, which would be equivalent in money to 2,000,000 rupees. This is partially expended by the State for the Church, and in distributing alms to the whole body of lamas belonging to the monasteries of Potala, Sera, Dabung, Gadan, etc. In every *djong* are kept registers, in which are entered the collections in previous years and the quality of the land under cultivation. The collector, after examining these, inspects the crops, and estimates the quantity of the yield, and by comparison with that of the five preceding years he fixes the tax for the current year. In very prosperous years the State takes two-fifths of the crop (the maximum allowed it).

Ulag consists in supplying to all those bearing a Government order for *ulag*, in which the number of animals, etc., is enumerated, beasts of burden—ponies, mules, yaks, and donkeys. If the *misser* have no ponies, they have to furnish yaks or donkeys instead. For stages along which neither yaks nor ponies can pass, porters must be supplied for carrying the traveller's goods. In default of these, the *misser* are required to pay a certain sum for carriage or conveyance. *Misser*, and all those who own more than one *kang* of land, must supply *ulag* and *ta-u*, consisting of either one coolie or pony, free of charge when the traveller produces his Government pass. The system of levying *ulag* is a kind of indirect taxation, accounts of which are kept by the village headmen. Some families supply a hundred *ulag* in a year, others only five or ten. If a *misser* fails to supply *ulag* once in a year, he is required to supply double the amount the following year. This duty is levied on all kinds of State lands and subjects, freeholds and private property granted to sacred personages alone being exempt from this hateful tax. Lands purchased from Government are also liable to it. Under the Lhasa Government there are about a hundred and twenty landlords, out of whom about twenty are very rich and powerful. The present Regent, Lama Ta-tsag Rinpoche, of Kundu ling, has upwards of 3,000 *misser* on his estates in Kharu and Tibet Proper. The ex-regent, whose estates lie in Kongpo, has about 5,000 *misser*, and other great lamas and laymen about 1,000 *misser* each. The greatest noble of Tibet, Phags-pa-sha, of Chab-mdo, is lord over 10,000 *misser*.

When questions arise about newly reclaimed lands, the tax-collector, having no register (*tsi-shi*) to guide him, measures the field and superintends the harvesting, when he fixes the amount due to the State. He is forbidden fixing his assessments otherwise than by personal examination. The land-tax may be paid in three instalments—in November, December, and January, at which latter date it is remitted by the Djongpon to Lhasa or Tashilhunpo, as the case may be. The tax-gatherer has authority to remit a portion of the tax when the crops have failed for some reason or other; in fact, as a Tibetan author puts it, 'as eggs are quietly taken from under a sitting-hen without disturbing the nest, so should the tax-gatherer collect the taxes without oppressing or disturbing the *misser*.'

The great monasteries at Lhasa and its neighbourhood, such as Sera, Dabung, Gadan, Samye, etc., have large freehold estates.

Besides these, there are more than 300 landholders, called *gerpa*, who pay a nominal revenue to the Government, varying from ten to thirty *doche* (1,250 to 3,750 rupees), and who are also called upon to furnish *ulag, ta-u,* and other indirect taxes. Cows and *jomo* belonging to the Government and tended by *dokpa* are calculated to yield at the rate of 5 pounds of butter per head per year. In the provinces of Kong-po and Pema-kyod numerous pigs are reared, and rich families count their pigs by the thousands. The Lhasa Government levies a tax of one *tanka* on every pig, and derives no inconsiderable revenue from these districts from this source. The tenants in each *djong* contribute ten days' labour per head for the ploughing or harvesting of the State lands. This service is called the *las-tal,* or 'labour-tax'.

There is in Tibet no fixed rate of duties on merchandise, nor is there a regular import duty. Rich merchants who come from foreign countries are required to pay annually a tax of fifty *srang* to the Government; large traders are charged twenty-five *srang,* and small traders three *srang.* Shopkeepers and pedlars pay five *sho* (1¼ rupee) annually, and itinerant Khamba hawkers who carry their own loads are charged half a *tanka* per quarter both in U and Tsang.

For crossing large bridges the charge is from one *kha* (one anna) to one *tanka* per head for a man, and a *karma* (two annas) to a *sho* (four annas) for ponies. For pasturing cattle on public lands there is a charge of from three to five *sho* yearly for every head. Besides these, there is a capitation tax of from two to three *srang* (7½ rupees) on people owning no land but only homesteads. The revenue-collectors (*Khraldupa*) and their servants get conveyance, ponies, and yaks at every stage free of charge, and the villagers are bound to furnish them in addition with attendants, water, fuel and lodgings. The revenue-collectors may accept for their own use all the *khatag,* butter, tea, and silver coin which the *misser* may see fit to offer them. They are also authorized, when on tour, to kill one out of every hundred sheep belonging to the *misser* for their own consumption. In all other matters they are guided by the usages and laws of the country. No Government official, revenue officer, or Djongpon may oppress the poorest *misser*. If one of these peasants fails to pay his taxes in money, he may offer the equivalent in tea, butter, or blankets; but livestock, except when nothing else is available, are not to be accepted. The property in cattle belonging to the Lhasa Government exceeds 1,000,000 head. There is a superintendent of this Government stock, who, at the end of every year, submits an account of the live animals and the number died or killed during the year. In order to satisfy the authorities, he is required to produce the entire dried carcasses of the dead animals with their tails and horns. These superintendents are appointed annually, and as a consequence they take every opportunity of making their fortune at the expense of the State before the expiration of their term of service.

Letters are carried by messengers and special couriers called *chib-zamba* (or *ta-zamba*), meaning, literally, 'horse-bridge'. The couriers generally discharge their duty with admirable efficiency, and everyone assists them with great promptness. All Government messengers are provided with the best and swiftest ponies, and at every halt are furnished with lodgings, water, firewood, and a man to cook their victuals. Couriers on foot usually travel from 20 to 25 miles a day, while those who ride do from 30 to 35 miles. The latter is the express rate, for which the Government generally gives an extra remuneration. Government couriers alone get *ta-u*, or ponies for travelling; private letters of officials are carried by them, while common people make their own arrangements for the conveyance of their letters, which are not, however, numerous.

The express couriers, or *te-tsi*, on the road between Lhasa and China are dressed in tight blue-coloured gowns, the tape fastenings of which are tied on their heads, and the knot sealed. They are required to subsist daily on five hen's eggs, five cups of plain tea, a pound of cornflour, half a pound of rice, and a quarter-pound of lean meat. They are forbidden to take much salt, and are strictly forbidden to eat onions, garlic, red pepper, butter, or milk. At midnight they are allowed to sleep in a sitting posture for three hours, after which they are awakened by the keeper of the stage-house. It is said that these couriers are in the habit of taking certain medicines to give them the power of endurance against fatigue. The letters are enclosed in a yellow bag, which the courier carries on his back, generally using some soft feathers to keep it from coming into contact with his person. They get relays of ponies at the end of every five *lebor*. Arriving at a stage-house, they fire a gun as a notice to the keeper of the next postal stage to make ready a post-pony. At every such stage a relay of five ponies is usually kept ready. The courier is allowed to change his dress once a week.

A special class of trained men are employed on this service. The distance between the Tibetan capital and Peking is divided into a hundred and twenty *gya-tsug*, or postal stages, of about 80 to 90 *lebor* each. This distance of nearly 10,000 *lebor* is required to be traversed in seventy-two days. Couriers are generally allowed a delay of five days, but when they exceed that they are punished. On occasions of very great importance and urgency the express rate to Peking is thirty-six days. During the last affray between the junior Amban and the people of Shigatse the express took a month and a half to reach Peking.

As regards the administration of justice and the laws of Tibet, the following peculiarities may be noted: Both parties in a suit make written statements of their case, and these briefs are read in court.

The judge has the evidence, depositions, and his decision written down, three copies of the latter being given to the parties concerned. Then he states the law fee (*tim teg*) and the engrossing fee (*myug-rin*), both of which vary with the importance of the case, and are borne by both parties to the suit.

The death punishment is only inflicted in certain cases of dacoity (*chagpa*), when those convicted are sewed in leather bags and thrown into a river.

Offences of a less heinous nature are dealt with by banishment to the borders, whipping, imprisonment, or fines.

Nothing can be more horrible and loathsome than a Tibetan jail. There are some dungeons in an obscure village two days' journey up the river from Tashilhunpo, where life convicts are sent for confinement. The prisoner having been placed in a cell, the door is removed and the opening filled up with stone masonry, only one small aperture, about 6 inches in diameter, being left, through which the unhappy creature is supplied with his daily food. There are also a few small holes left open on the roof, through which the guards and the jailor empty every kind of filth into the cell. Some prisoners have lived for two years under this horrible treatment, while others, more fortunate, die in a few months.

In cases of murder, there are four fines to be paid by the murderer: first, 'blood-money' (*tong jal*); second, a sum for funeral ceremonies for the benefit of the slain; third, a fine to the State; and fourth, a peace offering to the family and friends of the murdered person. These fines vary from the weight of the body of the slain in gold, to 5 ounces of silver, or the equivalent in kind. Should these fines not be paid, the murderer is thrown into prison.

When the murderer is insane, or a minor, aged less than eight years, the relatives or friends are only required to pay the funeral expenses of the victim; the same rule applies if any one is killed by a horse, yak or other animal, the owner paying the funeral expenses of the person killed.

When a husband kills his wife, or a master his servant, he is required to pay the usual fine to the State and the funeral expenses.

Thieves have to pay from a hundred to seven times the value

of the goods stolen, according to the social standing of the person from whom they have stolen.

When the thief is a recidivist, his hands *may* be cut off if it is his fifth conviction, and he may be hamstrung if it is his seventh. For the ninth conviction his eyes can be put out.

If a thief is punished by the person from whom he is attempting to steal, the courts will not take cognizance of the case; but should the thief be killed, blood-money, to the amount of 5 ounces of silver, must be paid to his family.

Children aged less than thirteen are not punishable for theft, but their parents are remonstrated with. When a woman commits a theft, the fines and possible corporal punishment are borne in equal proportions by herself and her husband.

No corporal punishment can be inflicted on a pregnant woman, nor on those suffering from an illness, who have recently lost parents, or who are older than seventy.

He who harbours a thief is held to be a greater culprit than the thief himself. If a person witnesses a theft and does not give notice thereof, he is held equally guilty with the thief. Thefts by one member of a family on another member should be punished by the head of the family alone.

The theft of a lock, a key, or a watchdog, is considered equivalent to robbing the objects they keep safe.

Rape on the person of a married woman of high degree is punishable by emasculation and fines. In case the woman belongs to the middle or lower classes, the culprit pays the husband a fine and gives the woman a suit of clothes.

If a man of low rank has intercourse with the unmarried daughter of a man of high standing, he must serve the father without wages for a term of years. If the offender is of high standing, he has only a fine to pay.

In all cases of assault and battery, fines, known as *song jal*, or 'life money', are alone imposed, to which may be added the amount necessary for medical treatment for the wounded party. The amount of the fine is fixed by the size and depth of the wounds, the importance of the bone broken or the organ injured.

When judges or arbitrators are unable to reach a decision, they may permit the plaintiff to challenge the defendant to make a deposition on oath, or undergo an ordeal. In Khams and Amdo this practice is dying out, but it is still in vogue in Central Tibet. On account of the nature of these oaths and ordeals, the law exempts certain classes of men from taking them. Lamas, teachers, *genyen* (semi-priestly laymen), monks, and novices are not allowed to take oaths and pass through ordeals, nor are Tantriks (religious sorcerers) and other practitioners of mystic incantations, who are supposed to be able to counteract the fearful consequences of breaking an oath by means of their powerful spells. Destitute and famished people, to whom food and clothing are all in all, and men who will do anything they like, regardless of the consequences in a future existence, are not allowed to make a deposition on oath, nor are wives and mothers, who can easily be persuaded to swear in the interests of their husbands and children. Besides these, young boys, lunatics, and the dumb, who do not understand the difference between good and evil, happiness and misery, are equally exempt. All others, not included in the above list, who are honest, know the difference between good and evil, believe in the inevitable consequences of one's actions (karma), are held proper persons to take oaths and undergo ordeals.

The challenger is required to pay the defendant the 'oath compensation' or 'oath blood' (*na-tra*), which varies from a trifling amount to a very large sum, according to the nature of the case; but for one of considerable importance the usual compensation is fifty silver *srang* (125 rupees), and a yak; besides this 'oath flesh' (*na sha*) is claimed.

The person challenged to take the oath first offers prayers to the all-knowing gods, the Buddhas and Bodhisattvas, to the gods of the land and to the goddesses called *Srung-ma* (protectresses), to the demi-gods of the land, and to the goblins and nymphs who live in the land, invoking them to bear witness to his solemn deposition. Then he speaks the following words: 'What I depose is the truth, and nothing but the truth.' He then seats himself naked on the skin of a cow or ox newly slain, smears himself with the blood of the animal, and places an image of Buddha, with some volumes of religious books, on his head. Next, after eating the raw heart of the ox, and drinking three mouthfuls of its steaming blood, he declares to the spectators, 'There is certainly no guilt in me, and if there be any, may the guardians of the world and the gods make me cease to exist before the end of the current month.' He then receives the oath compensation (*na-tra*) and the slain ox or 'oath flesh' (*na sha*).

It is commonly believed among the Tibetans that, should one perjure himself, he either becomes insane, or dies vomiting blood, before the expiration of a hundred and seven days. When this does not befall him, other misfortunes happen, such as the loss of his wife or children, quarrels, feuds, or the loss or destruction of his property. Death is believed to be the most common consequence of perjury.

The undergoing of such an oath liberates the swearer from the penalty of death, and from paying fines in all cases of robbery and murder, as well as from civil liabilities, such as debts and disputes about land, even though it involves thousands of *srang*. On the other hand it is believed that if the challenger be guilty of false and malicious accusation, all the evils reserved for the perjured swearer will fall upon him.

In certain cases the guilt or innocence of parties is decided by the throwing of dice, the person being exculpated who gets the greatest number of points.

Important cases of murder, dacoity, and theft are also decided by ordeals, of which there are two kinds—picking out white and black pebbles from a bowl of boiling oil or muddy water, and handling a red-hot stone ball. In the presence of the prosecutor, the witnesses, the judge, or his representative, and many other spectators, the accused person invokes the gods and the demigods to bear witness to his statement, and declares that he tells the perfect truth. A copper or iron bowl filled with boiling oil or muddy water is then placed before him, in which two pebbles of the size of an egg, one white and the other black, each enveloped and tied up in a bag, are thrown. The swearer washes his hands first with water, and then with milk, and, having heard read a section of the Law written on a tablet with the blood of a cow slain for the occasion, plunges his hand in the boiling oil or water, and withdraws one of the pebbles. If he takes out the white one without scalding his hand, he is believed to be innocent; but if his hand is scalded, he is considered to be only partially innocent. If he brings out the black stone and gets his hand scalded besides, he is pronounced guilty.

The second form of ordeal is performed by heating a stone ball of the size of an ostrich's egg red hot, and then placing it in an iron vessel. The person taking the oath, having washed his hands in water and milk, seizes the ball and walks with it to a distance of seven, five, or three paces, according as his challenger is of the first, second, or third class of social rank. After this, his hand is enveloped in a white cotton bag, which, in the presence of the spectators, is tied up and sealed. At the end of the third, fifth, or seventh day, the bag is opened and the palm examined. If it is found unscalded, with only a pale yellowish line or stain upon it, the accused is declared innocent; if there appear a blister of the size of a pea, he is thought partly guilty; if three blisters of that size appear, he is considered half guilty; but if his hand be burned all over, he is held guilty of all the charges.

According to the laws of Tibet, the interest on money, grain, or any other commodity is 20 per cent, or one measure for five measures yearly. The courts in a few cases admit contracts at even a higher rate of interest; but those who claim more according to their contract deeds may be punished as usurers, though sometimes their claims are allowed. In urgent cases 33 per cent have been known to have been agreed upon. All contracts are required to be made in writing, attested by witnesses, and duly signed and sealed. The interest must be paid at the end of the year. If the debtor absconds, the witnesses are called upon to make good the loss sustained by the lender; but if he dies, or becomes insolvent, and the money be not realized, the witnesses are not held responsible. If, however, the money has been lent by the Government, by certain monasteries, or lamas, or by the paymaster of the army, the amount is realized from the relatives, witnesses, and neighbours of the debtor. At every military station, a certain amount of money is generally lent out by the Government, on the interest of which the militia is paid by the quartermaster, who is one of the chief Government moneylenders. Usually when the person soliciting a loan is not known, or if doubts about his honesty are entertained, securities are required. Not so in Tibet, where the lenders have been known to use their power to collect debts from the heirs of debtors to the third generation. The more the debtor exceeds the fixed term for the payment of his debt the more urgent is the creditor in his demands. The court, when it sees that the creditor has extracted compound interest for many years from the debtor, can put a stop to the accumulation of further compound interest; but there is no fixed period mentioned in the law after which compound interest must cease to accumulate.

In Tibet such articles as household utensils, implements of husbandry or war, drinking cups, borrowed articles, articles held in trust, landed estates of which the revenue is paid to the State, and images of gold, are never given in loan or mortgaged.

When a man has a single pony, one milch cow or *jo*, one plough, one span of bullocks or yaks, or one suit of clothing, nobody can ask for a loan of any of these articles without committing the offence of 'impudence,' for which he may be severely rebuked. Creditors, whether the Government or private persons, cannot seize upon any of these properties for debt. This is the Grand Charter of the Tibetans. Nor can any creditor by force seize the property of his debtor. If without the debtor's permission he removes one *srang*, he forfeits his entire claim on a loan of a hundred *srang*; if he removes two, on two hundred srang, and so on in the same proportion. Nobody, be he a public officer, landlord, master, or creditor, can, for any kind of pecuniary claim, exercise violence on the people. If, while being in possession of means to do so, a man of the people refuses to pay off his liabilities or debts, his creditors may employ mediators, or institute proceedings against him in a court of justice; but if, without resorting to these means, they beat him or use any kind of violence on him, they forfeit all claims upon him.

If after buying an article the purchaser wishes to return it on the same day, he must forfeit one-tenth of the price. If he returns it on the following day he forfeits one-fifth; on the second, one-half; and if he keeps it beyond the third day it is not returnable. If a householder cheats a merchant lodger, he is required to pay compensation at the rate of five *srang* for every *srang*'s worth stolen. If a trader deceives his customers by using false weights and measures, or by selling adulterated goods, imitation gems or jewels, or by circulating counterfeit coin, he must be immediately handed over to the police, and committed for trial. If the merchant convicted be a Tibetan subject, all his goods are confiscated, and he is sentenced to penal servitude for a certain number of years. If he be a subject of some foreign Government, such as China, Mongolia, Kashmir, or Nepal, such fine, as is prescribed by law, is exacted from him. His goods are seized, examined, taken stock of, and after being securely packed, are sent with the owner in charge of the police to his own Government, together with a document complaining of his conduct, and stating the amount of the fine exacted from him.

The jealousy of the Tibetans towards Europeans is supposed to date from 1791–92, when English soldiers were believed to have taken part in the war which followed the incursion of the Gorkhas into Tibet; and as the English Government, then in its infancy in India, took no steps to cultivate the friendship of the Tibetans, that feeling took a lasting hold on their minds. The shock which China, Nepal, Bhutan and Sikkim have received from their reverses when at war with the British power, has also extended to the peace-loving Tibetans.

Throughout the nineteenth century the Tibetans have followed the Chinese policy of exclusiveness, not from fear of annexation, but because they had been shortly before nearly conquered, and were entirely under Chinese influence. This fear has been sedulously encouraged by an ex-minister of the Rajah of Sikkim, the Dewan Namgyal, who was expelled from that country for his treatment of Drs Hooker and Campbell, and subsequently obtained from the Grand Lama the post of frontier officer, to watch the 'encroachments of the Indian Government'. The attempts of Dr Hooker, Mr Edgar, and lastly of Sir Richard Temple, to enter Tibetan territory were described by him as instances of encroachment on the part of the Government of India, which he represented as devoting all its energies to the invasion of Tibet, and as having been foiled by his diplomatic skill and wisdom, aided by the zealous co-operation of the Djongpon of Khamba and Phari. On one occasion he even stated to the Lhasa officials, as a proof of his unshaken loyalty to the Grand Lama, that he had refused a pension of fifty rupees which had been offered to him by the Indian Government for supplying information respecting the state of affairs in Tibet! This functionary has, however, together with his coadjutor the Djongpon of Khamba, lately fallen into disgrace with the Grand Lama, and has also lost all influence at Tashilhunpo.

The exclusiveness of the Tibetan Government is to be chiefly attributed to the hostile and intriguing attitude of the frontier officials towards the British Government. Next to it is the fear of introducing smallpox and other dangerous diseases into Tibet, where the people, being ignorant of the proper treatment of this disease, die in great numbers from it. Death from smallpox is the most dreaded, since the victim is believed to be immediately sent to hell. Not the least important cause, however, is the fear of the extinction of Buddhism by the foreigners—a feeling which prevails in the minds of the dominant class, the clergy.

Besides jealousy of foreigners, there is another cause of great importance, being connected with the commercial interests of China. Peking is eight or ten months', and Silling (Hsi-ning) four months' journey from Lhasa, yet the Tibetans carry on a brisk trade with these and other noted cities of China in tea, silk, wooden furniture, and other commodities. The Government of Lhasa sends every year two or more caravans to purchase goods for the State from the commercial centres on the borders of China. An escort of 500 soldiers accompanies each caravan, for it is not unusual for mounted bands of robbers, from 200 to 300 strong, to attack the caravans. By the opening of the Darjiling railway, Calcutta, where most of the Chinese articles valued in Tibet may be easily and cheaply procured, will be brought within three weeks' journey of Lhasa.

The Tibetans thoroughly appreciate these facilities, and every Tibetan who has ever visited Darjiling warmly praises our Government for making the Jalep la road. The Chinese Government naturally fear that with the opening of free intercourse between Tibet and India, China will be a great loser so far as her commercial interests are concerned.

VIII

Return to Tashilhunpo and Ugyen-Gyatso's Visit to the Bonbo Sanctuary of Rigyal Sendar

The bells of the Jo khang were ringing and the great trumpets of Tangye-ling were summoning the lamas to early morning service, when, on June 13, I took from the roof of our house a last look at the gilded spires and red walls of Potala, and started out for Tashilhunpo. I noticed near our lodgings a number of women drawing water from a well in rawhide buckets. The water of Lhasa is excellent, and both abundant and very near the surface, most of the wells being not over 4 feet deep; and this is the reason for the belief that the town is over a subterranean lake.

Arriving at the foot of Chagpori, on the summit of which is the College of Surgeons of Tibet, I got off my horse and ascended the hill, as I had promised to visit an old doctor known as Amchi Rivola, who was afflicted with cataract. On the way up I was met by one of the Amchi's pupils, who presented me with *khatag*. I was led into a nice room containing a few neatly finished tables, on one of which was a cup full of delicate rose-coloured tea of the most delicious aroma. The ceiling was covered with silk, and satin hangings hid the walls, on which hung also pictures of the god of medicine and his attendants.

Amchi Rivola soon made his appearance, a man of commanding looks and heavily built. He was the Principal of the Vaidurya Ta-tsan of Chagpori, and physician to the Regent. He expressed his pleasure at seeing me, and said he had heard me most kindly spoken of by the Lhacham Phala, and he would be greatly pleased if I would postpone my journey to Shigatse and endeavour to cure his disease, which he thought curable by an operation, but he knew of no surgeon in Tibet able to perform it.

I was pained at my utter inability to help him, and told him that I would willingly prolong my stay at Lhasa if I had any means of curing him, but I had none whatever, and must take my leave. So saying, I rose from my seat, and left after the usual leave-takings.

Following the same road by which we had come to Lhasa, we stopped that night at Netang. On the 15th we reached Palti *djong*, and on the 18th arrived at Dongtse at 10 o'clock at night, and put up in Pador's house.

Early the following morning I went to the monastery, and was promptly led to the minister's apartments, where I found him covered with smallpox pustules, and hardly able to speak. The Lhacham's son was also ill with the same disease, but convalescing.

When the minister fell asleep, I went to the Tung-chen's room. He asked me if I had not met Phurchung on the road, as he had left for Lhasa only a week ago carrying my letters and a shotgun. As to Ugyen-gyatso, he had returned from Lachan with the luggage that had been left there, and was now waiting for me at Gyatsoshar near Shigatse. I remained at Dongtse until July 3, when, in company with Phurchung and Pador, I set out for Gyatsoshar, which place we reached the following day, and Ugyen gave me, to my infinite delight, a package of letters from India.

Ugyen told me that since his return from the Lachan barrier he had been busy collecting plants. He had also carefully kept a diary from which I culled the following details, which may prove of interest.

One evening a lama friend had called on him, and asked him if he would like to meet a Golog from Amdo. These Golog, his friend went on to say, are a nation of brigands living in Amdo in Eastern Tibet. Their country is nowhere cultivated, but they breed many ponies, which they use for making raids on the adjacent peoples. Their chiefs exact blackmail (*chag tal*) from all people, and rob all they fall in with, unless they have passports from the Golog chiefs.

The Gologs have a few lamaseries, the heads of which come from Tashilhunpo, and are appointed for a term of five years, after which they return to Ulterior Tibet. Not long ago one of these lamas returned to Tashilhunpo, after having enjoyed during his sojourn in Gologland the confidence of the people and chiefs. He had amassed considerable wealth, and he spent on his return several thousand rupees in entertaining all the Tashilhunpo monks, and in giving them presents of money. Two years ago the wife of the Golog chief, near whom he had lived, came to Tashilhunpo on a pilgrimage, and after visiting the temple, she expressed a desire to see their former lama, but he was nowhere to be found, though it was known that he was at Tashilhunpo. Among the Golog people it is customary to greet one another with a kiss, and whoever omits the kiss when meeting or parting with an acquaintance is considered rude and unmannerly.

The lama had kissed this lady hundreds of times in her own country, but how could he kiss her now before all the monks?—and particularly as the Panchen rinpoche was present at Tashilhunpo; how could he hope to escape unpunished if he committed an act of such gross immodesty?

The lady, however, before leaving Tashilhunpo, invited him to a dinner, and as soon as she appeared in the room he shut the door and greeted her with a kiss on the mouth, and explained to her the reason of his failing to see her at first, and the embarrassment he had felt in approaching her in public.

Ugyen's friend also told him that in the Bardon district of Khams, when two acquaintances meet they touch each other's foreheads together by way of salutation.

The same friend, who had imparted to Ugyen the preceding information, told him one day this fable: In times of yore, when beasts could talk, a leopard met an ass, and, though he had a strong inclination to kill him, he was impressed by his strength, of which he judged by his loud bray, so he offered him his friendship on condition that he would watch his den when he went out in search of prey.

One day the leopard sallied forth with a mighty roar by way of prelude to his day's work, and forthwith a wild yak rolled down the cliff overhanging his den, killed from fright at the sound. When the leopard returned and saw the dead *dong*, the ass said he had killed it, and stuck out his tongue, smeared with blood, in proof of his prowess.

The leopard believed him, and promised to help him when the time came. One day he told him to go and graze in the meadow on the other side of the hill. When the ass had eaten his fill he brayed twenty or thirty times in sheer wantonness, and the leopard thinking his friend in trouble, ran to his rescue, but the ass told him he was only braying for pleasure. A little while after a pack of wolves attacked the ass, when he brayed loudly, calling his friend to his help; but the leopard thought that he was only amusing himself, and did not go to his rescue, and the ass was torn to pieces by the wolves.

On the 7th of the eighth moon (June 23) a grand military review was held at Shigatse, when more than a thousand soldiers were present, and there was a sham fight in the presence of the general. There are two reviews (*mag chyang*) every year, one in summer, the other in winter; and besides these there is one whenever the Amban visits Shigatse on a tour of inspection.

On June 29 the summer prayer ceremony (or *monlam*) was celebrated. All the monks of Tashilhunpo, some three thousand odd, assembled at Chyag-tsal-gang. A satin wall or *gyabyal*, 1,000 feet in circumference, was erected, and inside it was a great State canopy, under which the Panchen rinpoche's throne was placed. He was unable to be present, but his stole and mitre were put on the throne, and round it thronged the lamas in order of precedence and rank. The people of Shigatse were there, some under tents, others under bowers of cypress and willow branches, all amusing themselves singing and joking. A mast about 120 feet high was erected, and ropes stretched from it to the great Kiku building, and on these were hung pictures of all the gods of the pantheon. At Shigatse, the while, there were racing and military manoeuvres and drill.

The following day was sacred to Dipankara Buddha, and his picture was made to occupy a prominent place in the exhibition. This representation of him was about 100 feet high, and skilfully worked in different coloured satins. On either side of it were gigantic representations of the Buddha.

All the lamas and nobles of Shigatse with their families made merry under the great tent in the Chyag-tsal-gang. Sumptuous dinners, cooked by the best native and Chinese cooks, were served to the great personages of Tashilhunpo and of the Government. Many persons had pitched tents near the great one, and were amusing themselves there with their families and friends. From morning to evening the deafening music of drums, cymbals, and trumpets never ceased.

No one was absent from the fete save the Grand Lama, who, it was rumoured, was laid up with smallpox at Tobgyal, where he had gone after a visit to the hot springs of Tanag. On either side of the great nine-storied building of Kiku, between Shigatse and Tashilhunpo, were two huge lions in which men were concealed; these were moved about from time to time to the great delight of the people.

The next day was the full moon, and was sacred to Sakya Buddha. The great picture of Dipankara Buddha was removed, and one of Sakya Sinha, of gigantic size, and surrounded by all the Buddhas of past and future ages, took its place. This picture was brought out from the lamasery to the sound of deafening music, and with great ceremony. Ten black priests (*Nagpa*), well versed in tantrik rituals, conducted a solemn religious service, and were assisted by 300 lamas from Tsomaling chanting hymns.

In the plain of Chyag-tsal-gang the lamas and people again feasted and enjoyed themselves as on the previous day.

On the morrow (July 2) the picture of Sachya tubpa was displaced for one of the Buddha who is to come, Maitreya (or Chyamba). It was brought out and hung up with the same ceremony as was observed on the preceding days. This day Tashilhunpo was open to women, and crowds of them in the gayest and richest apparel visited the temples and shrines. Ugyen estimated the value of the head-dress of one lady he saw at 40,000 rupees. In the evening every one went and touched with his or her head the picture of Chyamba, and thus received his blessing.

During my stay at Gyatsoshar I occupied the little pavilion belonging to the minister, which I have described previously. The flowers in the garden which surrounded it filled the air with their fragrance; the tall poplars, the widespread willows, the fragrant junipers, the graceful cedars, all contributed to make the place the most favoured of all the neighbourhood.

My health rapidly improved in these pleasant surroundings and genial temperature, and I worked diligently at transcribing works of great interest into the nagari character which had, though written in Sanskrit, been preserved in the (*Wu-chan*) script of Tibet. Ugyen devoted himself to botanizing, extending his excursions to considerable distances. Finally, to facilitate bringing in his collections, he bought a donkey and a pony for himself to ride.

July 19 was kept as a great holiday, it being the day on which the Buddha first turned the Wheel of the Law. The people of

Shigatse and neighbourhood visited the different chapels and sanctuaries and thronged in every corner of Tashilhunpo.

Two days later the Deba Shikha, of whom I have had so often to speak, gave a garden-party to a number of his friends in the garden surrounding the house in which I was living at Gyatsoshar. There were a dozen men and women; the former amused themselves the whole day at archery and quoits, in both of which they exhibited considerable skill. The same day Ugyen started on a botanizing trip, which took him as far as Sakya.

On July 26 I returned to Dongtse, and was pleased to find that the Minister had recovered from the smallpox. I found the Tung-chen busy preparing for the ceremony of consecrating a new house of the Seng chen, as the minister is called, now nearly complete, and built a little to the north of the Tsug-la khang temple. In the room given me were some five or six hundred balls of butter of about 2 pounds' weight each, and a number of bags of *tsamba* and wheat flour.

I had only been here four days when I was requested by the Chyag-dso-pa of Gyantse to visit him and see if I could not do something for the complaint from which he had now been suffering for some time. The invitation was so pressing that I could not refuse; so I set out at once, and was most kindly received by him and his family. I remained here until August 13, when a letter reached me from the minister, who was still at Dongtse, asking me to rejoin him there at once. This letter of the minister, though written in Tibetan, was in the Roman character, which I had taught him to write the preceding winter.

As I rode back to Dongtse I was greatly struck by the beauty of the vegetation; the little pools were frequently covered with lilies, and wild flowers were in full bloom.

The minister asked me if I would go to Tobgyal and see the Grand Lama, who was desperately ill. He had received a letter from him asking for some consecrated pills (*tsé-ril*); I could take this medicine along with me, and at the same time he would inform the Panchen that I was a skilful physician and might be able to cure him.

Hearing of the desperate condition of the Grand Lama, I naturally hesitated to undertake this commission, and so asked for time for reflection. The next day, however, I told the minister that I could not venture to wait on the Grand Lama unless he expressed a wish to see me; or, at all events, unless I was accompanied by the minister himself. He finally decided that he would send the *tsé-ril* by a confidential servant, and hint in his note accompanying them, that perhaps Indian medicines might prove beneficial.

On August 25 and 26, the final ceremonies of consecrating the new house built by the minister (and which had been going on for the last five days) were begun. The last ceremony is called the *chin-sreg*. The mask of the god of death (Shinje gyalbo), his weapons and armour were hung on a stake stuck close to the fireplace. Then bundles of sandalwood were arranged in six heaps, and melted butter poured over them to feed the flame; and a lama, chanting hymns, sat opposite each fire. Sesamum and barley were scattered about. At the termination of the first day's ceremony, a dinner was served to all the guests and monks.

The *chin-sreg* ceremony on the 26th was similar to that of the day before, and wound up with a long service. In the afternoon the Seng chen (the minister) took his position on a raised seat under a spacious awning spread on the roof of the Tsug-la khang, and ordered all the lamas, carpenters, masons, coppersmiths, gilders, etc., to assemble, when he distributed presents to them. To the lamas and monks he gave silver coins, *khatag* and blankets; and to the head labourers, rugs (*tumshi*), felt hats (*khamba*), and homespun cloth (*gyantse*).

On the 28th news reached us that two of the Grand Lama's

physicians had run away, another had gone mad, and the fourth was without hope or ability to do anything more for the illustrious patient, who had had a severe hemorrhage.

On the 31st the dreaded event took place, a letter was handed the minister announcing the Grand Lama's death. He had died on the day previous at Tobgyal, or, as it is the custom to say, 'He had left this world for repose in the realm of bliss (Deva-chan).'

A notice was issued to the people to assume signs of mourning; the women were forbidden to wear their headdresses or any other jewellery, and amusements and ornamenting of houses were prohibited. The people showed signs of deep distress at the untimely death of the Panchen; some attributing it to the sorrow he had felt at the disloyalty of his people, others said he had left this world on account of the discourtesy of the Dalai lama in not inviting him to his consecration.

At Dongtse, where I was, the minister was having performed as a termination to the ceremonies attending the consecration of the new building, a grand religious dance in the courtyard of the *Choide*. A great crowd, all in their holiday attire, was assembled on the roofs and balconies of the temple. The dance had but commenced; the minister's page, who impersonated the herald of the gods, had twice fired off a gun, and had proclaimed the arrival of the four guardian deities of the world; the devils and goblins had gone through their part of the performance, when the news of the death of the Grand Lama was made known to the minister. At once the dance was stopped, and the dancers and the crowd rapidly dispersed.

On September 3 it was reported to me that the Chinese commander of Shigatse had flogged several of the Grand Lama's servants for not having told him of the gravity of their master's illness. One of the physicians of the Panchen had been severely beaten, and the other medical attendant was found dead shortly after the Grand Lama had breathed his last. I thanked God I had not consented to the minister's proposal to go and attend the Grand Lama!

On the 6th Ugyen returned to Dongtse from his trip to Sakya, and from his journal I take the following facts, which may be of interest.

He had started, as previously stated, on July 21, and on the 23rd crossed to the left bank of the Tsang-po near Tashi-gang, and camped in the valley of Tang-pe. Thence he and his companion, a Mongol lama by the name of Chos-tashi, went to the Tanag district, where a fine quality of pottery is manufactured. They could not get lodgings anywhere, so afraid were the people that they might introduce smallpox among them, coming as they did from the infected city of Shigatse.

On July 26 they crossed the Tanag Tong chu by an iron suspension bridge, and, travelling westward, stopped for the night in the lamasery of Tubdan. Leaving Tubdan on the 28th, the travellers reached, after a march of 12 miles in a northerly direction, the famous hot springs of Burchu-tsan. A circular wall of stone encloses a portion of the springs, and here the Grand Lama takes his baths. The place where he camps is surrounded by a low turf wall. The Grand Lama had recently taken the baths, but it was supposed that the water gods (or *nagas*) had in some way or other been offended, as the water had but aggravated his complaint. To propitiate these *lu* a hundred lamas had been employed here until within a few days conducting religious services. In and near these springs are numerous black snakes which, though they are said to be venomous, do no harm to either man or beast. They enter houses in the neighbouring villages, but no one ever thinks of hurting them.

The next day they crossed the Jeh la and stopped for the night at the village of Keshong, but again they could not get lodgings. On the 30th they reached the old village of Shendar ding, near which is situated the famous Bonbo monastery of

Rigyal Sendar. Ugyen visited this lamasery the following day, and represented himself as a Bonbo from Sikkim on a pilgrimage to the sanctuaries of Bonbo Shenrab Mivo, the chief deity of this religion. He expressed a desire to give a general tea (*mang ja*) to the monks, presented the manager five *tanka* for the purpose, and it was arranged that the entertainment should take place on the morrow.

In the meantime he was shown about the temple. In the congregation hall the priests were reading the Bonbo scriptures. In the chapel of the upper story he noticed among the images of the various gods of the Bon pantheon that of Sakya Buddha.

The next day the *mang ja* took place. There were about thirty monks (*dabas*) present, and, on inquiring why there were so few, Ugyen was told that a large number of monks who are natives of Khams Gyarong had gone to the Chang-tang to look to the interests of the Bon church there.

Ugyen, in company with the head priest (*om-dse*), then visited the gloomy chapels of the monastery, only lighted by torches and butter-fed lamps, where he saw a number of curious pictures and tapestries on which were represented various terrifying gods. After this he was presented to the high priest, Je Khädub rinpoche, who received him most kindly. He was a man of sixty-eight years of age, but strong and hearty. He explained to Ugyen various points of the 'black water' (*chab-nag*) mysteries of Bonism, and lent him some books to read, a number of which Ugyen made copies of.

The Rigyal Sendar monastery is said to have been erected on the site of an ancient Bon temple, called Darding sergo tamo, and was built several hundred years before Tashilhunpo; and was sacked by the Jungar Mongols in the 17th century. When they demolished the chapel, the Bon high priest hurriedly concealed the sacred treasures and scriptures, written in silver on dark blue tablets, in the deep recesses of a cavern, and hence the sacred writings of the Bonbo are now in a confused state. The church furniture and other requisites of worship in the monastery are extremely ancient. Among them are the huge tambourines (*shang*), and gigantic cymbals made of the finest bell-metal, paintings representing the Seven Heroic Saints (*Pao-rab dun*), numerous old tapestries, and several volumes of scriptures written in silver and gold on thick dark-blue (card) boards. The roof of the great hall of congregation is supported by forty-two pillars, 6 feet apart, and all around the monastery are fine-looking *chorten*, *mendong*, and cairns, which visitors are allowed to circumambulate from right to left, instead of from left to right, as do Buddhists. When questioned respecting the reason for this custom, the priests replied that salutation, circumambulation, and the chanting of mantra being intended by the sages as processes to sanctify the body, speech, and mind, they did not at all benefit the divinity. It is, therefore, immaterial how and which way one salutes and circumambulates the sacred things, but it is the established usage of the Bon community to circulate from right to left.

The Bon monastery of Shendar is now in the joint possession of the four powerful members of the family of Shen-tsang. Though they are laymen, having wives and children, yet being the descendants of Shenrab Mivo, the illustrious founder of the Bon religion, they are venerated as lamas. The mother of the two leading members of this family was the elder sister of Sikyong, the late Rajah of Sikkim. The late Panchen rinpoche was the nephew of these brothers, in consequence of which they are addressed by the people as *Ku-shang*, 'Royal Maternal Uncle'. The late Grand Lama was of pure Bonbo stock, and the two families from which he sprang are known by the names of Shen-lug and Tu-lug. People inquire with wonder why the Vice-Regent of Buddha in the flesh should have been born in the family of Shenrab Mivo, the heretic. Some disaffected Tibetans were even in the habit of ridiculing this Grand Lama by calling him the offspring of Bon heretics.

In the monastery are two sections of monks, called

respectively the Tibetan Association (*Bod kham-tsan*) and the Khams Association (*Khamba kham-tsan*), the latter being the more numerous. The officers consist of one priest of the grand congregation (*Om-dse*), two discipliners (*Chos-tims*), two church directors (*Gekhor*), two general managers (*Chi-nyer*), and two chapel-keepers (*Kunyer*).

While conducting service the monks dress like the Gelugpa monks of Tashilhunpo. They wear tall mitre-shaped yellow caps, and a yellow cloak covering the bodies. The ordained monks hang the *chab-lug*, or badge of celibacy, from their waistbands like the Buddhist monks, and wear red serge boots. They are not allowed to wear anything that is blue, green, black, or white. During their residence at the monastery they wear the church costume, composed of the *sham-tab* and *tongu*, and red boots made according to the Bon fashion. When they enter the congregation hall for service they leave their boots at the door. The cost of the tea drunk during the services is borne for the most part by the Shen-tsang family. The monastery is maintained by a small endowment, supplemented by the donations and subscriptions paid by the Bon community of Chang.

The monks of the Khams Association, numbering about forty, go annually during the summer to conduct religious services in the houses of the Bon people of Chang. In the winter they remain in the monastery. During divine service the monks are allowed to drink as much tea as they like, there being no restriction in this respect, as in the great Buddhist monasteries.

The lamas here are divided into two sects, which differ slightly in their vows. In the one called Shen-tang srung-lug, a man may take vows when sixty years of age; while in the other, called Shen-tsang lug, he must take the vows of abstinence and piety as soon as he has finished his final clerical examinations. The high priest, or Je Kädub rinpoche, Yung-drung gyal-tsan by name, administers vows and ordains monks.

The rules of moral discipline, called *tsa-yig*, written on a broad sheet of pasted daphne paper, are posted in a conspicuous position in the monastery. When an ordained monk is found guilty of violating these rules, and particularly those of chastity, he is immediately punished and expelled from the monastery. Such punishments are, however, commutable into fines, such as the payments of money to the lama who ordained him, and providing entertainment and presents for the other monastic authorities and the members of the congregation.

The marriage ceremonies of the Bonbo are the same as those of all other Tibetans; so also the funeral rites, although some communities throw their dead into rivers and lakes. After death the body is kept in the house for twenty-four hours, after which it is removed to the temple or monastery. On the fourth day the ornaments and clothes worn by the deceased are placed before the gods, and prayers offered to them to take charge of his soul. At the end of the ceremony the corpse is removed to the cemetery, where it is cut into pieces to be devoured by vultures and dogs.

Ugyen left Shendar ding on August 5, and stopped at noon at the hot springs of Langpag, where the Tashi lama has a temple-like house in charge of an officer. The water is so hot that meat can be cooked in it in half an hour.

Proceeding thence they came to Non chu, where he saw the Non chu lama rinpoche, who made many inquiries about Calcutta, the railways, telegraphs, and telephones of which he had heard travellers speak. He himself, he said, had invented a telephone, and was just then engaged in making a new instrument with which he would be able to communicate with people at a distance by means of strokes of a hammer. He was also most curious to know about illuminating gas.

The next day Ugyen again called on the lama, who asked many questions about the resources of India, its government, commerce, laws, etc., and as Ugyen replied he noted down all he heard.

Taking leave of the lama the same day, the travellers reached Rag-tso ferry, where they crossed the Tsang-po in a rudely constructed boat, in which men and animals were ferried across. They halted for the night at Tondub ling, in the district of Jerong. They were unable to gain admittance to any house, and had to pass the night in a sheep-fold.

The next day they came to Phuntso ling, where there is a lamasery with 500 inmates. This was formerly the seat of the Taranath lama, and from here he went to Urga in Mongolia. Ugyen visited the cave where Taranath once lived as an ascetic. He also saw the printing-house of the Phuntso ling lamasery, which contained printing blocks for many valuable historical works.

Two roads lead to Sakya from this place, one via Tondub ling, the other by way of Lhartse. The travellers followed the latter, which is the shortest, arriving at Lhartse on August 10. Shakar *djong*, Ugyen learnt, can be reached from Lhartse in a day. The monks of Shakar are noted for their wealth, much of which is acquired by buying gold.

Lhartse castle (*djong*) is on a fine eminence overlooking the Tsang-po. It is the chief place of trade of Upper Tsang. Its monastery used to contain 1,000 lamas, but now the number is considerably smaller. Some distance from Lhartse is the famous monastery of Namring, whose monks are noted for their great learning.

Proceeding by way of Tana and Lasa, Ugyen and his companions reached Sakya on the 14th, and put up in a house belonging to the chief of the *ulag* department. There is a good market in this town, but with the exception of meat, all articles of food are dearer than at Shigatse. No good *tsamba* could be bought, and straw and hay were very dear, a *tanka* for a basketful of not over 5 pounds' weight.

Sakya is a notorious place for thieves and all kinds of bad characters, and the cattle have to be locked up at night in the stables and sheep-pens.

The next day, being the anniversary of the birth of Peme Chyungnas (Padma Sambhava), a grand religious dance took place in the courtyard of the temple, in the presence of the five surviving members of the royal Khon family of Sakya, who sat on chairs on a raised dais under a large Chinese umbrella, with attendants carrying the *gyal-tsan* or banners, and the sceptre.

Eighty gaudily dressed dancers (*chyampa*) danced the day long to the music of clarionets, trumpets, kettle-drums, tambourines, and cymbals, stopping only occasionally to partake of tea. When they finally stopped they carried off with them on their shoulders quantities of *khatag* flung to them by the audience.

This dance, called the 'club dance' (*phurpai kil chayam*), was performed in celebration of the birth, from a lotus flower in the lake of Dhanakosha, of the sage Uddayani. Two Timpon and a dozen policemen kept the great crowd in order with their whips.

When the ceremony of the day was over, the heir apparent of the Sakya Panchen took his seat in the maidan in front of the great temple, and gave his blessing (*chyag wang*) to all who approached. Ugyen visited the same day the famous library, where he saw many manuscripts written in gold, the pages some 6 to 8 feet long and 3 or 4 feet broad. On the board which covered these volumes were painted in gold and silver the images of innumerable Buddhas. There were also many books in Chinese, dating back to the early years of the Christian era.

The next day another kind of dance, called the *dsa-nag*, or 'black hat' dance, was performed in the court of the residence of Gong-sa. There were about eighty dancers. Seventy kept up the dance continually, while the ten remaining took refreshments. They danced with much grace, the movements of their arms and hands being especially curious.

On August 17 Ugyen left Sakya, and travelling by way of Lhadong, Shong-mar-tse, the Pa la and Chiblung reached Dobta on the 20th. This latter locality he found very poor, the people living in great squalor. The country is rocky and barren, yet the peasants have to give half the produce of their fields to the Sikkim Rajah.

Leaving Dobta, Ugyen came to the Tsomo tel-tung, or 'Mule's Drink Lake', which he went around, keeping it to his left, an heretical action according to Buddhist ideas.

Stopping at Naring for the night, he then passed through Tagnag and reached Targye on the 24th. Near here is the Dora chu-tsan ('Hot Springs'), in the neighbourhood of which he saw several carpet looms, on which excellent rugs, called *tum-shi*, were being made by women, who showed great taste in designing patterns.

Leaving Targye the travellers passed without any incidents through Kurma, Kyoga, Labrang-dokpa, and Luguri Jong, and reached Shigatse about noon on August 29.

Ugyen remained at Shigatse for seven days, drying the plants he had collected on his journey, and observing the different incidents which took place after the death of the Grand Lama.

The day after the Grand Lama's death, he and a friend had gone to Tashilhunpo to perform their devotions, but were refused admittance. No outsider was admitted into the lamasery, the inmates of which were now not allowed to see anyone or leave the monastery.

As they were coming back they passed in front of the palace of Kun-khyab ling, and saw a large pack of hounds and mastiffs, which the Panchen kept for hunting; for, though his sacred character forbade him shooting animals, he could indulge in this other form of sport.

While in the palace of Phuntso phodang, the lama's favourite residence, and where they were allowed to enter, an officer from the Labrang attached seals on everything belonging to the deceased, and on all the doors of the principal rooms in Kun-khyab ling.

The next day there was a report that the lama had come to life again, and every one was thanking the gods; the *tsamba* vendors on the marketplace were throwing handfuls of their ware heavenward as offerings to the gods who had restored their Grand Lama to them.

The Dingpon of Shigatse said, in the hearing of Ugyen, that last year, when the Government of Lhasa had consulted the oracle of Lhamo sung-chyongma, it had foretold great calamities for Tibet.

These were inevitable, in view of the perversity of the people who no longer had faith in the gods, but let themselves be led by demons in human shape.

Witchcraft was steadily increasing, he said, and in every village there were those who said they were in communion with devils. An edict had been issued forbidding witchcraft and fortune-telling. It was found that under the castle of Shigatse itself there were fifteen witches (*paonal jorma*). These had been brought to trial, and had been submitted to an examination which required them to describe the contents of several chests filled with a variety of things. Four alone were able to answer; the others were flogged and then released on condition that they should give up imposing on the public credulity and would furnish bonds for their good behaviour.

IX

Funeral of the Panchen Rinpoche—Visit to the Great Lamasery of Samye and to Yarlung

On September 19 the minister left Dongtse, and I despatched Ugyen once more to the Rigyal Sendar monastery to obtain further information on the Bonbos and their religion. I myself went to Gyantse, where I was most kindly received by the Chyag-dso-pa and his family.

The Chyag-dso-pa of Gyantse has under his superintendence a large rug and blanket factory in which about ninety women are kept constantly employed, some picking the wool, some dyeing it, and others weaving. The *tso*, or 'dye plant', grows in rocky soil and is collected by the Dokpas. It supplies a beautiful yellow colour. The leaves only are used in dyeing.

The people employed in this factory are kept under the strictest discipline. One day one of the women who was late beginning her work, was whipped by order of the Chyag-dso-pa. A boy caught stealing wool was also punished in the same way and imprisoned for a fortnight. I was rather surprised at seeing the Chyag-dso-pa thus taking the law in his own hands; but he told me that the Government allowed great landholders like his master, the Shape Phala, judicial power over their own serfs. I may here note that the pastoral tenants on this, and probably all other estates, pay the owners every year 2 pounds of butter for every she yak they own, and 2 pounds of wool for every sheep.

On September 25, corresponding to the 13th of the 8th moon, harvest began. This day was selected as it was a very lucky one. All the people turned out for the work, and I went to the roof of the castle to watch the reapers. While working they sang hymns and offered the gods bunches of barley, peas, and wheat, as first-fruit offerings.

Ugyen returned from his trip on the 1st of October.

On September 13, the day of the full moon, while he was still at Shigatse, the dead Grand Lama was brought from Tob-gyal to Tashilhunpo. First of all came a crowd of people on foot, followed by about a hundred men on ponies. After these came the officials of Labrang, followed by the chiefs, nobles, and high officials of Tsang, all on horseback. Behind them was carried the sedan containing the remains of his holiness, the Panchen rinpoche. The sedan was followed by the Chinese garrison, consisting of fifty soldiers. The lamentations of the people increased as the procession approached, and Ugyen said he cried like a child. Some prayed loudly, looking towards heaven: 'God and saints ordain that our beloved protector (*kyab-gong*), may soon return to this world for the good of all living beings.' No bells were rung, and the procession passed on in solemn silence, all, laymen and monks, dressed in dark red apparel, without any ornaments. When the procession entered Tashilhunpo, the sedan chair was placed on the State altar, in the Hall of Departed Saints. On the following day Ugyen went to make his obeisance to the dead Lama. He found the body (*ku-por*) wrapped in *khatags*, and placed in a sitting posture. It was very small, bearing no proportion to the stature of the Lama when living. Ugyen was told that this was the result of the embalmment.

The same day the period of summer retirement (*yar-nas*) for monks came to an end. It was observed as a holiday by the people:

there was racing and other sports, and all the people, lamas, men, women, and children bathed together in the Nyang chu. The only sign of mourning still observed this day was keeping the windows of the houses in town and at Tashilhunpo shut.

On the 17th Ugyen reached Shendar ding, where he put up in the house of a man whose wife had just been confined. A woman in Tibet, as in India, is held to be unclean (*kyedib*) for a month after her confinement, at the expiration of which time certain religious ceremonies are performed for her purification.

Ugyen remained in this place until the 26th, and obtained from the high priest of the lamasery much valuable information bearing on the theology and history of the Bon religion. He also copied many valuable works on these subjects, which were obligingly put at his disposal by the lama.

Having been prevented when at Lhasa, as previously narrated, from going to the celebrated monastery of Samye, the most ancient and famous, probably, of all Tibetan lamaseries, I now endeavoured to make arrangements for this much longed-for trip. I sent Ugyen to Dongtse, after his return from his trip to Shendar ding, to try and get a guide; but he failed, as rumours had got abroad that I was a British employé, and Phurchung was accused of having brought me into Tibet in violation of the express orders of the Nepal Durbar.

In view of these disturbing rumours, I left Gyantse on October 4, and returned to Tashilhunpo, where I was rejoined on the 13th by Phurchung, who had been sent with letters to India in August.

I now decided to send Ugyen back to India with the botanical and other collections he had made, while I would visit Samye, and the Lhokha country south of it. He bought ten yaks for a hundred rupees, and pack saddles, and engaged Lachung men to accompany him to Khamba *djong*. He started on the 17th, while Phurchung and I returned to Gyantse, arriving there on the 18th.

The people were now busy threshing their barley—cows, their muzzles covered with wicker baskets, treaded it out, and were kept to their work by two boys.

The Chyag-dso-pa lent me a man to guide me to Samye and the south country (Lhokha); his name was Gopon. He told me he was ready to start at any time, for his brother (*namdo pun*, 'joint brother'), as he called him, had now returned from Shigatse, and he could leave his wife. These two men had, though not related, one wife between them, and the three of them got on very well together.

On October 21 I finally started for Samye, and followed, as far as the ruined village of Ring-la, the high road to Lhasa I had travelled over earlier in the year. There is but one family now living in this once prosperous place. These poor people earn a precarious livelihood by making pottery. A concave wooden pan is used for the purpose, in which the pots are shaped with a piece of wood or the fingers, by turning the pan or mould around with the hand. This is the usual method employed in Tibet.

Leaving Ring-la, we travelled through the fine pasture-lands adjoining the Yamdo tso, and over desolate highlands with an occasional stump of a juniper or cedar tree, till we reached the village of Ta-lung, famous, as its name implies, for the number and breed of its ponies. Around the village the land is cultivated, and showed evidence of great industry on the part of the people.

We at first failed to secure a night's lodgings in any of the houses of the village, for the people took us for Lhopa or Bhutia, of whom they stand in great dread, as they frequently make raids on this district; but we were so fortunate in the end as to secure the good-will of a lama of the monastery, who got a friend of his to admit us to his house.

The next day (October 24) we resumed our journey by daylight, and crossing the Shandung chu bay of Lake Yamdo, followed along the base of the steep hills which overhang its shores. We got sight, on the way, of the Chong-khor monastery, from which come all the *amchi lhamo* dancers and mimes, some of whom annually visit Darjiling. Passing the Rivotag river some eight miles north of the *djong* of the same name, we ascended a ridge, from the top of which we saw the villages of Yurupe, Ke-utag, and Khyunpodo. The country was everywhere thinly populated; but large numbers of yaks, donkeys, sheep, and goats were grazing about.

We stopped at the village of Shari, prettily situated between the Yamdo and a little sweet-water lakelet, and put up in the *mani lha khang*, the centre of which was taken up by a great prayer-wheel about 6 feet high and 3 feet in diameter. An old man lived here whose sole occupation was to turn the wheel.

The next morning we crossed a low hill, the Kabula, and, skirting the northern extremity of the Rombuja lake, reached by eleven o'clock the village of Melung, thus called from the fire (*me*) stones found in the valley (*lung*) in which it is situated.

After a short halt at Melung, we resumed our march, the country opening a little as we advanced, and villages and hamlets becoming more numerous. That night we stopped at Khamedo, where there live about a hundred families.

We were off by sunrise, and passing some distance to the north of the large village of Ling, where the Djongpon of the Yamdo district reside, we soon after found ourselves in the broad pasture-lands of Karmoling, here some 10 miles broad, where hundreds of ponies, belonging to the Lhasa Government, were seen grazing.

We ate our breakfast at Shabshi, and then, passing through the hamlet of Tanta, we began the ascent of the Tib la, which marks in this direction the boundary between the Yamdo and Lhokha districts, and from the top of which I had a magnificent view of the whole lake country, the like of which I have seen nowhere in the Himalayas.

The difficulties attending the descent of the Tib la were infinitely greater than those of the ascent, and the violence of the wind, made it difficult even to stand erect. By five o'clock we reached the village of Tib, where there are about ten houses, around which grow a few stunted willows. The villagers were busy treading out their harvest with their cattle, and their merry songs, wafted by the night wind, fell pleasantly on my ears till I dropped asleep.

Tib is under the authority of the Gongkhar Djongpon, who, with his two lama assistants, or Tse-dung, usually resides in the neighbouring town of Tosnam-gyaling.

October 27—Our road led us down the course of the Tib chu. The valley was covered with willows (here called *nyamyam shing*, or 'mourning trees'), cypresses, junipers, and a species of silver fir, and though the way was stony, it was pleasant on account of the forest growth through which it led.

We reached Tosnam-gyaling *djong* early in the afternoon. This place is celebrated for the serge and broadcloth manufactured here. The Tib chu, as it flowed through the town between low banks covered with flowers, and the tall poplars and walnut trees surrounding the high, well-built houses, gave this place a most attractive appearance. We met here a party of Horba with a caravan of yaks laden with salt, which they had brought from the north for sale in this country.

Before reaching the town we passed by the little nunnery of Peru, and shortly after leaving it we came to the large lamasery of Toi Suduling, with about 500 monks of the Gelugpa sect.

We stopped for the night at Khede-sho, a small town with two castles, and situated near the Tsang-po. The town looks like a fortress, with its old-fashioned solid houses, its narrow streets, the Dombu choskhor, or lamasery, with encircling walls painted blue and red, and an old monastery on top of the hill commanding the town.

It seemed to be a prosperous place; there were flower gardens and groves of trees, and in nearly every window and doorway flowers were growing in pots. Two Nyerpa are stationed here, who administer the town and supervise the manufacture of serge and cloth for the Dalai lama and Panchen rinpoche.

The next morning we passed through 2 miles of soft sand, and finally came to the mighty Tsang-po, and after much shouting to the boatmen on the farther side to bring over their junk (*shanpa*), and after a couple of hours' waiting in the cold and fog, it came slowly across, rowed by three women and two men, who sang lustily as they pulled.

The river is here about half a mile broad, very deep, but with a sluggish current. We were soon landed at the Dorje-tag ghat, where we paid a *tanka* for each of our ponies, and five *karma* (or two annas) for each man as ferry charges. The ferry belongs to the Dorje-tag lamasery near by, one of the oldest and holiest of the Nyingma sect. The incarnate lama who rules this lamasery died about a year and a half ago, but he has reappeared recently in the flesh at Darchendo. This convent is at the foot of a range of hills which stretches along the river to beyond Samye, and a large grove extends from near it to the high road.

We stopped for tiffin on the riverbank, where I noticed the ground covered with fish-bones and shells. Gopon told me that all the small fry which the people of this country catch are used to manure the fields with, as they are too bony to eat.

Gopon, who, by the way, was a most loquacious fellow, told me while we drank our tea that when a newborn child dies in this country the body is packed in an earthenware jar or wooden box, and is thus kept in the storeroom, or hung from the ceiling of its parents' house. In Upper Tibet the body is usually kept on the roof with a little turret built over it; though the people who cannot afford to do this keep it also hung from the ceiling, the face turned upwards.

The road now led over sand hillocks and spurs of rock, in some places close to the edge of the river, where great care was necessary in getting the ponies along.

We stopped at Tag, behind which rise the forest-covered mountains, and where we got quarters in a fine new house, and were made most comfortable by the owners.

The next day we were off before sunrise, and after a few miles through heavy sand, came to Songkar with about 200 houses, and around which grow walnut, willow, peach, poplar, and other varieties of trees. It is said that Prince Lhawang, son of King Me agtsoms, was drowned here, and the king, furious at the river gods for having caused the death of his heir, ordered the river to be whipped. The *nagas* were terrified when they learnt the order, and repairing to the king, told him that if he would forbear, they would show him many good omens. 'Tis for this that this place is also called Songkar (or Zungkhar) lha-tag, or 'Zungkhar of the gods' omens'.

Near the village passes the road to Lhasa by the Songkar la and Dechen, over which a great deal of timber is carried on yaks to Dechen and thence by boat to Lhasa.

From Songkar to Samye most of the way is over a great sandy plain called Nagshu chyema, which stretches from the base of the rugged Lomda hills to the Tsang-po. Reaching the top of a low hill, Samye stood before me, its gilded domes glittering in the sun, and the hillock of Haboi ri rising amidst the sands to the south of the great monastery.

Passing under some willow trees growing through the sand just outside the lamasery walls, we entered by the southern gate, over which was a *chorten* made somewhat in the shape of a *dorje*. The guide led us to the house of the mother of the Om-dse (head priest), and we were most hospitably received by the old lady, who gave us her oratory to lodge in. Before the rooms assigned us was a little flower patch, and other plants were growing here and there in pots. There were also two singing-birds in cages.

Tung-ma, our hostess, was a fine-looking old lady of about sixty years of age. She wore as a necklace a number of silver ornaments and charm boxes set with turquoises. Her headdress differed from any I had seen, being in shape like a pointed cap.

Phurchung was delighted with Samye; he had not only reached the holiest of Tibetan sanctuaries, but a place where *chang* was extraordinarily good and cheap; what more could he ask for?

After taking tea I went with my two companions to visit the chief temple of Wu-tse (Amitabha). I inquired of the beadle (Kunyer) the whereabouts of the celebrated library with the famous Indian books which Atisha had found here when he came to this monastery 800 years ago. I was told, to my great disappointment, that 'for our sins the great library was destroyed by fire about sixty years ago, and there are at present but modern reprints in it.'

In the great congregation hall the Dalai lama's throne occupies the northeastern corner of the chapel of the Jo-vo. Near this latter is an image representing the first Dalai and statues of the principal disciples of the Buddha.

In the second story of this building are images of Tsepamed (Amitayus) and of the historic Buddha, besides many others of minor interest. In the third or upper story are images of the three Buddhas of the present cycle. From this story I had a splendid view of the Tsang-po, which is very wide here.

On the wall surrounding the Wu-tse temple are painted various mythological and historical scenes, also pictures of the principal sanctuaries of Tibet. The monks attached to the temple live close by in a two-storied building.

The next day (October 30) I visited the four *ling*, or minor temples built around the Wu-tse, and the eight *ling-ten* or lesser shrines. In some of the smaller chapels were life-size images of

Indian sages who had visited Tibet in the early ages of Buddhism in this country, and these images are said to have been made by Hindu artists. I also noticed growing in some of the courtyards some stunted bamboos and Indian shrubs.

After visiting the white *chorten*, we went outside the temple walls to see the chapel built by the wives of King Tisrong detsan, which resembles in style the Wu-tse, though much smaller than it.

We made an excursion the next day to the famous cave called Chim phug, where Padma Sambhava and other worthies gave themselves up for a period to abstraction.

We passed through the village of Samye, in which there are probably a thousand people and a few Chinese and Nepalese shops, and then for a few miles travelled through cultivated fields, with here and there a little village, till we came to the foot of the Chim phug hill. The range of which it forms a part is a thousand feet or so high, well covered with fine timber, and inhabited, so some of the numerous woodcutters we met told us, by wild goats, sheep, deer, and snow leopards.

We reached the temple before noon. It is a two-storied, flat-roofed building built on the rock. In the rock underneath the temple there is a fissure about 15 feet long and 6 feet broad, and varying in height from 3 to 6 feet. In this there is a little chapel where the image of Padma Sambhava, flanked by two female attendants, is to be seen. In the building above are images of a host of deities and saints, as also that of King Tisrong. The books I looked at in the temple belonged to the Nyingma sect, and were of no special interest.

Leaving Chim phug after a couple of hours' rest, we returned to Samye by another road, passing three little temples, or rather hermitages, where Indian pundits are said to have lived in times of yore. Flocks of pigeons were hovering about them, and walnut and willow trees grew around, giving them a peaceful and secluded appearance.

The sands are slowly but surely burying Samye, and a large portion of the town, including some of the temples, is already lost under them. There is a prophecy attributed to Padma Sambhava, to the effect that Samye will be engulfed in the sands, and it is in a fair way of being accomplished.

November 1—I again visited the Wu-tse. The principal room in the *gong khang* (upper hall) is full of all kinds of weapons and armour sacred to the gods, protectors of religion (Darmapalas). In the beautiful temple of Behor and Noijinhamara is a room called the *wu-khang*, where the breath of the dying is kept in a jar specially consecrated to this purpose.

A few notes on the famous lamasery of Samye and Padma Sambhava find place here.

The temple was built by King Tisrong detsan, whose capital was on the hill of Haboi-ri, just south of where Samye now stands, at the suggestion of the Indian sage Santa Rakshita, and with the assistance of Padma Sambhava, the originator of monasticism in Tibet. It was a copy of the great temple of Odantapura in Central India. Its three stories were each in a different style of architecture, one Tibetan, another Indian, and the third Chinese: so it was after a while given the name of San-yang or 'three styles', which in Tibetan is pronounced Samye, though it was originally named Mi-gyur lhun-grub Tsug-lha-khang, 'the temple of the unalterable mass of perfection'.

Both Santa Rakshita and Padma Sambhava were unable, on account of the open hostility of the Bonbo, to remain long in Tibet. It is said by some that the latter sage remained there six years, others make his sojourn there eighteen years, after which he returned to India; but, however long he stayed, he firmly implanted mysticism in Tibet.

King Tisrong gathered together at Samye sacred images and treasures from India and the borderlands of China; but of all the collections made here the most valuable was the great library of

Indian works, of which Atisha, who visited Samye in the eleventh century, said that there were more Indian books here than in the great Indian convents of Buddhagaya, Vikramashila, and Odantapura united.

Samye has experienced, since the days of its foundation, many vicissitudes: it was partly destroyed by King Langdharma, and again later on by other followers of the old religion. Then it was partially destroyed by an earthquake, in 1749, and in 1808 the Wu-tse itself was destroyed by fire. To rebuild it the people of Tibet gave a hundred thousand ounces of silver, and the Shape Shada Dondub dorje, who had charge of the works, occupied 500 workmen for seven years in reconstructing the temple. Again, in 1850, an earthquake caused great damage to the temple, the dome fell in and the frescoes, floors, etc., were irreparably injured. But the damage was again repaired by means of public subscriptions and grants from the state, amounting together to about 1,75,000 ounces of silver in value,

On November 2 I left Samye for a visit to Yarlung, the early home of the first Tibetan kings, if tradition is to be believed.

The road we followed led eastward, over a sandy plain and by numerous villages, the most important of which was Do, until we reached Taga-sho, around which were many walnut (*taga*), peach, plum, poplar, and willow trees, all planted with great regularity. Here we put up in the house of a friend of our guide, who himself was from the neighbouring village of Do.

I was pleased to find mutton selling here at a very low price, a result of the presence of a party of Hor Dokpa from Radeng, who had brought large quantities of salt, wool and meat. Their yaks were the largest I have seen in Tibet.

Leaving Taga-sho the next morning, we passed by the ruins of Tagkar-sho, probably at one time the residence of the kings of the Phag-modu dynasty, who derive their name probably from a village nearby still called Phagmodu. Near this place, in a commanding position, is the lamasery of Nari ta-tsang, founded by the Dalai lama Gedun-gyatso.

At the village of Jong we began the ascent of the steep hill on whose summit is the old lamasery of Densa-til, the principal building nestled amidst frowning crags, on which grow here and there a few firs and juniper trees. In the adjacent cliffs were numerous caves for recluses.

This temple differs somewhat from all other buildings of this kind I have seen in Tibet, the plan of it approaching rather that of a modern public building in Bengal. I noticed here eighteen beautiful silver and copper *chorten*, the finest specimens of such metal work I have seen. Six tablets of gold, each 6 feet long and 6 inches broad, hung from the ceiling, besides six piles of similar but smaller tablets in a corner.

Of all the monasteries in Tibet, this is perhaps the richest in religious treasures, and the Government of Lhasa takes particular care of it. Among the curious objects placed before the images of the gods in the principal temple, I saw some bowls filled with various kinds of seed and some fossils, among which were some grains of barley.

The next day we resumed our journey. The road at first led through a forest said to have sprung from the hairs of Je Phagmodu, the founder of the Densa-til lamasery.

All the way to Samdub phodang, the capital of the Phagmodu kings, was a gentle descent over gravel and mica-schist rock. Crossing a fine wooden bridge about 50 yards long, with railings running along either side, we found ourselves in the principal street of the town, in which a large number of Dokpa traders were camped under some walnut trees.

The three-storied castle, once a royal residence, is now occupied by the Djongpon and the two Tsedung from Lhasa. Samdub phodang is now a *gon-shi*, or 'Crown Demesne' of Lhasa.

A few miles beyond this town we came to the Sangri khamar

lamasery, situated on a beautiful eminence overlooking the Tsang-po, whose surface is broken here by huge masses of rock. Around the grand lamasery stretched broad fields of barley, now ripe for the sickle, and the beauty of the crops surpassed anything I have ever seen in Tibet.

Here at Sangri khamar once lived Saint Machig labdon, an incarnation of Arya Tara. I visited the cell she lived in, and saw her tomb and an image of her. There are now two ascetics living here, who have made vows never to come out nor to speak a word so long as they live. When I approached them they smiled and seemed pleased with the little present I made them. The beadle who accompanied me said they had been immured in their cells for ten years.

Resuming our journey, we passed by Sangri Jong, and following a narrow path, scarcely a yard wide, overhanging the eddying river, reached Logang ferry; but, though we shouted for an hour to the boatmen on the other side, we could not get them to come over for us, so we had to return to the village of Jong at the western base of the Densa-til mountain. Here we got lodgings for the night in the house of the headman.

November 5—A little before dawn we left Jong and made for the Nango ferry. There is an iron suspension bridge at this place, but it is so much out of repair that it cannot be crossed over, and we were ferried across in a large boat, together with a number of traders and their donkeys. The river is very narrow here, scarcely a hundred yards in breadth. Passing through the village of Khyungar we entered Tse-tang, the capital of Yarlung, and formerly a place of great importance. Our guide procured lodgings for us in the house of a woman whose husband, a Kashmiri, had died a year or so before and who was now living alone with her husband's son. The Kache (Kashmiri) received us very kindly, but after a short conversation with me he became alarmingly suspicious of my true character, and kept continually turning the conversation to the *Shaheb-logs* (Englishmen) he had known at Katmandu, and the greatness of the *Engrez Maharani* (Queen of England). As often as he spoke of these subjects, so often did I rejoin with some inquiry about Buddhism or a lamasery I wished to visit.

I soon began to feel excessively nervous, and told my men that we had better leave Tse-tang as soon as possible; but Phurchung assured me that I need have no fear, that furthermore the ponies absolutely required rest, so that we must stay here a few days.

The day after our arrival at Tse-tang I went on the roof of our house, and was able to see a broad stretch of the surrounding country. To the north of the town was the Gonpoi ri, one of the favourite resorts of Shenrezig (Avalokiteswara), and where, according to tradition, the monkey king and the goblin raised their family of monkeys, from which ultimately descended the Tibetan race.

There are four lamaseries around Tse-tang, and in the town are some fifteen Nepalese, twenty Chinese, and ten Kashmiri shops, besides native traders from all parts of Tibet. Mutton and butter were abundant, but barley, though cheap, is of inferior quality.

I left Tse-tang on November 17 for a visit to the Yarlung valley and its monuments.

A short distance to the south of Tse-tang we passed through Ne-dong *djong*, where resides the Djongpon of this district, and which used to be a royal city of the Phagmodu kings. Save the lamasery of Benja, little remains but ruins to attest its past importance.

Following up the course of the Yarlung river, we came after a few miles to the temple of Tandub, one of those said to have been built in the seventh century by King Srong-btsan gambo, and to which a monastery was later on added by Tisrong detsan. It is a copy, on a small scale, of the Jo khang of Lhasa, and contains many objects of interest to the pious pilgrim.

Three hours' ride from Tandub brought us to Ombu lha-khang, the most ancient of Tibetan palaces. It is situated on the side of a range of bare hills, and is about a hundred yards from the village of Ombu, which derives its name from the number of *ombu* trees (tamarisks) which grow around it. Ombu lha-khang, though it has temples and shrines, is more properly a kind of memorial hall. The images in it are not those of gods and saints, but of kings, nobles, and ministers. The building itself is a curious mixture of the Indian and Tibetan styles of architecture, and the interior arrangement of the rooms and their decorations were unlike those of Tibetan buildings. The rooms, I may add, all face eastward.

After taking our lunch under a tamarisk tree, we remounted our ponies and rode on to Phodang *djong*, the most ancient town in Tibet. As all the kings of the dynasty which sprang from this place bore the title of Chos-gyal, or 'Catholic majesty', this town is also called Chos-gyal phodang. The present chief of this place claims descent from this very ancient line, but even his own people do not believe much in his pretended genealogy.

A few miles over gently rising ground brought us by sunset to the top of a hill, on which is situated the Tag-tsan bumba, or 'Dome of Good Omens'. We were kindly received by the young monk in charge of the shrine, who presented me with a basket of splendid white potatoes, which vegetable he assured me had grown around this place from time immemorial.

November 8—We left before daylight, and, crossing the Yarlung, reached the Rachung lamasery on the top of a steep hill, where we gained admittance after a good deal of trouble, the keeper being away and the incarnate lama, Rachung, confined in a cell performing certain vows. A little below the monastery we were shown the cave in which the original Rachung, the greatest of Milaraspa's disciples, dwelt for three years, three months, and three days.

We rested here for a while, and then went to the village of Rachung at the foot of the hill, where we found good lodgings for the night in the house of an old acquaintance of our guide, Gopon.

Formerly this broad valley of Yarlung, or Gondang-tangme, was covered with innumerable populous villages, and in no other part of Tibet was there such opulence. But one day the snows melting on the Yarlha-shampo and torrential rains caused a mighty flood which submerged the whole plain for many days. The villages were utterly destroyed, and the people all perished, and when the waters had retired, a deep deposit of sand covered everything. In course of time the country was reclaimed, and has now reached a certain degree of prosperity, but it has never recovered its primitive flourishing state.

The next day we rode across the northern slope of the Shetag mountains, or 'Black Crystal' (*Shel-tag*), thus called from the glistening black rocks exposed to view along the road, and after a few miles came to the great cemetery which adjoins the lamasery of Yarlung-shetag. Phurchung and Gopon rolled themselves on the blood-stained stone slab, on which corpses are cut up, and mumbled some mantra.

In this lamasery there live forty monks and as many nuns: their children are brought up to the professions of their parents. This arrangement has been sanctioned by the Nyingma Church, as the lamasery was so lonely that no monks could be induced to reside in it till this privilege was conceded them.

Beyond this lamasery the trail led along the edge of a precipice where we passed a number of little cells occupied by hermits (or *tsampa*), who, as we passed, stretched out their hands for alms through the little opening left in the front of their dens. Some of these men had been immured five years, and many of them had also made vows of silence.

A little way beyond this point, and about 500 feet below the summit of the hill, we reached the cell of Padma Sambhava, near which is a chapel called the Upper Lha-khang of Shetag. The keeper led us to a heavy door under a huge rock; unlocking it we entered the cavern, which is held the most sacred shrine of the Nyingma sect. In it I saw a silver reliquary in which is kept a silver image of the saint, representing him as a boy of twelve. There was a plate before the image filled with rings, earrings, turquoises, pieces of amber, gold and silver coins, the offerings of pilgrims.

Passing the Shetag, we came to the village of Ze-khang shikha and thence by a gentle descent we reached the famed temple of Tsandan-yu lha-khang, 'the temple of sandalwood and turquoise'. It was thus called, it is said, because its founder, King Srong-btsan gambo, only used in building it sandalwood, and the blue tiles which covered it were glazed with melted turquoises. It is a rather Chinese-looking structure, but one of the handsomest I have seen in Tibet. Every month six monks come here from Tse-tang to hold service.

A very short distance to the west of this sanctuary is the Lha-bab-ri, or 'the mountain of the descent (of the king or god)' (*lha* having both meanings), where the first king of Tibet, Nyakri-btsanpo, was seen for the first time by Tibetans. There is a little plateau on this hill, called the 'King's Plain' or Btsan-tang, where a temple has been built called the Btsan-tang lha-khang.

Leaving this interesting spot behind, we rode on across the fields which the peasants were ploughing and irrigating for the autumn crops, and came, after a few hours, to the sanctuary of Gadan namgyal-ling, where Tsongkhapa took his final vows of monkhood. It is a fine building in the midst of a grove of trees, through which flows a brook.

From this point we retraced our steps to Tse-tang, which we reached the same day, recrossing the Yarlung chu by a long stone bridge near the monastery of Tse-chog-pa, where we saw a number of the monks bathing in the river.

The Yarlung valley appeared to me to be a most prosperous one, the people gentle and good-natured. The soil produces grain and fruit in greater abundance than any other part of Tibet; *chang*, butter, meat, oil, barley, wheat, and fuel were everywhere plentiful.

On November 10 we left Tse-tang, on the return journey to Tashilhunpo.

We forded the Yarlung river, in which there was but little water, nearly all of it having been drawn off by irrigation ditches higher up the valley, and passing to the villages of Yangta and Gyerpal, we came to the old sanctuary of Yarlung, called the Chyasa lha-khang, or 'the resting-place-of-birds temple', for the vast flocks of birds which pass here in their migrations make it a resting-place. It is situated on the banks of the Tsang-po, and is a finely built and well-kept edifice, with a courtyard and beautifully frescoed walls. The image of Sakya Buddha in the temple is said to be made with an alloy of gold, silver, copper and iron.

Following the bank of the Tsang-po, through heavy sands or over low hills, we came towards evening to Chincho-ling, a secluded and desolate little hamlet, the houses surrounded by low walls of stone to keep off the drifting sands, and here we put up for the night.

The next morning there was a heavy fog—quite a rare phenomenon in these parts—when we started. We breakfasted at the little fisher village of Dong-sho, and a mile or so beyond this entered a well-cultivated valley containing numerous villages and fine trees. Near the first village we came to stands the monastery of Chongdu-chog. We reached, before evening, the famous Nyingma lamasery of Mindol ling, in a dale opening on the west side of the valley; a little below it is a very large village, where we found, after some difficulty, accommodation in the house of a well-to-do man.

The next day we visited the temple, which is very beautiful, though the lamasery itself has never recovered from the pillage by the Jungars in the seventeenth century; and the Nyingma Church being at present, moreover, persecuted by the dominant Gelugpa, no longer enjoys its former wealth. The neatness of the stonework and the finish of all the masonry about the temple were very remarkable, and the courtyard was regularly paved with stone slabs.

To the south of the monastery is the residence of the abbot, who is always selected from the Tertalingpa family, in which this office is hereditary.

I left Mindol-ling on November 12, returned to the Tsang-po, and reached the village of Cho by dusk. Quite early the next morning we entered Khede-sho, where our route joined that we had taken when going to Samye.

We left Khede-sho by daylight the next morning, and continuing along the bank of the Tsang-po, crossed the long meadow of Ding-naga, which is covered with a fine, short, moss-like sod. Then passing through the villages of Kyishong, Panza, and Gyatu-ling, we came to where the Gonkhar mountains abut on the river. On their farther side is the town of Gongkhar, still surrounded by imposing, though ruined walls. Here, after much difficulty, we managed to obtain shelter in the house of a fisherman, who gave us leave to pass the night in a hovel half-filled with yak hides. He and his wife were very kind to us, and looked, to the best of their ability, after our wants and those of our ponies.

We resumed our journey at 4 in the morning, and pushed on slowly and with considerable difficulty, for the path was over rocks, in places overhanging the roaring river. At daybreak we passed by the village of Shyati-ling, and shortly after the sun pierced the fog which had enveloped us. A low *col*, called Yab la, was next passed, and we joined the high-road between Lhasa and Shigatse, which I have previously described. We stopped for the night at Tamalung.

The next day (November 16) we reached Palti *djong*.

On the 18th, a mile or so to the west of Oma-tang, where we had passed the night, we fell in with the Chinese Amban and his train on their way to Lhasa. First came numerous parties on horseback, then about 300 men on foot carrying all the paraphernalia common to Chinese processions, and finally the Amban's chair carried by Chinese and sixteen Tibetans, the latter only holding strings attached to the poles to show that they were assisting in the work. Two Chinese armed with whips kept the way clear.

On November 24 I found myself once more at Tashilhunpo, and immediately set to work to prepare for a trip to Sakya, from whence it was my intention to proceed directly to India. A day or so after my arrival I was delighted at the receipt of a passport from the new Shape of Shigatse, permitting me to proceed to India and return to Tibet. It had been obtained at the instance of my friend, the minister.

X

Visit to Sakya and Return to India

On November 30, 1882, I said farewell to Tashilhunpo, and, accompanied by Phurchung and Gopon, my recent guide to Samye, I started for Sakya, from which place I proposed returning to Darjiling by way of Khamba *djong* and the Kongra lamo pass.

The country was now bare, the brown rocks, the gravelly soil, and the distant snow-covered mountains, gave additional bleakness to the scene. We reached the village of Nartang the same evening, and were kindly received by some old friends of Phurchung.

A little before daylight the next morning we set out, following the great high-road which leads to Upper Tibet, instead of taking the direct road which leads there by the Lang la, but which is infested by highwaymen.

At the little hamlet of Chagri we stopped to make some tea, and had to pay three annas for a little water, as the people have to bring all they use from a very considerable distance.

The wind was blowing violently when we resumed our journey, and the dust was so thick that we had to stop at Ge-chung, a little village to the west of the Singma la.

At daybreak we set out again, and after crossing the Re chu (here called Shab chu), along whose banks are numerous hamlets, we came to Lhimpotse, near which is a large lamasery built on a rocky eminence.

We stopped for the night at Samdong, just beyond which village is a long wooden bridge. We got accommodation in the house of a rich villager, the younger of the two husbands (and they not brothers) of the woman of the house. The other husband was the headman, or *Sa-yong*, and when he appeared, he obligingly sold us very good *chang*, mutton, onions, and other vegetables.

December 3—After drinking a cup of steaming *chang* we set out, and following the course of the Shab chu, came to where the Tsarong chu empties into it, when we took up the course of this stream and followed it to its source.

Several miles above the village of Sikya, where cultivation practically ceases, we came to the large Dokpa village of Jig-kyong, where we stopped for the night. In all the villages smallpox was raging, and where the people were free from it, they showed great apprehension about letting us in, lest we should introduce the dreaded disease among them.

The next day (December 4) we crossed the Shong la, which, though quite high, was of easy ascent, and traversed the Tao valley. After taking lunch at the Kham-yol we came to the Aton la, from whose summit Sakya is visible, with all its red-walled buildings and gilded spires, bearing in a northwesterly direction.

We secured lodgings in a house in the town, near the bridge over the Tom chu, and from the window of my room, which opened to the south, I had a gorgeous view of the town by which the river gently flows; also of the great temple, and beyond these, of the snow-covered peaks of Tinki (Tingri) and Pherug.

In the evening I strolled about the clean, though narrow streets, where the market people were still busy selling their wares.

Sakya is built on the eastern flank of Ponpoi ri, along whose base flows the Tom chu. Facing the town, but on the other side of the river, is the Lha-khang chenpo with its famous library and temple.

The appearance of Sakya is different from that of most Tibetan towns. The walls of almost all the public buildings, temples, and dwelling-houses are painted red with a clay obtained from the neighbouring hills. Black and blue stripes about 9 inches broad cut the walls perpendicularly.

The four Labrang temples, built with Chinese roofs and gilded spires, are especially noticeable. They are called Labrang-shar (or 'eastern'), Labrang-nub (or 'western'), Labrang khung, and Khansar chenpo, and in their general arrangement they do not differ from the temples I had seen at Tashilhunpo and elsewhere.

In the palmy days of the Sakya hierarchy there were four abbots under the hierarch who ruled these four Labrang. The rank was hereditary in their families, and all those abbots, the hierarch included, were allowed to marry. This system of hereditary hierarchy was known as *dun-gyu*. At the present time the abbots are Tantrik lamas from Khams. I was told that neither the lamas nor the nuns of Sakya are held by the people to be exceptionally virtuous, and, to tell the truth, the laity of Sakya has a similar unsavoury reputation in Tibet.

The Emperor Kublai made the hierarch Phagpa ruler of Tibet, and it was the latter's deputy (or Panchen), Kunga zangbo, who began building the Lha-khang chenpo of Sakya, which was completed by one of his successors in office, Anglen tashi. This latter proved himself an able and vigorous administrator, and annexed Tagpo to the Sakya principality. Zangpo-pal, the then reigning hierarch, sent him on a mission to the Emperor of China, Buyantu, who granted to him and his heirs in perpetuity the Yamdo lake country. The Sakya Panchen have, down to the present time, been taken from this family. The last Sakya Panchen, Kunga nyingpo, died on June 20, 1882; his tomb, at the time of my visit to Sakya, was almost finished, and his wife was still wearing mourning.

It is told of the late Sakya Panchen that, some sixteen years ago, after the death of the two famous Dayan khanpo, the treasurer of the Gadan gomba of Lhasa, when his wicked spirit was causing various dire calamities to Tibet, every endeavour to expel it from the country proved abortive. So finally the Government of Lhasa, at the suggestion of the oracles, requested the Sakya Panchen to visit Lhasa to drive the fiend away. At the foot of Mount Potala he had lighted a great fire, and, by the potency of his charms, drove the evil spirit into a lay figure prepared for the occasion, whereupon it fell straightway into the fire. Then the Panchen drove his charmed *phurbu* into the image, but while so doing the flames of the pyre surrounded him, and all thought he was dead; but lo! after an hour or so he came out of the flames dressed in rich satins, and with not even so much as a hair of his head scorched.

Panchen Jimed wang-gyal, or one of the other sons of the late Panchen, will succeed him as ruler of Sakya. One son is an incarnate lama and superior of the Tanag Donphug lamasery, but he is obliged to reside continually at Sakya on account of a rule which prescribes that when the re-embodiment of a lama takes place in Sakya, the reincarnation cannot return to the locality he occupied in his preceding existence. The names of the four other sons of the deceased Panchen will shortly be sent to Lhasa, and the Nachung oracle will decide who shall become the ruler of the principality.

These princely lamas wear long hair, ordinarily plaited in two queues hanging down their backs and tied at the ends with white cotton handkerchiefs. Over their ears they wear covers of gold studded with turquoises and emeralds, and almost reaching to their shoulders. To the lower part of these are appended earrings.

In the Lha-khang chenpo (or 'great temple') are five seats of equal height, on which the princes take their places when conducting religious services; the one reserved to the hierarch remains vacant so long as the successor to the title has not been chosen.

Under the hierarch there is a Shape, or minister, who attends to all the temporal affairs of Sakya. The monks are divided into two orders, according to the locality of their birth; those from Tibet proper forming one set ruled by a Gekor, and having their cells near the great temple, and those from Khams (or Eastern Tibet), also with a Gekor over them, who live in the town.

As to the great library of Sakya, it is on shelves along the walls of the great hall of the Lha-khang chenpo. There are preserved here many volumes written in gold letters; the pages are 6 feet long by 18 inches in breadth. On the margin of each page are illuminations, and the first four volumes have in them pictures of the thousand Buddhas. These books are bound with iron. They were prepared under orders of the Emperor Kublai, and presented to Phagpa on his second visit to Peking.

There is also preserved in this temple a conch shell with whorls turning from left to right, a present of Kublai to Phagpa. It is only blown by the lamas when the request is accompanied by a present of 7 ounces of silver; but to blow it, or have it blown, is held to be an act of great merit.

On December 5 I left Sakya, and passing by the Choskhor-lhunpo monastery, entered the broad Yalung valley, in which stands the big village of Lora and numerous scattered hamlets. We stopped at Lora to eat our breakfast, but so intense was the fear of the people of smallpox, of which there were several cases in the village, that they would have absolutely nothing to do with us, not even to sell us firewood.

After crossing the Yalung river we ascended the Dong la, from whose summit we saw the Chomo kankar (Mt Everest), and the endless ranges of mountains which jut out from it westward. At the Dong la the Arun and the Kosi have their sources.

The descent of the Dong la was very gradual, the country extremely bare, not a single tree was to be seen anywhere. We reached Chu-sho, at the foot of the pass, at about five o'clock, and it was only after much persuasion that we gained admittance to a poor hut occupied by an old woman and her son.

The next day we followed for a while the course of a little stream, called the Chu-shu, and then came upon a broad, barren plain, on either side of which rose bleak and lofty mountains.

Leaving the village of Map-ja, in which there are about one hundred houses, we breakfasted at Donkar, and then made our way towards the Shong-pa la, following up the course of the Shong chu. The ground in many places was riddled with holes made by a burrowing animal called *srimong*, and our ponies had many tumbles by putting their feet in them.

On descending from the Shong-pa la we found ourselves in the broad Chib-lung valley, and towards six o'clock we reached the village of Dogang, and found shelter for the night in the hut of some poor people.

The following morning we passed through Tashigong and breakfasted at Gure, a village belonging to my friend the minister. Leaving this place, we began the ascent of a high range which separated us from lake Tel-tung, or 'Mule's Drink'. This pass is known as the Dobta Lachan la, and one commands from it a most gorgeous view of a wide expanse of country, the Nepalese and Sikkimese Himalayas, with lake Tel-tung and Dobta *djong*, belonging to the Sikkim Rajah, on a hillock beside the lake in the foreground.

We stopped for the night at Chorka, a part of Dobta, where a villager gave us the use of a yak-hair tent standing in his courtyard. We only remained here a short while, leaving before daylight, as we wanted to reach Khamba *djong* the same day. The cold was intense, and the violent wind which blew made it more piercing. Our way led along the margin of lake Tel-tung, now completely dried up and more resembling a broad pastureland than a lake. The country was alive with game; wild sheep, goats, and asses were specially numerous.

Leaving this broad plain, we entered the valley of the Che chu by a low *col* between the Dobta and Yaru la ranges. Crossing the river, we stopped for a while at Targye, while Phurchung went on ahead to Khamba *djong* to secure lodgings for us.

At five o'clock we reached the village of Khamba, and were received most kindly by Phurchung's friend, Wang-gyal, who, together with his wife, did everything in their power to make us comfortable.

After tea I went with Phurchung, who had put on his best clothes for the occasion, to visit the Djongpon. The Djong stands on a hillock, the ascent of which is rather steep, and is made by flights of stone steps. The fort is a spacious two-storied building, and is supplied with water brought there through clay pipes from the mountains to the north, a piece of work of which the people are not a little proud.

The Djongpon were reading religious books when I entered their presence, and the lama asked me questions about myself and the object of my journey, all of which I managed to answer satisfactorily. I showed my passport, to which they put their seals, retaining a copy of the document. When I left they presented me with a dried sheep's carcass, 10 pounds of rice, and a rug, and expressed the hope that they would see me again the following year.

On returning to our lodgings I hired two ponies and a yak-hair tent for our use as far as Gen-pang tang.

We left early in the morning, after saying farewell to our faithful guide Gopon, who left us here to return to his home at Gyantse, and breakfasted at Geru. On the way we saw several flocks of wild sheep and some foxes. Leaving Geru, we ascended, one after the other, the foothills of the Kongra lamo pass, through a wild but beautiful country, till we finally reached the snow-covered summit, near which we camped on a bare rock. Thanks to the yak-hair tent and the good fire of argols which

Phurchung kept burning, we did not suffer from the intense cold and piercing wind.

The following morning (December 10) we reached, at an early hour, Gen-gang, which forms the boundary between the territories of the Grand Lama and the Rajah of Sikkim, a vassal of the British Raj. From this point my way lay through Sikkim by a route followed by various European travellers, and concerning which I need say nothing here. I reached Darjiling and my home on December 27, after an absence of over a year.

XI

Social Divisions—Marriage—Funerals—Medicine—Festivals

In Tibet there are three distinct classes among the people, lay and clerical, which are determined by birth and social position, and each of these has three sub-divisions. They are as follows:
First, or highest class, *Rab*:

1. *Rab-kyi rab*: The King, members of the royal family, and incarnate lamas who have appeared many times on earth.
2. *Rab-kyi ding*: The Desi, or Regent, ordinary incarnate lamas, ministers and councillors of state, learned lamas, or abbots, professors at important monasteries.
3. *Rab-kyi tama*: Secretaries to the Government, Dahpon, Djongpon, and inferior lamas, or abbots.

Middle classes, *Ding*:

1. *Ding-kyi rab*, or 'upper middle class', including families who have for generations possessed great wealth, landlords who do not claim descent from illustrious ministers or warriors; Dungkhor, old families and men who have personally contributed in a marked degree to the welfare of the country; and lastly, the Don-nyer.

2. *Ding-kyi ding*: This class includes the Dung-yig, or clerks, stewards, chamberlains, head grooms, head cooks, and other petty officers.
3. *Ding-kyi tama*: Soldiers and subjects.

Lowest class, *Tama*:

1. *Tamai rab*: Grooms, menials engaged in domestic service, and other hired servants.
2. *Tamai ding*: Those who have no fixed homes, men who keep concubines, but no wives, loose women, professional beggars, vagabonds, and paupers.
3. *Tamai tama*: The lowest of the low are butchers, scavengers, disposers of dead bodies, blacksmiths and goldsmiths.

In Tibet there are no caste restrictions with regard to marriage as in India. The rich may bestow their daughters on the poor, the daughter of a poor man may become the bride of the proudest noble of the country. But the girls of the royal family and those of high rank are not generally bestowed on the low classes; but in the event of their not finding a suitable match, they are sent to convents. The daughters of commoners do, however, occasionally become the wives of nobles.

The nuptial ceremonies are alike for all classes, the only difference being in the amount of money expended in the festivities. In the first place, the friends of the bridegroom employ a go-between to make the first overtures to the parents or guardians of the girl. Should the latter entertain the proposal, the parents of the would-be bridegroom either take or send presents to them, consisting of *khatag* and wine (called *long chang*, 'proposal wine'), and formally make an offer of marriage. The girl's parents make excuses, saying that she is neither handsome nor accomplished, and will be of no service to the suitor. The go-betweens thereupon more and more earnestly press their suit. After these conventional phrases have been exchanged, the girl's parents say, 'If you are really in earnest, and believe that she will be of service to you, we shall consult with our friends and relatives, and let you know our decision.'

A few days later their consent to the union is formally conveyed to the suitor's parents, when the latter, taking with them twenty or thirty gallons of wine, proceed to the home of the bride, where they entertain not only all her relatives, but also the servants and neighbours, and present each with a scarf. The purchase-money (*rin*) is then paid, which, for the middle classes is usually five or six *doche* (625 to 750 rupees), and about fifty gallons of wine. Another scarf is then presented to each of the elder members of the bride's family, and also to prominent persons among her friends and neighbours.

After an auspicious day has been fixed for the wedding, the parties make the arrangements necessary for the occasion. On the appointed day the bridegroom's parents depute some seven or eight respectable men to go as their representatives to bring home the bride. They remain at her father's house three days, during which they are engaged in making negotiations and in assuring their hosts, by whom they are provided during this period with all necessaries, that their daughter will be happy in her new home. At the end of the three days the bride is told by her parents to go to the bridegroom's house. They give her a good milch-cow or yak, a pony, four or five oxen, two suits of summer and winter dress, a complete set of jewellery according to the custom of the country, a piece of stuffed carpet and a small dining-table, cups, plates, cooking vessels, and other articles for domestic use, 50 ounces of silver, and a female attendant. All those who have received scarves now come to present her in return with a scarf and a piece of money. The nearest relatives and friends of the parents, the chief of the country, and other people of position, present her with scarves, clothes, blankets, etc., and silver coins.

Presently about twenty of the bridegroom's friends arrive to conduct the bride to her new home. For the first half of the journey the arrangements are made and expenses defrayed by the bride's parents; for the second half by those of the bridegroom, and it is made on horseback, the bride riding in the middle of the party. Arriving at their destination, the bride is seated on a cushion placed on a raised stand by the side of her husband in the middle of the bridal party. At an auspicious hour a short religious service is performed by the village lama, and the parents or sponsors of the parties offer prayers for the happiness of the union. The bridegroom's parents then beseech the gods to witness the ceremony of their son's marriage, and declare that henceforth the bride will be owned by the bridegroom and his brothers alone. For three days the festivities continue, during which time as much as fifty *chupan* of wine, three oxen, and three pigs are sometimes consumed. The notables among the bridegroom's friends arrive with presents of scarves, and are entertained by his father.

On the third day the bride exchanges the clothes and jewellery she wore on her arrival, for others supplied by the bridegroom. After a short prayer to the gods the pair are left together for the first time, and on the following morning the bride begins to apply herself to her household duties. Her brothers and relatives who have accompanied her, return home at the expiration of seven days.

Some three months after the wedding her parents, accompanied by the chief men among their friends and by servants, arrive with presents of food, and request that their daughter may pay them a visit. After being entertained for ten or twelve days, they return home, and are followed some weeks later by the young couple, who are accompanied by a number of female servants bearing presents of scarves, provisions, wine, etc. They remain a month, and on their departure the bride receives from her father a new costume and jewellery, and the husband a complete suit of clothes and the inevitable scarf.

Among the very poor the proceedings are much simplified, the negotiations being conducted by the parents in person.

There is no fixed limit of marriageable age in Tibet. The average age, however, for both sexes, is from fifteen to twenty-five, and frequently the bride is older than the bridegroom.

When parties are desirous of dissolving the marriage bond, the reason for so doing must first be investigated. If the husband be found entirely blameless and willing to live with his wife, but she be resolved to divorce him, she is required to pay double the *rin*, or price paid for her, as a fine for the dissolution of the marriage contract, called *borche* and *den yo*, that is, 'divorce fine' and 'innocence fine'. In the absence of a marriage contract, the divorce fine fixed by law for the wife to pay amounts to eighteen gold *sho*, equal to 135 rupees; and for the husband three gold *srang*, equal to 180 rupees. If the husband's innocence be doubtful, but the wife's charges remain unproved, the wife is required to pay as divorce fine a complete suit of clothes, a pair of shoes, a bed-carpet, bed-rug, and a wrapper, and the husband must present to his wife a second scarf and a third article of any kind.

On the other hand, if a wife be found perfectly innocent, and willing to live with her husband, but the husband be resolved to divorce her for no fault of hers, he is required to pay to her twelve gold *sho*, equal to ninety rupees, as divorce fine, and also *yog la*, 'service wage', amounting to 6 pounds of barley for every day and six for every night which she has spent with him from the day of marriage to the date of separation. The husband is also required to return the price of all the clothes and other gifts made to the wife by her friends since the time of their marriage. The divorced woman also takes away with her all jewellery given her by her relatives, but not that given to her by her husband. The wife cannot demand the 'innocence fine'. If there be children at the time of separation, the father takes the boys, and the mother the girls. If the husband be a man of property, the court may order him to give the divorced wife a certain share of his possessions for the maintenance of the girls. On the other hand, if the wife be possessed of property, she may be required to give something for the maintenance of her sons.

Again, when a marriage is contracted between a man of noble blood and a woman of humble rank, or *vice versa*, with the definite understanding that they shall share each other's good and adverse fortune, their property in case of divorce is to be divided between them according to their faithfulness or guilt, and their amount of mutual presents at the time of union. In cases of divorce between parties who were united at their own wish for the enjoyment of pleasure or merriment, the court should, without regard to the nature of their guilt, divide their property equally between them. In cases of marriage between slaves or serfs, the owner decides their separation or continued union. A man of this class is, for instance, married to a woman who, the owner thinks, might be of some service to him. When the woman is found useless, she is dismissed, being given one-sixth of her husband's belongings, and her place is supplied by a new wife chosen by the owner.

In Tibet members of the same family are forbidden by law to contract matrimonial alliances with their kindred within seven degrees. This rule is, however, nowadays disregarded by the people, who are known to make alliances with their kinsmen who are distant only three or four degrees of consanguinity. Among the Pobos and Khamba marriage is promiscuously contracted, the brother marrying his sister, the nephew his aunt. Among the common Tibetans, so long as the parties do not claim a common father, there is no objection to the marriage; the uterine brother and sister may be united, and a man may marry his stepmother or aunts.

The custom of several brothers making one woman their common wife, to keep the ancestral property entire and undivided, is said to have had its origin in Khams, where it is at this day extensively practised. The Tibetans of U and Tsang have borrowed it from their cousins of Khams, but it is not universal with them. The wife is claimed by the younger brothers as their wife only so long as they continue to live with the eldest one. When they separate from their eldest brother, they cannot ask him to pay compensation for their share in the wife, and she remains the lawful wife of the eldest brother. It is not unusual for a father or uncle to live with his son's or nephew's wife, and even in high life a father makes himself a partner in the marital rights over his son's wife.

The cessation of the pulse and the suspension of breathing are not considered tests of the extinction of vitality. The Tibetans consider that the spirit (*nam she*) usually lingers in the mortal frame for not less than three days, though the spirits of those who have attained to some stage of holiness quit the body immediately after the last breath has been drawn, for communion with the dwellers in Paradise, called Gadan or Tushita; but instances of such saintly personages are of very rare occurrence. It is consequently considered a very sinful action to move or dispose of the corpse immediately after death. Nowadays in Tibet and Mongolia the dead bodies of all classes of men are carefully kept within doors for three days, during which time their friends and relations attend on them and make prayers for their future well-being. On the morning of the fourth day the horoscope of the deceased, and that of the man who is selected to be the first to touch the corpse for removal, are consulted. A lama is employed to perform certain funeral ceremonies, with a view to cause the spirit of the deceased to pass out through a certain slit in the skull. If this ceremony is omitted the soul will make its exit by some other passage and go to a state of damnation. The lama remains alone with the corpse, all the doors and windows being closed, and no one is allowed to enter until he declares by what passage the soul has fled. In return for this important service he receives a cow, yak, sheep, or goat, or a sum of money, according to the means of the deceased.

Before the dead body is removed from the house, an astrologer notes the dates of birth of the friends and relations present. If any among them were born under the same constellation and planet as the dead person, they are said to incur the risk of being ridden by his ghost, and are consequently not allowed to attend the funeral. The astrologer also receives his reward in money or kind. Then the corpse, tightly wrapped in clothes, is placed on a stretcher facing the direction which has been declared auspicious by the astrologer, and is placed in a corner of the house. Five butter lamps are lighted near the head, and a screen is drawn around it, within which his usual food and drink, together with a lamp, are placed. Early on the morning of the day appointed for the disposal of the body, it is carried to the nearest cemetery. At the time of its removal the relations make profound salutations to it. Two men carrying wine or tea, together with a dishful of *tsamba*, follow the bier. The family priest, or lama, of the deceased throws a *khatag* on the litter and walks behind at a slow pace, holding a corner of another scarf tied to it. As he proceeds he mutters funeral mantra, turning a hand-drum (*damaru*) with his right hand, and with his left ringing a bell. It is inauspicious to place the litter on the ground before its arrival at the cemetery. If by accident this should happen, the body must be disposed of at that spot, instead of in the cemetery. In the neighbourhood of Lhasa there are two sacred cemeteries, Phabongka and Serashar. Those who dispose of dead bodies at the former pay two or three *tanka* for tea to the monks of Phabongka monastery; and at the latter they pay one *tanka* to the cemetery keeper, who also gets the bedding and clothes of corpses.

In every cemetery there is a large slab of stone, on which the corpse, stripped of its coverings, is placed face downwards. The officiating lama then crosses it with lines, and while repeating *mantras*, cuts it in pieces. The first pieces are flung towards the biggest and oldest vulture of the flock, called *tankar*, and the remainder to the rest. They are so tame that they come one by one at the call of the priest. Last of all the head of the corpse is crushed, and the bones pounded together are mixed with the brain and distributed among the vultures. Then a new and unused earthen bowl, filled with fire of *argol* (dried cowdung), with some butter and barley flour burnt in it as incense, is presented to the departed by being placed in the quarter towards which he is supposed to have gone. The funeral attendants now wash their hands, and retiring to a short distance from the cemetery, breakfast, and at about midday return home. During forty-nine days after the drawing of the last breath, food and drink are offered to the departed in his favourite dish; and incense, consisting of barley, butter, and juniper spines, is burnt.

During this period of *bardo*, as the interval between death and regeneration is called, the departed spirit is believed to wander, and in order to prevent its being subject to misery, on the forty-ninth day some of the clothes, shoes, headdress, coins, etc., which belonged to the deceased, after being washed and sprinkled with saffron-water, are presented to some incarnate lama for his blessing. The last service is conducted by a Tantrik lama, with a view to expelling all the evil spirits and hungry ghosts which haunt the house of the departed.

On the seventh day after death, prayers are moreover offered for the deceased's well-being, and alms in coin, food, tea, gold, and silver are distributed among religious men. This is repeated on every consecutive seventh day until the forty-ninth day, when a grand feast is given to the congregation of lamas. Nowadays, however, the rich people of Lhasa generally distribute alms, at the rate of one *tanka* each to the monks of Sera, Dabung, and Gadan, dispensing with the other costly ceremonies. They also present the clothes belonging to the deceased to the professors and heads of those monasteries. Some bequeath the whole of their property to these monastic institutions or to Lamas of great repute.

The practice of making wills has been followed by the Tibetans from very remote times. Every man of property leaves a will bequeathing his movable property to his children or friends, and leaving instructions for the performance of his funeral obsequies and other pious works.

The cutting up and distributing of a corpse is a practical illustration of the Tibetan belief that charity is the highest of all the moral virtues. That man is said to be most virtuous whose funeral is attended by the largest number of vultures, while if his corpse attracts but a small company, the very dogs not deigning to touch his defiled remains, he is judged to have led a sinful life.

The dead bodies of pregnant and barren women, and also of lepers, are packed in leather bags and thrown into the waters of the great Tsang-po. A Tibetan proverb says, 'She whose son dies after birth is white barren (*rab-cha karpo*); she whose daughter dies after birth is partly barren (*rab-cha tavo*); she who has borne no children is black barren (*rab-cha nagpo*).' The corpses of such and of lepers are considered particularly unclean, and should not be kept within the limits of the country, but must either be thrown beyond nine hills and dales, or packed in horses' or oxen's skins and thrown into the river.

The dead bodies of incarnate lamas are occasionally burnt, and their ashes and bones deposited in *chorten*. The remains of saintly personages, such as pretend to have emanated from Bodhisattvas and Buddhas, are preserved like the Egyptian mummies, being embalmed or salted and placed within gold, silver, or copper *chorten*, where they are seated in a meditative posture, like the conventional image of Buddha. These incarnate lamas, at the time of death, mention the time when and the place and the family where their souls will subsequently find re-embodiment, and also the name and race of the family, and instruct their friends to perform rites and ceremonies for their well-being after death.

On the demise of the Dalai and Tashi lamas, the work in all the public and private offices, all business, and market gatherings are suspended for seven days. For thirty days women are forbidden to put on their jewellery, and men or women may not wear new apparel. Lamas and monks must, on such occasions, mourn for ten days, during which they must not shave their heads, or wear their church headdresses during services. All classes of people refrain from amusements and festivities, and from going into groves for pleasure, sports, or love-making. It is only in honour of the death of these two great hierarchs of Tibet that the whole country goes into mourning. The mourning for abbots of other monasteries and heads of families is confined to the friends and monks who are near to them. Rich and respectable men do not, within a year after the death of their parents, take part in marriage ceremonies and festivities; and do not undertake journeys to a distance.

Among the Sikkim Buddhists, dead bodies are burnt. On the fourth day after cremation, a lama performs the *tusol*, or washing ceremony, which consists in removing the relics, ashes, etc., and washing the place of burning with water. The relics are placed in an urn and deposited, in a *chorten*. The ashes are thrown into a mountain stream, such as the Tista or Rungit. The relics of lamas and important men, after being pulverized, are mixed with clay and cast in moulds into miniature *chorten*. These relic *chorten* are deposited in sacred places, such as monasteries, temples, caverns, etc. On the seventh day the funeral ceremony, called *Tenzung*, is performed. All relations and neighbours are invited to this funeral feast. At dusk all the evil spirits which are believed to have been invited to the departure of the deceased, are expelled by a Tantrik priest, assisted by the deafening yells of the guests.

The physicians of High Asia have, I am told, discovered such remarkable properties of vegetable drugs, and of the flesh and bile of certain animals, and of some sorts of excrements in healing different kinds of sores, that if the statements of my informant be true, the surgeons of civilized countries would be struck with wonder at their marvellous performances. For this remarkable success, the Tibetans do not appear to be indebted to their Chinese or Indian neighbours. Their medicines are mostly indigenous, and their discoveries in surgery have resulted from their own experience. They supply the greater number of physicians and surgeons to the Mongols and other neighbouring peoples.

The treatment of smallpox is very little understood by Tibetan doctors. Inoculation is, however, resorted to, and a new method of performing this operation has been discovered by the Northern Chinese physicians. It consists in selecting the best lymph from the white pox pustules of a healthy child, which, mixed with camphor powder, is blown with a pipe into the nostril of the person to be inoculated. Great care and experience are required in selecting the lymph, on which alone depends the safety of the patients. Chicken-pox occurs only in a mild form, and is generally left to take its course.

Hydrophobia is very prevalent in Tibet, Mongolia, and China, and its effects are considered to manifest themselves, according to the colour of the dog, at periods varying from seven days to eighteen months, and also according to the time of day at which the bite was received. The remedies are, however, sufficiently practical. As soon as possible tie a ligature four fingers above the wound; draw out the poison by means of the sucking apparatus, called *rnyabs-ras*, similar to the cupping-glasses of the Indians, and then bleed the wounded part. If the patient presents himself to the physician a day after having been bitten, the latter should only cauterize the wound, and then apply an ointment made of butter, turmeric, a poisonous bulb called *bon-nya*, and musk.

In Lower Kongbo, Pobo, Pemakyod, and other mountainous districts of Southern Tibet, and in Nepal, Sikkim, and Bhutan on this side of the Himalayas, goitre is the most prevalent disease. It owes its origin to the calcareous nature of the water drunk by the natives. Six varieties of goitre are recognized by Tibetan physicians, which are variously treated by cauterization, bleeding the jugular vein behind the ear, and also the swollen muscle of the goitre, and the administration of nostrums composed of the dried gullet of the yak or sheep, dried fish, different kinds of salts, *Piper longum* and pepper, and powdered conch-shell, burnt in a hermetically closed vessel.

Snake-bite is of rare occurrence in Higher Tibet, but in the lower valley of the great Tsang-po, great numbers of snakes are found, and also on the western frontier of China bordering Tibet. Snake-bites are treated like hydrophobia, by tying a ligature above the part bitten and cupping. The wound is then washed with curd or milk, camel's milk being the most efficacious. It is believed in High Asia that if a snake bites a camel, the snake dies immediately without injuring the camel. If there be no burning heat as a consequence of the bite, the wound should be cauterized. Internal remedies are also taken, consisting of cardamom, musk, pepper, and other native drugs. The Glak-los (wild people) of Pemakyod immediately cut off the bitten portion, or the bitten limb, if possible, after which they apply musk and bear's bile to the wound and bind it up. The Lalos eat snakes, of which, however, they reject the head and tail as injurious.

During the months of January and February, when the great *mon-lam* (or prayer-meeting) fair takes place at Lhasa, the city is occasionally visited by a highly infectious disease which causes great havoc among the people when the crowd is great. When the disease is not properly treated the patient generally dies before the tenth day, but those cases which have passed the thirteenth day are considered hopeful. Tibetan physicians, by watching this disease in its different phases, have achieved remarkable success in treating it with their indigenous drugs.

In Lhasa, Shigatse, and other towns and monasteries of Tibet, the principal disease from which people suffer and die is paralysis.

Five different kinds of this disease are recognized by Tibetan physicians, who also profess to have observed that the first symptoms generally show themselves on the 4th, 8th, 11th, 15th, 18th, 22nd, 25th, or 29th day of the lunar month. Persons who have passed their sixtieth year seldom survive a paralytic stroke of any kind. All other cases in their milder forms are curable by proper and regular medical treatment.

Leprosy is prevalent in most of the countries of High Asia. It is variously called *glud-nad*, 'the nag's (serpent's) disease', and *mje-nad*, the 'corroding malady', and is believed to originate from various causes, fanciful and real. By digging in pestilential soil where snakes live, turning up stones under which these reptiles lurk, felling poisonous trees, throwing tea, water, or cooked food and other refuse on the blazing hearth, men are said to excite the wrath of the *Nagas* and mischievous spirits of the upper and nether worlds, who delight in working the ruin of the human race. They spread this hateful malady by the exhalation of their breath, by their poisonous touch or malignant glance, or even by the power of their malignant wish. The 'charmed banner' is a great preventive of these evils. The people of High Asia generally fix banners with printed charms thereon near to or on their houses, as they are believed to prevent the *Nagas* entering them. Leprosy is likewise assumed to be the consequence of the sins of former lives. It also originates from disorders produced by irregularity and intemperance in food and habits, whereby the black and yellow fluids of the body are increased, and give rise to this distressing malady. Eighteen different kinds of leprosy are recognized. The chanting of charms and mantras of Vajrapani Buddha by the patient or the physician is resorted to, that wrathful deity being a mighty subduer of all malevolent demons and *Nagas*, and various native drugs are also administered in the form of pills.

Dropsy, though rare in High Asia, prevails in the southern and eastern districts in Tibet, and is caused by drinking much water after exercise, lying down in damp places, taking cold, or by light unsubstantial food, by which the digestive powers are deranged. Twelve varieties of this disease are recognized, which are divided into two main groups, characterized as 'the hot' and 'the cold fluid' respectively. Bone-ash is believed to be the best remedy; but other medicines, consisting of grapes, cinnamon, oxide of iron, pomegranate, lime, and other ingredients, are also prescribed.

Dyspepsia (*pad-kau*) is one of the commonest diseases in Tibet, and forty-three different varieties of this malady have been observed by native physicians.

Toothache is also a very general complaint of the people of Tibet, due to the extreme rigour of the climate and the coldness of the water. The inhabitants of the remote province of Chang-tang usually lose their teeth before reaching the age of thirty.

Among the games played by the Tibetans, there are some such as *mig-mang*, or 'many eyes', resembling chess; *srid-pai khorlo*, or 'the circle of life', and dice, which even the clergy are permitted to amuse themselves with. Others, as, for instance, wrestling, archery, polo, foot and pony races, are confined to the people; nor are the lamas allowed to amuse themselves with singing and dancing except at stated times, as, for example, during the New Year holidays.

At midsummer the people and nobility dress tents, and for several days amuse themselves under them, picnicking, dancing, and singing.

In the 8th moon the *jon-gyu* festival takes place, lasting for seven or fourteen or even twenty-one days. On this occasion the lamas and people amuse themselves with sports, games, dancing, and feasting. This festival is observed in all northern Buddhist countries.

Again, in the latter part of the 12th moon, there is a lama dance in every monastery, after which the evil spirits arc exorcised. Sometimes the 4th of the 6th and the 22nd of the 9th moons are observed as feast days; the latter as the anniversary of the Buddha's descent from the Tushita heaven.

In the summer, commencing with the full moon in July and lasting for a period of forty-five days, all lamas make a retreat in their monasteries, during which time they are not allowed to go without the lamasery walls, or take part in any amusement. This is known as the *yar-nas*.

The birthdays of the Dalai and Tashi lamas are also kept as holidays, and on their reaching the age of three, twenty-five, forty-nine, sixty-one, seventy-three, or eighty-five, there are also great festivities.

When eclipses of the sun or moon occur, the Tibetans hold religious ceremonies similar to those of the Hindus.

Of all feasts, that of the New Year is probably the most popular. At Lhasa the State makes arrangements for the celebrations, beginning them about a month beforehand.

The kitchen of the Grand Lama is in a large yellow building called the Phodang serpo, or Jag-ming khang (*ljags-ming khang*), situated to the east of the palace. The cooking-stoves are ornamented with gold, silver, and precious stones, estimated to be worth Rs 20,000, and all the cooking utensils are of solid gold. All the butter and milk used here is obtained from the herd of 500 *jomos* (half-breed yaks) belonging to the Dalai lama, which herd the people salute as it passes, taking off their hats or kotowing to the animals. Twenty Tse-dung (lama officials) herd these cattle, milk them, and churn the butter.

Here, when New Year is approaching, five lamas prepare cakes and dainties for the Grand Lama, their mouths covered with eight thicknesses of silk, so that the food may not be polluted by their breath. In the village at the foot of Potala, called the Shedo khang, two or three hundred men make cakes and biscuits for the officials, lamas, and people; and every one, whether rich or poor, has some prepared for the festival.

On the 15th of the 12th moon 200 workmen begin white-washing the walls of Potala, which work occupies them for three days; and then, but only then, people are at liberty to have the walls of their houses whitened, and there is no one so poor that he does not at this season renovate the exterior of his dwelling.

On the 18th all public offices are closed for fifty days. Booths are erected to supply the crowds which assemble for the *monlam chenpo*, or 'grand prayer-meeting', which, beginning on New Year's day, lasts for a month, and many of the officials visit Tsedung linga, a beautiful park to the south of the city, where there is a Chinese restaurant and singing and dancing girls, called Tungshema, or 'drinking ladies'.

On the 22nd in all lamaseries and in many houses of the people *torma* offerings are made, to be offered the following day to the household gods. Then the people bathe and get themselves ready to make visits of congratulations, which they begin doing on the 27th. On the 29th each householder has a general house cleaning, and the dust and dirt is thrown in a cross-road, and thus all impending misfortunes are got rid of with the rubbish.

Early on the morning of the 29th large and gorgeously decorated tents are erected in the great courtyard of Potala and other temples, in each of which three or four hundred people can be seated. In the centre of each tent are *estrades* of carved and gilt sandalwood, on which the abbots, head lamas, and guests of distinction take their seats, while on lower seats are the other guests. A number of lamas, with little tables of sandalwood in front of them, on which different instruments of music, and implements used in church ceremonies, such as *dorje*, bells, *damaru*, etc., are placed, occupy another portion of each tent. When the preliminary service is over the grand 'black hat' dance, of which I have previously made mention, begins.

The dancers are eighty in number, and their gowns are made of white, red, and green satin. Each one holds in his left hand a wooden skull, and in his right a short club, from which hang five silk scarves of different colours. They prance about, wildly waving their arms, for half an hour or so, when suddenly there is heard wild shrieking, and a second set of dancers, or masks called *Kambab*, come in. They are dressed to represent the various gods, most of them extraordinarily hideous to look at. These continue the wild dance to the music of cymbals, drums, and flutes for a couple of hours.

When the *Kambab* have stopped, four skeleton-like figures appear: they are the *Durdag*, or 'lords of cemeteries', and they dance in their turn. These are followed by sixteen figures representing Indian *atsaras*, who, by their dress and contortions, excite wild mirth among the people. A number of dancers wearing stag heads then appear, and finally the 'black hat' dancers come out once more, each with a cymbal or a drum in his hand, and the dance comes to an end.

At the termination of the dance the lamas who performed the religious service earlier in the day form in a procession and proceed to throw away the *torma* offering.

500 soldiers and twenty-four flag-bearers accompany the procession. Three lamas carry on an iron tripod the *tsamba torma*, which is of pyramidal shape, about 10 feet high and painted red, with projecting edges to represent flames, and frequently surmounted by a skull moulded in *tsamba*. Three other lamas bear on a large iron tray supported by a tripod a skeleton also made of *tsamba*. The procession goes to about a mile from the temple to where a shed, or *hom khang*, of straw or brush has been made, in which the *torma* and the skeleton are placed and then set on fire.

When the flames break forth the flag-bearers lower their flags and run back to the lamasery with all speed, to escape the devil's assaults, and the soldiers fire off their guns at the burning mass to prevent the evil spirits escaping from the fire in which they are now supposed to be roasting.

On the 30th day of the moon, New Year's eve, all house decorations and furniture are renewed or cleaned, and offerings and oblations made in every domestic chapel. The walls, pillars, posts, lintels, etc., are washed with whey. A lotus, finger-marks or marks of animals' claws are painted on the wooden floors of the rooms, or a sheep's head is scorched, and its eyes, ears, and nose painted with the five colours mixed with butter: this is said to be a certain means of insuring good luck, and is believed to be a pre-Buddhist custom of the country.

In the evening the whole city is illuminated, and this is kept up for three successive nights.

New Year's day is called Gyalpo lo sar, or 'the King's new year', and the Grand Lama holds a levee on this occasion. The Donyer chenpo, or Grand Chamberlain, opens the ceremony by wishing the lama all happiness (*tra-shi de leg phun-sum tsog*), and presenting him some wine and *tsamba*. The Grand Lama replies, '*Tan-du de-wa tobpar shog*,' and dipping his finger in the wine, sprinkles a little about as an oblation, and then tastes the *tsamba*. Then the great trumpets sound, and the Dalai lama takes his seat on the throne in the great hall, and all the ministers and church dignitaries take their places according to precedence. Tea is then served, followed by *toma*, a kind of red potato of Tibet, cooked in butter and sugared. When they have finished eating, every one presents His Holiness with *khatag* about 18 feet long, and he gives each one in return his blessing.

In the meantime 'the good luck dance' (*tra-shi-gi gar*) is going on outside the hall, in which some twenty little boys, of eight years of age, take part, the lower officials, such as the Dungkhor, forming the audience.

In every house of any importance the master, his wife, and children are offered the compliments of the season by all their relatives, dependents, and friends, who, in their turn, are treated with wine by them. When the New Year's wine has been drunk, the *misser* (serfs) sing some hymns or glees.

At the New Year the Tibetans watch out for omens for the forthcoming year, the best of which, if one is to start soon on a journey, is to see a young woman with a child in her arms. To see flags, banners, milking of cows, persons carrying vessels filled with water or any other liquid, or timber for house-building or firewood, is lucky, as is also the sight of a corpse on a bier. To meet well-dressed persons, to be greeted by friends, to hear a lucky name, are also held to be signs of good luck; but to see beggars, ragged persons, empty vessels, a person descending a hill, or carrying shoes in his hand, a saddled horse without a rider, to hear impolite or rough language, are portends of bad fortune.

On New Year's day dancing beggars (or *Dre-kar*) make their appearance in the streets and houses. They wear masks, usually representing a black devil, with a shaggy, white beard, with cowries for eyebrows and encircling his face, and sometimes with a cowrie for either cheek. They dance and crack jokes to the delight of the guests assembled in each house for the New Year's breakfast.

In the afternoon there is further feasting in most of the houses, and the guests, both male and female, frequently end the entertainment with a dance (*shabdo*); first, the women dance alone, then the men, and finally, both sexes together.

The New Year's festivities terminate on the third day at noon, when the monks of the great lamaseries all meet in the Kyil khording (or Jo khang) to hear the Grand Lama expound the faith. On each succeeding day, till the 24th of the moon, they hold the great prayer-meeting, or *mon-lam chenpo*.

In the afternoon of the third, the Tsog-chen Shalnyo of Dabung assumes the government of Lhasa for the next month and a half, previously informing the police magistrates of the fact, and henceforth all authority, even that of the Kalon, as far as the city is concerned, is vested in him alone.

ALSO FROM SPEAKING TIGER

NO PATH IN DARJEELING IS STRAIGHT: MEMORIES OF A HILL TOWN

Parimal Bhattacharya

'Parimal Bhattacharya's outstanding prose elegy captures the essence of Darjeeling, for me the Queen of Hill Stations, a place of many happy and sad memories.' —Mark Tully

'It is difficult to pigeon-hole [*No Path in Darjeeling Is Striaght*] into a neat genre: it is not *only* a memoir, or a history, or natural history, or anecdote—it is everything at once, and more.' —*Business Standard*

For a few years in the early 1990s—at a time when a violent agitation for Gorkhaland had just ended—Parimal Bhattacharya taught at the Government College in Darjeeling. No Path in Darjeeling Is Straight is a memory of his time in the iconic town, and one of the finest works of Indian non-fiction in recent years.

Parimal evocatively describes his arrival at a place that was at odds with the grand picture of it he had painted for himself. And his first night there was spent sleepless in a ramshackle hotel above a butcher's shop. Yet Darjeeling grew on him. He sought out its history: in villages, on its roads and footpaths, among old-timers and the newly arrived. And in the enmeshed lives of his neighbours—of various castes, tribes, religions and cultures—lived at the measured pace of a small town, Parimal discovered a richly cosmopolitan society which endured even under threat from cynical politics and haphazard urbanization. He also found new friends.

With empathy, and in shimmering prose, *No Path in Darjeeling Is Straight* effortlessly merges travel, history, literature, memory, politics and the pleasures of ennui into an unforgettable portrait of a place and its people.

ALSO FROM SPEAKING TIGER

HIMALAYA: ADVENTURES, MEDITATIONS, LIFE

Edited by Ruskin Bond and Namita Gokhale

'[*Himalaya* is a] delicious hoard; more a larder rather than a buffet. You might well pick and choose the sequence of what you wish to read, with the energy and particular appetite of your moment. But you can also go back to it repeatedly over time, for much more.'
—*India Today*

'The poet Ko Yun wrote: "One thing alone is beautiful: setting off./The world's too vast,/to live in a single place/or three or four." *Himalaya* makes you feel like that.' —*Business Standard*

'From the most widely read to texts inaccessible in the public domain are stitched together for a perfect winter read ... This certainly is no book for a hurried reading. It demands meditation. It kindles philosophical understandings and musings; and waits upon poignant pauses.' —*Muse India*

With over fifty essays, this comprehensive volume of writings on the *Himalaya* brings together a dazzling range of voices—among others, Fa-Hien, Pundit Nain Singh, Heinrich Harrer, Fanny Parkes, Dharamvir Bharati, Arundhathi Subramaniam, Rahul Sankrityayan, Amitav Ghosh, Jawaharlal Nehru, Frank Smythe, Paul Brunton, Edmund Hillary, Mark Twain, Sarat Chandra Das, Dom Moraes, Manjushree Thapa—and the two editors themselves—in an unparalleled panorama.

Edited by Ruskin Bond, India's most-loved writer, and acclaimed novelist Namita Gokhale, this anthology spans the entire range, from the foothills to the highest peaks, and from its easternmost to its westernmost ends. *Himalaya* will keep you riveted.

ALSO FROM SPEAKING TIGER

IN A LAND FAR FROM HOME: A BENGALI IN AFGHANISTAN (DESHE BIDESHE)

Syed Mujtaba Ali

Translated from the Bengali by Nazes Afroz

'*Deshe Bideshe* [is] one of the most enthralling books in Bangla literature.' —*Financial Express*

An intrepid traveller and a true cosmopolitan, the legendary Bengali writer Syed Mujtaba Ali from Sylhet (in erstwhile East Bengal, now Bangladesh) spent a year and a half teaching in Kabul from 1927 to 1929. Drawing on this experience, he later wrote *Deshe Bideshe* which was published in 1948.

Ali's young mind was curious to explore the Afghan society of the time and, with his impressive language skills, he had access to a cross-section of Kabul's population, whose ideas and experiences he chronicles with a keen eye and a wicked sense of humour.

His account provides a fascinating first-hand insight into events at a critical point in Afghanistan's history, when the reformist King Amanullah tried to steer his country towards modernity by encouraging education for girls and giving them the choice of removing the burqa. Branded a 'kafir', Amanullah was overthrown by the bandit leader Bacha-e-Saqao. *Deshe Bideshe* is the only published eyewitness account of that tumultuous period by a non-Afghan, brought to life by the contact that Ali enjoyed with a colourful cast of characters at all levels of society—from the garrulous Pathan Dost Muhammed and the gentle Russian giant Bolshov, to his servant, Abdur Rahman and his partner in tennis, the Crown Prince Enayatullah.

ALSO FROM SPEAKING TIGER

TIBETAN CARAVANS: JOURNEYS FROM LEH TO LHASA

Abdul Wahid Radhu

Foreword by His Holiness The Dalai Lama

Born into an eminent merchant family in Ladakh in 1918, Khwaja Abdul Wahid Radhu, often described as 'the last caravaneer of Tibet and Central Asia', led an unusual life of adventure, inspiration and enlightenment. His family, and later he, had the ancestral honour of leading the biannual caravan which carried the Ladakhi kings' tribute and homage to the Dalai Lama and the Tibetan government. *Tibetan Caravans*, his memoir, is an unparalleled narrative about trans-Himalayan trade—the riches, the politics and protocol, the challenging yet magnificent natural landscape, altitude sickness, snow storms, bandits and raiders, monks and soldiers. The book also contains rare and fascinating details about the close connections between Ladakh, Tibet and Kashmir, the centuries-old interplay between Buddhism and Islam in the region, the Chinese occupation of Tibet, and life in Lhasa before and after its takeover by China.

In this rich and insightful memoir, Abdul Wahid Radhu reminisces about a bygone era when borders were fluid, and mutual respect formed the basis for trade relations across cultures and people. As his son, Siddiq Wahid, says in his introduction, *Tibetan Caravans* is a testimony to the organic relationships between 'societies who have learned how to hear each other out, argue, even do battle and yet remain hospitable to each other.'

www.ingramcontent.com/pod-product-compliance
Lightning Source LLC
Chambersburg PA
CBHW050855160426
43194CB00011B/2168